...

THE COMPLETE WORKS

Compendium of the Nottingham Panthers ice hockey team

Michael A Chambers

...

This would normally be a page to dedicate this book 'for' someone but this time I'll be a bit different and offer this to ME.

Yes, after previous books written *for* someone else, it's about time I put myself in the lime light and first.

Always have done things for others but this time I'm proud to have produced this third book on the Nottingham Panthers and most probably it will be the last.

One book each on Great Britain Ice Hockey, The History of Ice Hockey in the UK and a fictional story set around the sport 'Ice Cold Murder' were other publications.

But now I will bow out and hopefully someone else will tread the path of collating statistics, facts and worthy detail in order to reveal the clubs history to the public domain, as time goes by.

This one is larger than normal to include an update of facts and a few more statistics if not to recap on previous.

****

Some people who are volunteers sell 50/50, shirt of the players back and Chuck a puck tickets. Let's mention them.

50/50
Brian and Sue Bailey, Natalie Bashton, Paula Cruikshank, Wendy Martin, Erika Read, Sharon Richards, Helen Westray-Cawthan
Shirt
Adrian Bashton, Keith Colley, Saf Fairweather (+ 50/50), Catriona and Dorothy McGowan, David Smith and Karon (unknown)
Chuck a puck
Sophie Platt and Sophie Utton

www.icehockeyreview.co.uk

...

Publishing History 1ˢᵗ Edition

Independently published in December 2022
And distributed via the Kindle Direct Publishing platform

© 2022 Michael A Chambers

Collated and edited by M A Chambers

Editorial consultant: Paul Breeze

ISBN: 9798365711198

Front cover image: painting by J K Muddiman
Cover design by Esra Kelham

Back cover image: Cartoon by Merv Magus

SPECIAL THANKS TO…
Fraser Shaw, Matt Bradbury and Simon Hopkins for their help in answering queries
David Parker and Robert Hicklin for the same as regards the statistics and fixtures
J.K.Muddiman (cover picture) available as prints at **www.jkmartwork.com**

Last time on the (c1939) stadium's ice

...

CONTENTS

Page 10 Acknowledgements
Page 11 Introduction and notes
Page 12 KEY to abbreviations
Page 13 Foreword by Paul Breeze
Page 14 'when it all began'
Page 19 Black and White Pictures galore of the first era
Page 30 The Second era's first 40 plus seasons
47 Catch up Seasons 2007-08 to 2022-23
144 Competition Titles
147 Season by Season Tournaments
156 Nottingham European entries
169 Players in the Great Britain National team
175 Nottingham All Time statistics (lists and registers)
251 All time top lists
253 University players, Para hockey and the Women's team
262 Honours and All Star team players
264 'spotlight' on Matthew Myers
265 Quiz Time
266 Jerseys
270 Who's Who in Officialdom
273 'Bits and Pieces'
277 Quiz Two

279 Appendixes
a) History of Ice Hockey
b) Cup, League and Play-offs

291 My plan for the future
292 Signing off

ACKNOWLEDGMENTS

Mike Smith for his invaluable help as regards photos once again

Paul Breeze for easing me through the checking process and production onto Amazon

Sue Bailey…..for contribution of photos

Sources
IIHF website
Wikipaedia
My personal documents

Nottingham Bibliography

The Nottingham Panthers – A Pictorial History by the club 1982
Official Year books 1982-83 and 1983-84 by the club
Rebel - free A4 leaflet newsletter – 4 issues by myself
Upfront Newsletter – 4 issues by Hugh Stanley
Black and Gold – The rebirth of Ice Hockey in Nottingham 1988 by David Litchfield
The Cool Cat fanzine 1992-93 to March 1997 – 10 issues by the fans
The Cat's Whiskers Fanzine October 2000 to March 2003 - 5 issues Jono Bullard
EIHL Challenge Cup Champions pictorial 1907-08 by Dave Page
SHMYR pictorial 1907-08 by Dave Page
Panthers Italian Job – job done 2017 by Gary Moran
Panther's Annual 2000-01 through to 2018-19   Edited by Gary Moran
Broken Heart 2020 by Gary Moran
Panthers quiz Annual 2020

INTRODUCTION and notes

Welcome to this third read on the statistical and factual events of the Nottingham Panthers Ice Hockey Team.

It has come about with a few years passing since the last two books called 'Factual Scrapbook' 2007 and previous to that the 'Statistical Guidebook' back in 2000

I won't be around forever so thought it a good time to roll out a last one to round up the seasons from 2007-08 to 2022-23.
Interest in sitting at the computer has waned due to the hours spending time on it all, plus I now have a family to give time to.

To note that with statistics you'll find that each and every account 'may' be different. 'That should not be the case' you'll say because what happens should be noted and set in stone as a record. However, people may record in error, as I have found even with the official numbers. Or the source you have used has printed them in error. This has happened as I wrote this book, realising something did not add up and checking the work to find for some inexplicable reason a list combining several tournaments had some players totals calculated different to others, again because of slight human error, so time has been taken to rectify as best could be done.

There is the obvious error when a player was adjudged to be a goal scorer but someone actually saw different and has changed numbers accordingly. Many times game record sheets are altered post game but not to the public knowledge and reason for some differing figures. Also those changes might not have been added to the end of season total.

These are few but I'm keen to see mine are as watertight as possible. I'm happy but wanting to hear from anyone of possible glitches in the 'works'. So get in touch if you feel there is something amiss.

Regards photos, bar the period when a picture can be re-produced without consent/permission, I have still taken it as my duty to always pen who took the photos when known. Apologies if some are missed.

Michael Chambers

spikc2004@yahoo.co.uk

KEY to abbreviations

Found on these pages and seen thereafter repeated within the book

Page 14 ft - feet, m - metres, VIP - very important person
Page 15 RAF – Royal Air Force
Page 48 n/m – net minder
Page 51 GP – Games played, RW – Regulation win, OW – Overtime win, PW – Penalty shot win, RL – Regulation loss, OL – Overtime loss, PL – Penalty loss, GF – Goals for, GA – Goals against, GD – Goal difference, Pts - Points
Page 52 GPi – Games played in, Mins – Minutes, Sts – Shots, GAA – Goals against average, %sv - percentage save, Pims – penalty in minutes, SO – shut out
Page 122 Dir.of Hoc – Director of Hockey
Page 129 OT – Overtime
Page 130 SF1/2 – Semi-Final ½
Page 147 USA – United States of America
Page 148 RCAF – Royal Canadian Air Force
Page 154 UQTR – University Quebec three rivers Patriots?
Page 156 AUG – August, Oct – October, NOV – November
Page 175 SOG – shots on goal, GLS – goals, GA% - goals against percentage.
Page 178 Reg. - register, APP – appearances
Page 189 Mids – midlands
Page 190 G – goals, A – assists, CH – challenge
Page 257 Para – Paraplegic
Page 273 ED (ed) – Editor (me)
Page 280 LIGH – Ligue Internationale de Hockey sur Glace (French term), GB – Great Britain, SC – skating club? HC – Hockey Club, IHC – Ice Hockey Club
Page 282 Switz – Switzerland, chech – Chechoslovakia, CAHA – Canadian Amateur Hockey Association
Page 283 IIHF – International Ice Hockey Federation
Page 287 EIRE – Gaelic name for Ireland (Irish Republic – Southern Ireland)

Those early years in the second era

In picture: left to right in white… Robin Andrew, Leyton Erratt (foreground), Dwayne Keyward and in goal Chris Keyward.

FOREWORD by Paul Breeze (My consultant for this book)

Michael has asked me to write a Foreword for his new 'meisterwerk' about the Nottingham Panthers and, while it's a great pleasure and an honour to do so, it is also rather perplexing as, despite having watched British ice hockey now for 40 years (yes – I know, I don't look old enough...!), I am NOT, in fact, a Panthers fan and nor have I ever actually been to watch a match in Nottingham.

I have, however, over all those years seen Nottingham teams play on numerous occasions – the Panthers when they were regular visitors against the Peterborough Pirates in those halcyon days of the Heineken British League in the 1980s and early 1990s, the Trojans in Division 2, an Under 16 team in a Junior match at Blackpool once, various recreation teams and, most recently, the Lions team in the NIHL and women's Vipers team in games at Widnes that I have officiated at – and, while I was almost certainly rooting for the opposing teams on each of those occasions, I dare say that I will be able to think of something to say about the Lace City contingent.

Ice hockey in Nottingham, of course, dates back to the late 1940s when the first Panthers team was brought over "en masse" from Canada and gave the British game such legendary names and long term servants as Chick Zamick and Les Strongman. They won a couple of English league titles in the early 1950s and were then part of the innovative, but relatively short-lived, British League of 1954 to 1960, where they won the play off title in its final year.

I think it is safe to say that the return of ice hockey to Nottingham in 1980 was a key factor in the renaissance of the game in this country in the 1980s and the fact that top level hockey has been played there ever since – along with the club's enviable record in producing local home grown players through their highly successful junior development system - is an indication of the dedication and passion for the game in the city.

The local derby tussles between the Pirates and the Panthers in the old days were always great fun to watch and, at just 60 miles away, Nottingham were Peterborough's nearest opponents. The Panthers would always bring a good travelling support with them and I always found Nottingham fans to be very knowledgeable about the game, very polite, perfectly well mannered and easy to mix with.

In fact, I remember numerous occasions when the Panthers were away in Scotland for a "double header" weekend (do they still have those? Ayr on a Saturday, Murrayfield on a Sunday – probably not...) and groups of Nottingham fans would come along to Peterborough, complete with all their shirts, scarves and flags, to watch whoever the Pirates were playing against that night - just to have a game to go and watch, so that really is dedication to your sport!

So - those are a few thoughts from me about the Panthers and Nottingham ice hockey in general. I will now pass you back into the - much more - capable hands of Mr Michael Chambers to get on with the nitty gritty!

Paul Breeze   Editor, Ice Hockey Review

WHEN IT ALL BEGAN

1939

The Nottingham Ice Stadium, Lower Parliament Street, Nottingham, England. NG1 1LA. Built by Messrs Sims, Sons & Cooke Ltd
Sold to The Nottingham Corporation in the summer of 1957

Opened	10/4/39	Ice 185ft x 85ft (56m x 26m)
Re-opened	31/8/46	spectator capacity 2,950
Closed	27/3/00	(originally 3,000)
		Seating 2,850

First game - Challenge   12/4/39   7.30pm
(2/-, 3/-& 4/- prices including tax & skating)
Result: Harringay Greyhounds   10   Harringay Racers   6

Second Era...... The Sheffield Lancers re-located to the City of Nottingham playing two games behind closed doors. This was the re-birth of the "Panthers" after a twenty year absence of Ice Hockey. Playing officially on the 20/9/80, a Challenge versus Solihull in front of 850 spectators, winning 7-4.
The ice pad was replaced in 1983.
In May 2000 Robinsons disused fruit and vegetable cold store on Handle Street NG3 1JE... 100ft x 80ft (30m x 24m) enclosed mainly by walls was used as a temporary training pad. This facility closed in June 2001.

NATIONAL ICE ARENA INFORMATION NG1 1LU
Opened 1/4/00 - with a second pad by 7/4/01 197ft x 98ft - (60m x 30m) Seating 6,500 with 48 VIP boxes.
Designed by owners Nottingham City Council (Design & Property Services)
Construction by Laing at 40 million (m) pounds of which 22.5 million pounds funded by Sports Council Lottery, 11.1 m by Charitable Trust and one from English Partnerships.

****

Nottingham's debut game 15/11/39

Versus R.A.F (Grantham)

Attendance approximately: 1500

Match Result: Lost 4-7

The team are mentioned in Phil Dracketts book "Flashing Blades" and were unquestionably recruited from Canadians serving over here in the RAF.
Another source for information being the Ice Hockey World publication 1939/40.

Further to this, Jo-Jo Grabosky is mentioned as a player within the Ice Hockey Annual 2002/03 by Stewart Roberts. hockey historian Martin Harris a member of The Society for Hockey Research notes Jo-Jo who lived in Kingstown, Ontario came to Nottingham to play for the Panthers but returned to Canada at the outbreak of World War II without playing any games.

Team

Block.H
Block.J
Brown.R
Jones
Keller.Max
Lee
Raines
Rivett
Spencer
Torgalson
White

02/12/39   Panthers   8   RAF (Canadian section)   7

03/02/40   Panthers/RAF Canadians   12
                Cambridge Canadians   1

22/11/46 was the first domestic game in The English National League with the team winning 3 – 2. Players were:- Warwick, Lyons, <u>Westman</u>, Howard, <u>Herriott</u>, Stevens, Burke, McLachlan, <u>Strongman</u>, Mollard, Young,
          Coyston.--- *the underlined having long UK careers*

ICE HOCKEY AGAIN

CANADIAN R.A.F. TEAM BEATEN IN NOTTM.

Though the large crowd of spectators at Nottingham Ice Stadium, on Saturday night, did not witness an exhibition of ice-hockey so skilful as that when the Harringay Racers appeared, they had full enjoyment in a match between Nottingham Panthers and the Canadian R.A.F.

In the Panthers side the two most notable players were Brown and Rivett. Brown had several goals to his credit, and no player on the rink had such speed and control of the puck as Rivett.

In the first session Rivett assisted Brown in scoring a fine goal. This success was short-lived for the R.A.F. took command and goals by Ready, Lewis and McIntyre gave them a substantial lead.

The tables were turned in the second session and the R.A.F. scarcely knew how to counter the Panthers' attacks. Brown reduced the arrears, and Keller added a third goal with the assistance of Sargent to equalise. This was followed by a capital goal by Brown, and Lea added a fifth before the end of the session.

In the final spell Rivett was soon in action again and scored a goal from long range. A minute later Ready reduced the arrears. Soon the R.A.F. goal was in trouble and twice fell to shots by Sargent and Lea. Three quick goals followed for the R.A.F. by McIntyre and Lewis (2) and the Panthers won by the odd goal in 15. Result:

NOTTM. PANTHERS 8
CANADIAN R.A.F. 7

Panthers.—Hanson; J. H. Block, R. Block, Spencer, Rivett, Lea, Brown, Keller, Sargent, Davidson, White. Canadian R.A.F.—Torgalso (Vancouver), Lewis (Battleford), McIntyre (Arnprior), Kyle (Edmonton), Davis (Port Cosborne), Ready (Prince Edward Island), Wooll (Peterborough, Ont.), Lavicheliere (Montreal), Jones (Vancouver), Holyoke (Frederickstowns), Puncheon (Toronto).

4th December 1939 Nottingham Guardian Newspaper report
(Courtesy of Nottingham Evening Post)

CANADIAN ICE HOCKEY PLAYERS IN NOTTINGHAM

ICE hockey still has a big following in Nottingham, although the war vetoed league games, and there was an appreciative crowd at the ice stadium on Saturday night when a combined team of Nottingham Panthers and Canadian R.A.F. opposed Cambridge University Canadians. The combined side was much stronger, and deserved their win by 12 goals to one.

It was not the hockey of experts but it was full of enthusiasm. There were, however, one or two notable players, particularly Rivett, Ready and Lewis. Rivett was remarkably fast, and is without doubt a real "local find."

The Cambridge attacks were too easily broken up by reason of the forwards' lack of combination. In the first session the combined team was prominent and their raids were held off by capital goalkeeping by Hood. He was eventually beaten by a fine shot by Ready, and this was followed by goals by McIntyre and Lewis.

Solo efforts by Rivett were a feature of the second session and Hood brought off many great saves. There was greater life in the exchanges.

A Cambridge attack broke down when a goal seemed in the offing, and the combined side advanced and Lewis added a fourth goal. After a fine run by Lea, Davidson scored a fifth goal.

The last session had not been in progress more than a minute when Wool took the Cambridge goalminder by surprise with a rising shot which found the net. Lea quickly followed with another goal.

Further goals were scored for the combined side by Davidson, McIntyre, Lewis (2), Ready. Cambridge's only goal was obtained by Masser.

R. Johnson, of the Cambridge side, was struck on the head with the puck and was taken to the General Hospital for treatment. Result:

NOTTM. POACHERS & R.A.F. CANADIANS 12
CAMBRIDGE UNIVERSITY CANADIANS 1

Nottm. Panthers and R.A.F. Canadian Section.—Pilot-Officer Torgalson; Pilot-Officer Lewis (capt.), Benson; Lea, Pilot-Officer Davidson, Rivett; Pilot-Officer Davies, Pilot-Officer Ready, Pilot-Officer Wooll. Reserve Pilot-Officer MacIntyre.

Cambridge University Canadians.—H. Hood; J. Philips, R. Johnson; R. James, J. Knapp, G. Ashton (capt.); J. Roberts, D. Masser, A. Powell. Reserve, G. Oppenheim.

5th February 1940 Nottingham Guardian Report (Courtesy of Nottingham Evening Post)
The Nottingham Post also made similar articles in its sports section

Chick Zamick left with family early on and on the right here (centre) with friends in latter times.

17

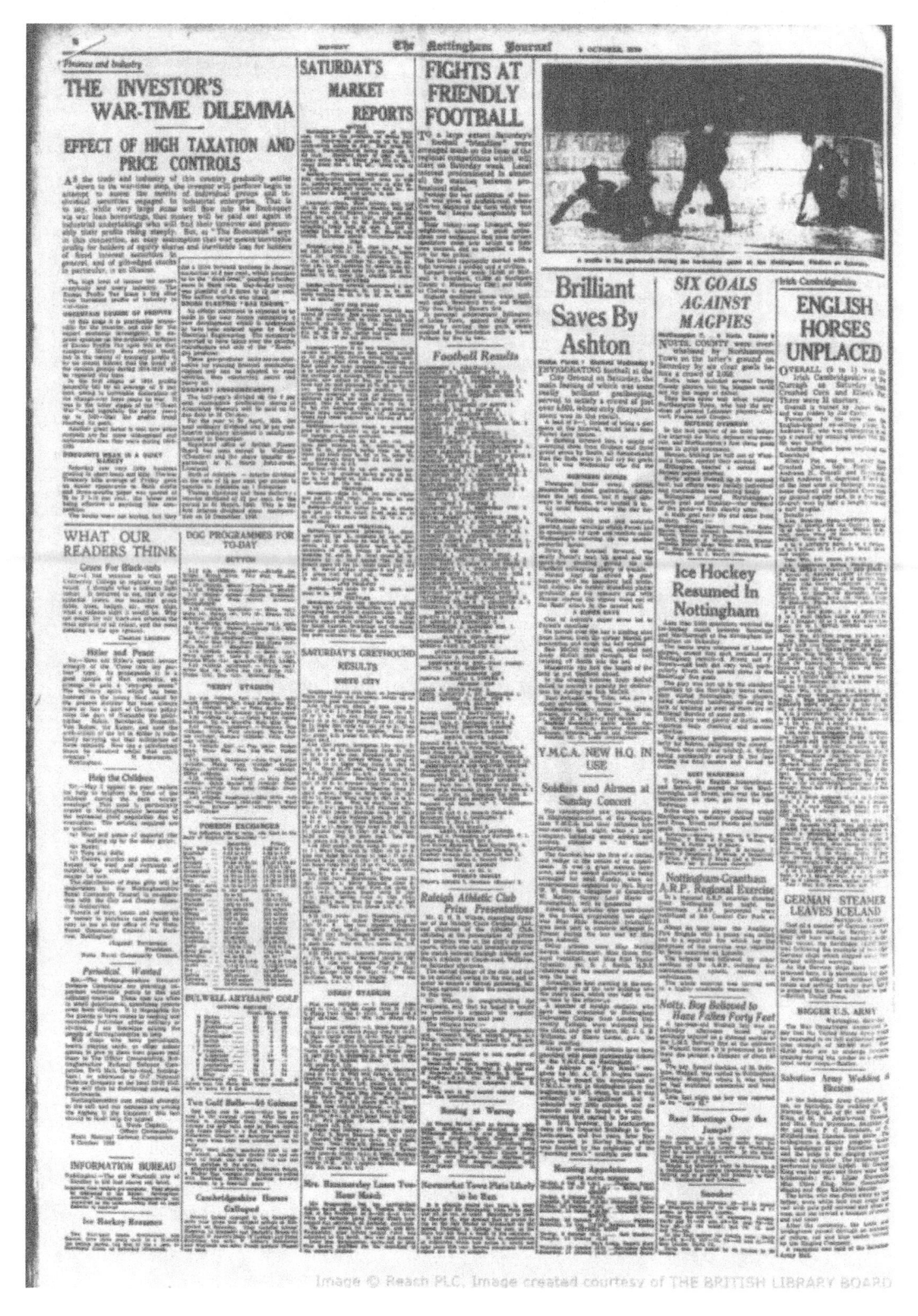

The 9th October 1939 Nottingham Journal report on a match between the Redwings and Marlborough. London sides with two Panthers 'Rivett' and 'F.Brown' included on either side. (Newspaper clip courtesy of Nathan Greasley)

BLACK and WHITE
Pictures galore of the first era

From Warren Goodman, son of Nottingham player Roger (these two photos)

Grand photos of the players in that first jersey ever worn

Visiting the capital

Back at home in Nottingham at the council house

The ship HMS Aquitania used to transport players and sailed from Halifax to Southampton. Picture here taken 1914

For those foreign tournaments travel was more private

Away abroad as tourists

(Photo: Warren Goodman)
Roger Goodman 'in' the sin bin

22

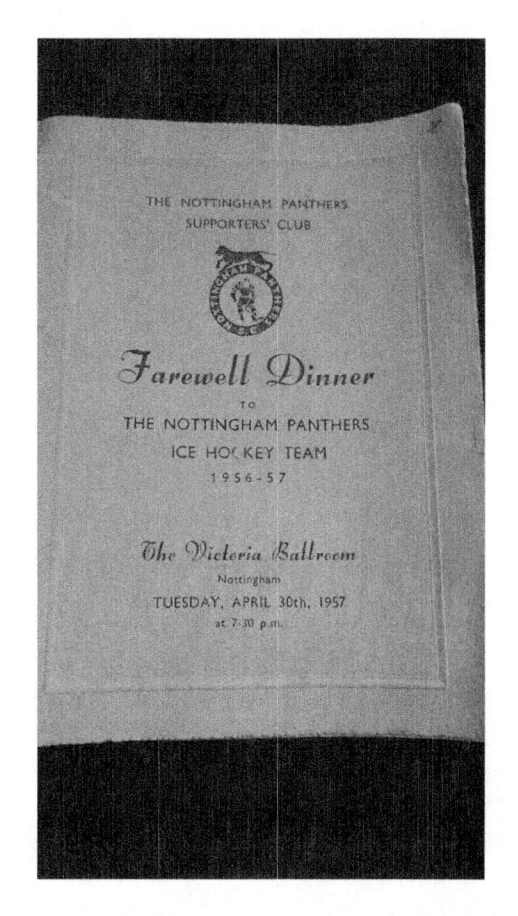

An early 'end of season' awards evening and (below) the 'enticing menu and events'

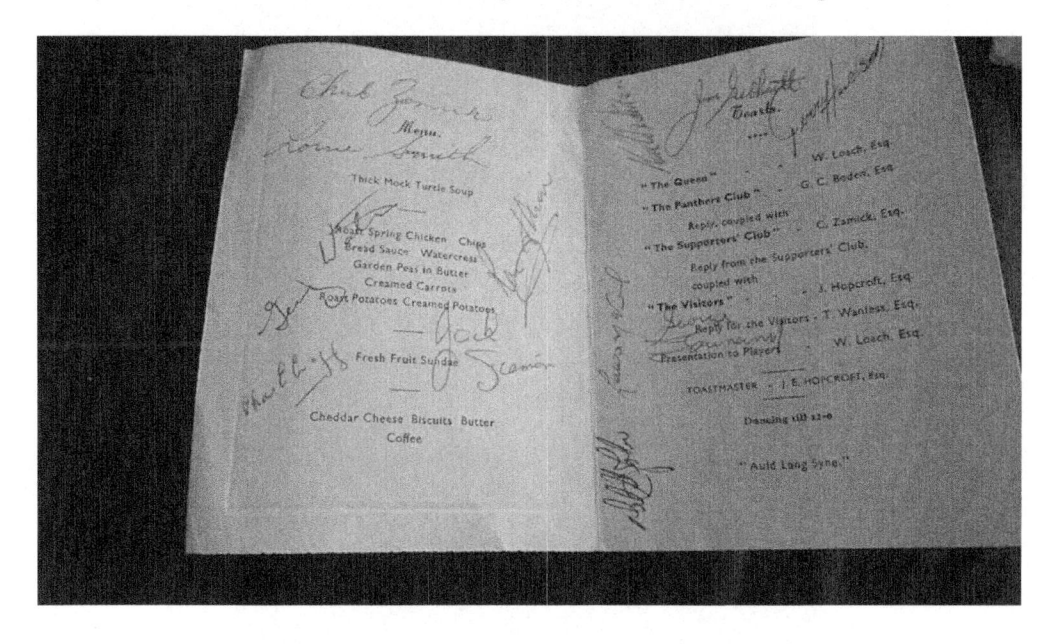

Nottingham Panthers

What seems like the first bit of merchandise? A metal pin badge and below the supporter's club committee listed.

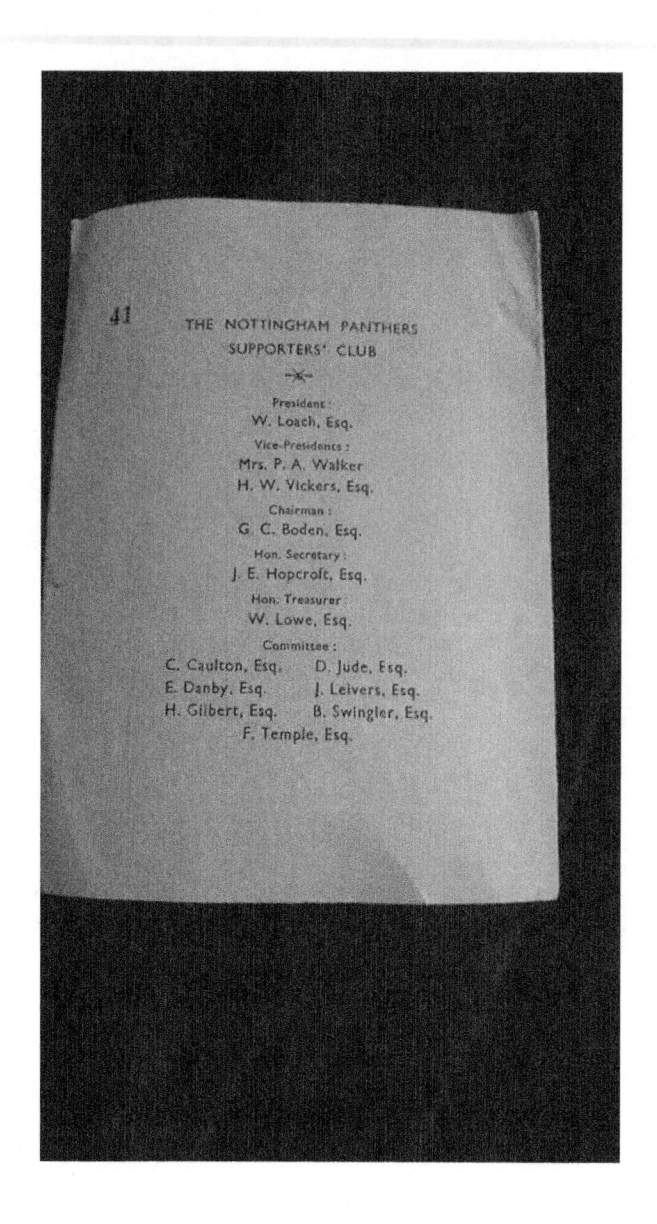

41 THE NOTTINGHAM PANTHERS
SUPPORTERS' CLUB

President:
W. Loach, Esq.

Vice-Presidents:
Mrs. P. A. Walker
H. W. Vickers, Esq.

Chairman:
G. C. Boden, Esq.

Hon. Secretary:
J. E. Hopcroft, Esq.

Hon. Treasurer:
W. Lowe, Esq.

Committee:
C. Caulton, Esq.   D. Jude, Esq.
E. Danby, Esq.   J. Leivers, Esq.
H. Gilbert, Esq.   B. Swingler, Esq.
F. Temple, Esq.

KENNY WESTMAN

Outside the old Stadium
1953-54?

Doug Wilson, Bill Ringer and Lorne Smith

1950-51 Pete Moulden, Gyle Woods and Bill Ringer

Returning aboard the Cunard white star ship September 1951-52
Les Strongman, Bill Ringer (he sent me a few pictures) and Bill Innes

End of season Ball 1951/2/3 (unknown season)
Bill and wife Gloria plus Archie Stinchcombe

'Panthers Ball' 1951-52
Ringer, Red Matthews, Bill Innes and Tony Malo

Action 'shots' around the net

Even the Midlands club can beat the mighty Russians so no wonder that the public rushed to join the club.

The second era's first 40 plus seasons
THE 1980's when Panthers came back after a 20 year hiatus
 Introducing:

(top photo:Sue Bailey)
Kurtenbach, Adey, Durdle / Dwayne Keward then Terry Gudzuinas
Below: Frankie Killen with supporter's chairman /Leyton Erratt

Photo:Nottingham Post)

Presenting the 'Midlands Cup' to Darryl Easson

(Photo: Sue Bailey)

Jamie Craiper and on ice Todd Bidner

31

Top: David 'stef' Litchfield presents a trophy to Gavin Fraser

Photo:Sue Bailey

Middle: All-Time 'Most appearances' Randle Weber

Below: Nigel Rhoads and Jimmy Keys

THE 1990's and this second era of hockey extends beyond the first era's 14 seasons. Let's see some close up action.

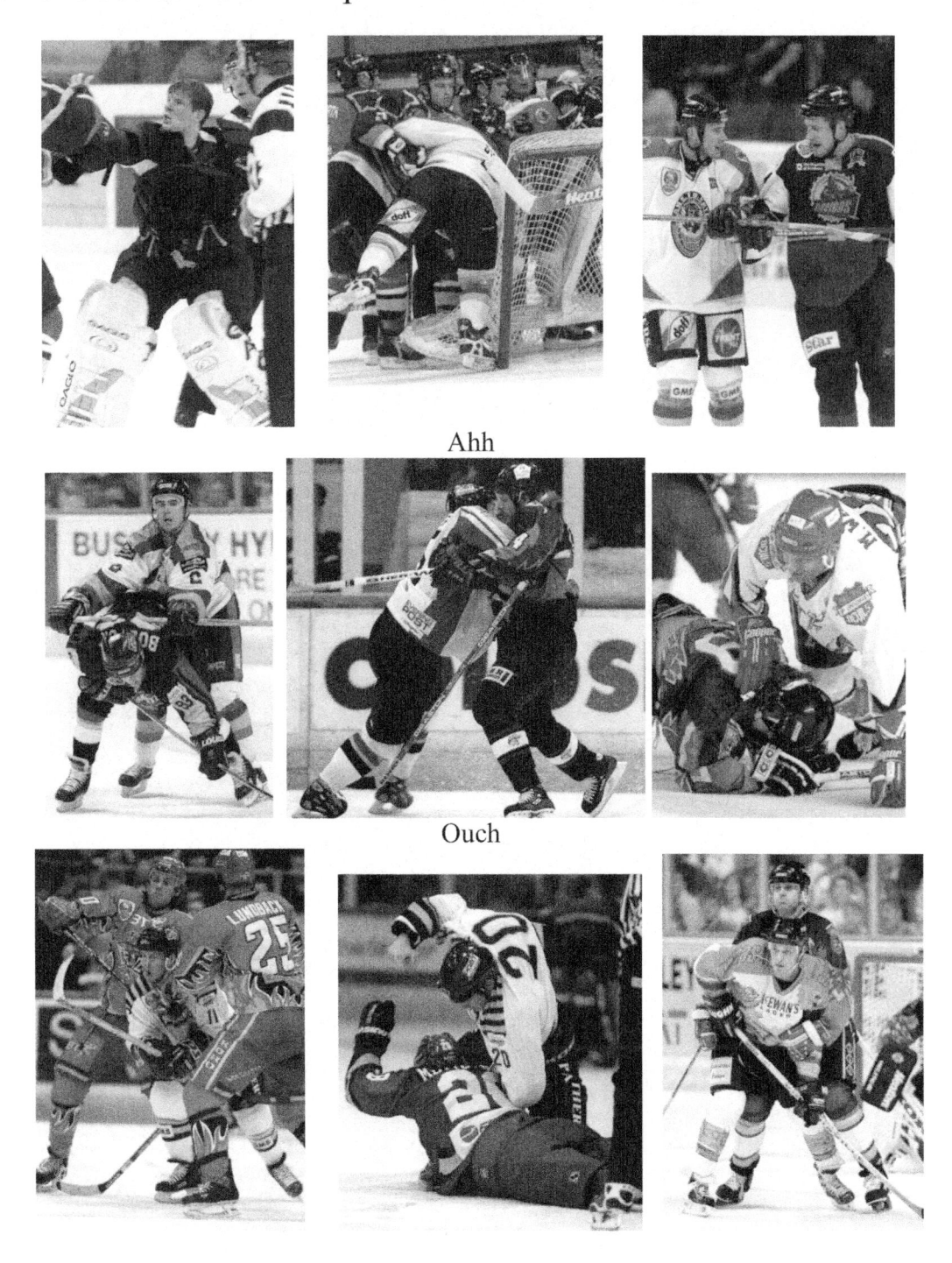

Ahh

Ouch

ALL photo's in this section (six pages) courtesy of Mike Smith (icepix)

33

1. making sure that angle is closed down and 2. Blaisdell getting in front of that net

Tait 'This is just not on'

Well, that's me past him says Steve Roberts

Opps I'm caught says Darcy Lowen

Ahh ha, handy stick work by Aaron Cain and Graham Garden

36

We missed something? Marcus Adolfsson on top of things

Where's that puck Says Trevor Robins

37

Corey Beaulieu, Blake Knox, Mike Zanier and Trevor Robins

Strutch 'talking'

THE 2000's and Ice Hockey is here to stay and in a new Arena

Welcoming:

(photo x3:Sue bailey)
Calle Carlsson / P C Drouin -both returned for addition seasons.

Below: Most penalised player on average per game,
Barry Neickar

(photo: Geraldine Ellis)

NHL Korean player Jimmy Paek

(photo: The Yardley's)

The family Yardley
'Shaun, his wife and children

Steve Moria in his national kit

Below, award winning Kim Alroos and John Craighead

(photo:Sue Bailey)

THE 2010's and the silverware cabinet expands this decade with Cup, League and Play off success plus European glory

Jeff Dimmen    Brad Moran

Three players who hold the honour, in their career, of being a winner of the Continental Cup

Moran (second top point's scorer) as Captain lifted the 'plate' away on foreign ice in Italy.

Stephen Schultz, the top point's scorer of the season. Dimmen during that super final along with Robert Farmer was joint penalty taker. (Photos:Lisa Atkin)

****

The club and Jeremy Welsh showing their appreciation to volunteer 'sellers'. With flowers for Wendy Martin and Helen Westray-Cawthan on their 42nd year (photos these two pages:Nat Bashton)

More celebration with themed events, here is Paws looking a bit spooky.

Fans have sent me their photos as supporters are encouraged to be a sponsor too, here on an invited training session to meet the players

The 2021-22 players celebrating themselves at a sponsors own venue. Do you think that is Annie?

PAUL BREEZE Publications

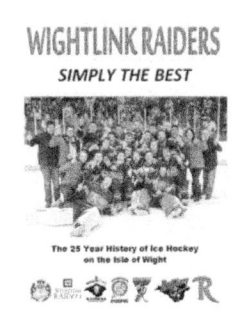

NIHL Yearbooks 2012 to 2018 also available

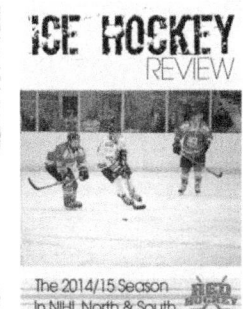

Mail Order via Amazon, www.poshupnorth.com,
www.icehockeyreview.co.uk and other quality outlets

STUART LATHAM books

List :
Ice Hockey in Solihull – ISBN No - 978-1-8384609-5-2
The History of Ice Hockey in Peterborough ISBN No: 978-0-9530608-6-3
The History of the Swindon Wildcats 1986 – 2016 ISBN No: 978-0-9530608-7-0
The History of the Swindon Wildcats 1986 – 2012 ISBN No; 9780953060832
The History of the Bracknell Bees ISBN No 978-0-9530608-8-7
60 Years of The Altrincham Aces ISBN No: 978-1-8381165-0-7
The Deeside Dragons ISBN No: 978-1-8381165-3-8
Ice Hockey in Bristol ISBN No: 978-1-8381165-2-1
The Manchester Storm ISBN No: 978-1-8381165-4-5
The Rise and Fall of the Manchester Phoenix ISBN No: 978-1-8381165-6-9
The Cardiff Devils – ISBN No: 978-1-8381165-9-0
Ice Hockey Memories – ISBN No: 978-1-8383328-0-8
The Slough Jets – ISBN No 978-1-8383328-2-2
More Ice Hockey Memories – ISBN No: 978-1-8383328-4-6
Ice Hockey in Edinburgh – ISBN No: 978-1-8383328-5-3
Stars Wars– Oxford City Stars – ISBN No: 978-1-8383328-9-1
Swindon Ice Hockey Statistically Speaking 1986-2021 – ISBN No: 978-1-8384609-0-7
In Their Own Words - Swindon Ice Hockey Memories – ISBN No: 978-1-8384609-1-4
Hockey in Haringey – ISBN No: 978-1-8384609-3-8
From Vikings to Devils - Ice Hockey on the Solent – ISBN No: 978-1-8384609-4-5

Email interest to:
Stuartlatham65@sky.com

CATCH UP – those recent seasons

2007-08

One International match
An International tournament
Non entry to the Knock Out Cup
A Charity Shield match

Challenge Cup Winners
League placing 3rd
Play-Off quarter finals

Charity Shield winners

Elite All-Star chosen - Shaun McAslan

Seasons Iron men: McAslan, Myers, Neilson, Pelltier and Shymr

Player's Player of the Year – Patrick Wallenberg

Returnees: M.Ellis, J.Ferrara, Lachowicz, A.Levers, McAslan, Meyers, Myers, Neil, Neilson, Rovnianek
Shmyr, Woolhouse

Also, Nottingham Lions win the English National League

Players in	Players not returning
ASKEY Tom n/m	BELL Jonny
BERGIN Kevin	CARDERELLI Joe
BULLAS Sam	COOKE James
CALVERT Ashley	CLARKE David
COLEMAN Jon	EMERSIC Blaz
DROUIN P.C.	FOORD Matt
FERRARA Robert	GALLANT Trevor
GRAHAM Joe	GRIFFITHS Richard n/m
HARTLEY Mark n/m	KRAJICEK Jan
HUTCHINSON James	LINDSEY Evan
JASZCZYK Andrew n/m	MORAN Paul
LEVERS Alan	PETRICKO Marcus
LEVERS Marc	PRINCE Jack
MOLIN Johan	REES Mike
NELSON Eric	SIMOES Steve
NORTON Tom	STEVENS Rod
PELLETIER Steve	
REYNOLDS Kurt	
RICHARDSON Mark	
SHEPHAERD Jim	
SMITH Julian	
STANCOK Robert	
THOMPSON Shaun	
WALLENBERG Patrick	

Rastislav Rovnianek and, on the right, equipment assistant Ramon Marvin

2007-08

CHALLENGE CUP QUARTER

DATE	VERSUS	SCORE			HOME/AWAY
SEPT	28 Belfast	4	-	3	A
	30 Cardiff	3	-	0	A
OCT	07 Basingstoke	4	-	4	H
	27 Coventry	1	-	0	H

semi-final

| NOV | 20 Newcastle | 5 | - | 4 | H |
| | 30 Newcastle | 5 | - | 1 | A |

Final

| JAN | 23 Sheffield | 6 | - | 3 | A |
| FEB | 20 Sheffield | 3 | - | 4 | H |

Nottingham win 9-7 on aggregate

BRITISH LEAGUE

DATE	VERSUS	SCORE			HOME/AWAY	
SEPT	08 Manchester	2	-	0	H	
	09 Newcastle	2	-	4	A	
	12 Sheffield	2	-	4	A	
	15 Cardiff	3	-	2	H	
	16 Hull	1	-	5	A	
	22 Belfast	6	-	4	H	
	23 Manchester	1	-	2	A	
OCT	02 Edinburgh	6	-	4	H	
	06 Basingstoke	2	-	1	A	ps
	13 Sheffield	1	-	2	H	
	14 Edinburgh	5	-	2	A	
	20 Newcastle	1	-	4	H	
	21 Coventry	0	-	4	A	
	24 Basingstoke	5	-	2	H	
NOV	03 Hull	8	-	2	A	
	04 Cardiff	1	-	2	H	
	10 Hull	5	-	2	H	
	11 Cardiff	2	-	6	A	
	18 Manchester	4	-	2	A	
	25 Edinburgh	5	-	4	A	
DEC	02 Cardiff	3	-	2	A	ps
	05 Manchester	2	-	0	H	
	09 Newcastle	4	-	0	A	
	14 Belfast	2	-	1	A	
	16 Edinburgh	3	-	2	H	OT
	22 Newcastle	4	-	2	H	
	23 Coventry	2	-	5	A	
	26 Coventry	3	-	1	H	
	29 Sheffield	2	-	3	H	ps
	30 Hull	5	-	2	A	

JAN	04 Hull	2	–	0	H		
	05 Belfast	1	–	2	A		
	12 Cardiff	5	–	3	H		
	13 Edinburg	0	–	3	A		
	19 Basingstoke	5	–	4	A		
	20 Belfast	2	–	6	H		
	26 Coventry	6	–	2	H		
	27 Manchester	4	–	3	A		
FEB	02 Sheffield	1	–	2	A		
	03 Cardiff	5	–	1	A		
	09 Edinburgh	1	–	2	H		
	10 Newcastle	3	–	0	A		
	13 Basingstoke	2	–	3	H	ps	
	16 Sheffield	6	–	1	H		
	17 Basingstoke	2	–	1	A		
	23 Belfast	5	–	1	H		
	24 Coventry	3	–	4	A	ps	
MAR	01 Coventry	1	–	5	H		
	04 Newcastle	6	–	2	H		
	07 Belfast	6	–	3	A		
	11 Basingstoke	7	–	0	H		
	15 Hull	4	–	2	H		
	16 Sheffield	1	–	3	A		
	22 Manchester	2	–	4	H		

BL Play-Offs

Quarter Final	Cardiff	3	–	4	H	
	Cardiff	3	–	3	A	

OTHERS

CHARITY SHIELD

SEPT	05 Coventry	7	–	6	Nottm	

INTERNATIONAL CHALLENGE GAMES

AUG	29 Morzine Penquins	3	–	2	OT

Epinal 4 Team Tournament

AUG	31 Les de Dijon	6	–	3	
SEPT	02 Epinal	5	–	4	

Red Bull Salzburg -2nd (u23) team
nb: declined match v Nottingham

Domestic season
Challenge Cup
Semi-Finals – aggregate score
Nottingham 5 Newcastle 4, Newcastle 1 Nottingham 5
Cardiff 4 Sheffield 4, Sheffield 2 Cardiff 0
Final-aggregate score
Sheffield 3 Nottingham 6, Nottingham 3 Sheffield 4

Nottingham win the Cup

*****

League table
2007-2008 Elite

	GP	RW	OW	PW	RL	OL	PL	GF	GA	GD	Pts
Coventry Blaze	54	36	3	2	11	2	0	217	127	90	84
Sheffield Steelers	54	33	1	4	14	0	2	190	128	62	78
Nottingham Panthers	54	30	1	2	18	0	3	172	133	39	69
Belfast Giants	54	29	2	2	19	2	0	184	150	34	68
Newcastle Vipers	54	24	0	4	22	3	1	159	174	-15	60
Cardiff Devils	54	23	1	2	25	1	2	164	174	-10	55
Manchester Pheonix	54	20	3	0	28	2	1	162	179	-17	49
Edinburgh Capitals	54	16	3	0	32	2	1	155	208	-53	41
Basingstoke Bison	54	13	1	2	33	3	2	172	224	-52	37
Hull Stingrays	54	12	1	0	34	1	6	119	197	-78	33

Play-offs

Quarter final
Cardiff beat Nottingham 7-6 on aggregate
Coventry beat Edinburgh 4-2 on aggregate
Sheffield beat Manchester 9-8 on aggregate
Newcastle beat Belfast on shoot-out after 6-6 tie

Semi final
Coventry 4 Newcastle 2
Sheffield 2 Cardiff 1

Final
Sheffield 2 Coventry 0

Player stats

Name	GP	GPi	Mins	Sts	GA	GAA	% sv	Pts	Pims	SO
Tom Askey	36	34	2050	950	77	2.26	91.89	0	4	4
Rastislav Rovnianek	26	24	1445	639	68	2.82	89.36	0	26	3
Geof Woolhouse	58	9	430	194	15	2.09	92.27	0	0	1
Andrew Jaszczyk	4	0								
Alan Levers	3	0								
Mark Hartley	3	0								

Name	Games	Goals	Assists	Points	Penalties
Sean McAslan	65	41	56	97	114
Patrik Wallenberg	64	34	46	80	74
Corey Neilson	65	17	50	67	156
Johan Molin	62	30	32	62	28
Kevin Bergin	52	24	20	44	49
Matthew Myers	65	10	21	31	76
Steve Pelletier	65	8	24	32	83
Marc Levers	63	10	16	26	52
Danny Meyers	63	1	21	22	51
Mark Richardson	47	8	14	22	16
Ryan Shmyr	65	6	13	19	279
P C Drouin	21	8	14	22	36
James Ferrara	63	2	9	11	14
Jon Colemen	19	4	5	9	12
Eric Nelson	19	1	8	9	20
Robert Stancok	39	4	5	9	115
Mike Ellis	20	1	3	4	16
Jim Shepperd	7	0	3	3	35
James Neil	61	1	1	2	0
Sam Bullas	26	1	1	2	0
Shaun Thompson	3	1	1	2	0
Robert Lachowicz	31	1	0	1	0
Joe Graham	29	0	0	0	4
Julian Smith	5	0	0	0	0
Tom Norton	4	0	0	0	0
Kurt Reynolds	2	0	0	0	0
James Hutchinson	2	0	0	0	0
Robert Ferrara	1	0	0	0	0
Ashley Calvert	1	0	0	0	0

Johnathan Boxhill played in French tour only

2008-09

> One International Match
> Two UK Challenge games
> Non entry to Knock Out cup
> Did not qualify for Charity Shield match

Challenge Cup quarter final
League placing 3rd
Play-off runners up

Seasons Iron men: Bergin, Cook, Neilson, Richardson, Toneys

Player's player of the year – Johan Molin

Returnees:
Bergin,Bullas,J.Ferrara,J.Graham,Lachowicz,M.Levers,Meyers,Molin,Myers,Neil,Neilson,Norton,M.Richardson,Woolhouse

Also, Nottingham Lions win the English National League play offs

Players in	Players not returning
CLARKE David	ASKEY Tom
COOK Brendan	BOXHILL Jonathan
GABRAITH Jade	CALVERT Ashley
GOLICIC Juri	COLEMAN Jon
HILL Ed	DROUIN P.C
LeCLAIR Corey	Ellis Mike - coach
N'DUR Ityoruman	FERRARA Robert
PARLEY Davis	HARTLEY Mark n/m
RICHARDSON Bruce	HUTCHINSON James
ROBINSON Michel	JASZCZYK Andrew n/m
TESSIER Dan	LEVERS Alan n/m
TONEYS Nick	McAslan Shaun
	NELSON Eric
	PELLETIER Steve
	ROVNIANEK Rastislav
	REYNOLDS Kurt
	SHEPHERD Jim
	SHMYR Ryan
	SMITH Julian
	STANCOK Robert
	THOMPSON Shaun
	WALLENBERG Patrik

(photo: Geraldine Ellis)

Bruce Richardson

2008-09

CHALLENGE CUP QUARTER

DATE	VERSUS	SCORE			HOME/AWAY
SEPT	28 Hull	2	-	2	A
OCT	26 Coventry	3	-	3	H
NOV	13 Cardiff *(Also a League fixture)*	4	-	1	H
	22 Basingstoke	3	-	5	A

BRITISH LEAGUE

DATE	VERSUS	SCORE				HOME/AWAY
SEPT	06 Newcastle	3	-	2		A
	07 Hull	6	-	2		H
	13 Edinburgh	6	-	0		H
	14 Manchester	5	-	3		A
	20 Sheffield	5	-	4		H
	21 Coventry	5	-	6		A
	27 Cardiff	5	-	1		H
OCT	4 Edinburh	6	-	1		A
	5 Edinburgh	6	-	5		A
	11 Hull	7	-	4		A
	12 Sheffield	3	-	6		A
	18 Manchester	1	-	4		H
	19 Cardiff	0	-	1	ot	A
	28 Basingstoke	4	-	6		H
NOV	01 Manchester	5	-	4		H
	02 Coventry	3	-	4	ps	A
	13 Cardiff Devils *(Also a Cup game)*	4	-	1		H
	15 Belfast	6	-	7		H
	16 Newcastle	3	-	1		A
	23 Hull	5	-	4	ps	H
	29 Newcastle	6	-	3		H
DEC	7 Newcastle	2	-	1	ps	A
	12 Belfast	3	-	4		A
	14 Belfast	7	-	2		H
	17 Basingstoke	3	-	2		A
	20 Cardiff	5	-	4	ps	H
	21 Coventry	4	-	0		A
	26 Sheffield	2	-	5		A
	27 Sheffield	2	-	1	ot	H
	30 Newcastle	3	-	0		H
JAN	3 Coventry	4	-	1		H
	4 Manchester	2	-	4		A
	7 Basingstoke	7	-	3		H
	11 Edinburgh	6	-	0		A
	17 Basingstoke	7	-	1		A
	18 Hull	2	-	3		H
	24 Cardiff	5	-	3		A
	25 Coventry	1	-	3		H
	31 Manchester	3	-	2		H

FEB		1	Manchester	4	-	2	A
		7	Edinburgh	5	-	2	H
		8	Hull	5	-	1	A
		13	Belfast	4	-	5	A
		14	Sheffield	3	-	4	A
		17	Coventry	5	-	6	H
		21	Newcastle	5	-	2	H
		25	Basingstoke	3	-	0	A
MAR		1	Hull	4	-	6	A
		7	Sheffield	4	-	2	H
		8	Basingstoke	7	-	2	a
		13	Belfast	7	-	5	A
		14	Edinburgh	3	-	2	H
		18	Belfast	4	-	3	H
		22	Cardiff	0	-	3	A

BL Play-Offs

Quarter Final

mar		28	Manchester	6	-	3	H
		29	Manchester	2	-	3	A

semi-final

	Coventry	5	-	2	nottm

final

	Sheffield	0	-	2	nottm

OTHERS

INTERNATIONAL CHALLENGE GAMES

NOV		9	Geneva	2	-	5	H

League games tied go into 5mins ot before possible ps for result
(thus 1pt for 60min game before extra point)
Cup games only played to regulation time of 60 mins
Play-Off games-

CH assumed Manchester (A) 31/08/08
Lost 7-5

Peterborough (A) 03/09/08
Won 5-0

Domestic season
Challenge Cup
Semi finals-aggregate score
Coventry 1 Belfast 1, Belfast 4 Coventry 1
Basingstoke 2 Manchester 5, Manchester 6 Basingstoke 1
Final-aggregate score
Belfast 3 Manchester 4, Manchester 1 Belfast 3

Belfast win the Cup

*****

League Table
2008-09 Elite

	GP	RW	OW	PW	RL	OL	PL	GF	GA	GD	Pts
Sheffield Steelers	54	35	3	3	6	2	5	201	115	86	89
Coventry Blaze	54	34	2	2	14	2	0	228	151	77	78
Nottingham Panthers	54	33	1	3	13	1	3	225	153	72	78
Belfast Giants	54	29	3	3	15	3	1	216	170	46	74
Cardiff Devils	54	21	4	3	19	1	6	172	141	31	63
Manchester Phoenix	54	22	3	2	23	2	2	198	179	19	58
Newcastle Vipers	54	14	2	5	29	0	4	146	183	-33	46
Edinburgh Capitals	54	18	0	1	29	3	3	179	243	-64	44
Hull Stingrays	54	13	1	2	33	3	2	154	243	-89	37
Basingstoke Bison	54	5	1	2	43	2	1	131	272	-141	19

Play-offs

Quarter final
Cardiff beat Belfast 6-5 on aggregate
Sheffield beat Edinburgh 12-7 on aggregate
Nottingham beat Manchester 9-5 on aggregate
Coventry beat Newcastle 6-4 on aggregate

Semi final
Sheffield 5 Cardiff 2
Coventry 2 Nottingham 6

Final
Sheffield 2 Nottingham 0

Player stats

Name............	GP	GPi	Mins	Sts	GA	GAA	% sv	Pts	Pims	SO
Michel Robinson		36	2181	1107	86	2.37	92.2	1	18	4
Geof Woolhouse		5	260	133	13	3	90.2	0	2	0
Davis Parley		21	1251	599	66	3.17	89	0	4	1

Name.......	Games	Goals	Assists	Points	Penalties
Brendan Cook	61	34	41	75	39
Jade Galbraith	59	23	52	75	53
Dan Tessier	53	21	53	74	99
Corey Neilson	61	16	52	68	145
Kevin Bergin	61	29	37	66	126
Bruce Richardson	61	14	47	61	133
Johan Molin	53	28	32	60	20
David Clarke	41	28	21	49	48
Matthew Myers	51	13	32	45	85
Marc Levers	57	11	19	30	54
Danny Meyers	55	6	16	22	55
Nick Toneys	61	3	8	11	84
James Ferrara	57	7	3	10	16
Mark Richardson	45	4	6	10	10
Ed Hill	20	0	7	7	16
Ruman Ndur	36	2	4	6	198
Robert Lachowicz	36	1	3	4	2
Juri Golicic	6	2	1	3	8
James Neil	28	2	0	2	0
Corey LeClair	6	1	1	2	4
Joe Graham	36	0	2	2	25
Tom Norton	16	0	0	0	2
Sam Bullas	22	0	0	0	2

****

NOTTINGHAM PANTHERS SOCIAL MEDIA

For the latest news on the team check out the club website

https://www.panthers.co.uk/

Merv Magus Cartoon

2009-10

20/20 hockey fest held in Sheffield
One International match
An International tournament in Hull
A Charity Shield match

Challenge Cup winners
League pacing 3rd
Play-Off semi final
Charity Shield runners up

Elite All-Star chosen: Jade Galbraith

Seasons Iron men; Galbraith, M.Levers, McAslan, Neilson

Player's player of the year –M.Levers

Returnees: Bergin, Bullas, D.Clarke, J.Ferrara, Galbraith, Lachowicz, M.Levers, Meyers, Molin, Neil, Neilson, Norton, B.Richardson,Toneys,Woolhouse

Players IN	Players NOT returning
BOWLEY Callum	COOK Brendan
DAGLIESH Ross	GOLICIC Juri
D'AMOUR Dominic	GRAHAM Joe
GASCON Mark	HILL Ed
HARPER Tristan	LeCLAIR Corey
HARTLEY Mark n/m	LEVERS Alan n/m
HENDERSON Jay	MYERS Matthew
LAROCQUE Mario	N'DUR Ityoruman
LEE Stephen	PARLEY Davis n/m
McASLAN Sean	RICHARDSON Mark
MANN Cameron	ROBINSON Michel
St.PIERRE Kevin n/m	TESSIER Dan
SOAR Tom	
WARD Josh	
WELDON Will	

(photo: Geraldine Ellis)

Geoff Woolhouse

2009-10

CHALLENGE CUP QUARTER

DATE	VERSUS	SCORE			HOME/AWAY	
SEPT	6 Coventry	5	-	3		A
	27 Hull	4	-	2		A
	30 Cardiff	3	-	2		A
OCT	10 Hull*	2	-	2	60 mins	H	also L game
	18 Coventry	3	-	1		H	
	25 Cardiff*	6	-	5		H	also L game

semi-final
| FEB | 3 Sheffield | 4 | - | 2 | A |
| | 10 Sheffield | 3 | - | 1 | H |

Final
| FEB | 28 Cardiff | 4 | - | 2 | A |
| MAR | 9 Cardiff | 4 | - | 5 | H |

nottingham win 8-7 on aggregate

BRITISH LEAGUE

DATE	VERSUS	SCORE				HOME/AWAY	
SEPT	5 Belfast	4	-	1		H	
	12 Coventry	2	-	1		H	
	13 Newcastle	3	-	5		A	
	19 Newcastle	4	-	3		H	
	20 Edinburgh	4	-	3	OT	A	
	26 Sheffield	5	-	2		A	
OCT	3 Belfast	6	-	2		H	
	10 Hull*	3	-	2	OT	H	also CC game
	11 Coventry	2	-	5		A	
	17 Cardiff	2	-	6		A	
	24 Belfast	0	-	3		A	
	25 Cardiff*	6	-	5		H	also CC game
	28 Newcastle	2	-	3		H	
	31 Edinburgh	5	-	3		H	
NOV	1 Edinburgh	4	-	5		A	
	7 Sheffield	6	-	3		H	
	8 Newcastle	1	-	2		A	
	10 Edinburgh	4	-	3		A	
	14 Hull	5	-	2		A	
	15 Cardiff	5	-	3		A	
	20 Belfast	3	-	6		A	
	21 Belfast	0	-	4		H	
	29 Cardiff	2	-	1		H	
DEC	5 Coventry	6	-	2		H	
	6 Coventry	4	-	6		A	
	12 Newcastle	3	-	2		A	
	13 Hull	4	-	3	PS	H	
	19 Edinburgh	7	-	3		H	
	20 Hull	4	-	5		A	
	26 Sheffield	2	-	1		H	
	27 Sheffield	5	-	3		A	
	30 Cardiff	5	-	0		H	

JAN	2	Hull	4	-	1		H
	3	Edinburgh	1	-	5		A
	9	Edinburgh	4	-	3	OT	H
	10	Hull	6	-	3		A
	16	Newcastle	10	-	3		H
	17	Cardiff	2	-	3	OT	A
	23	Sheffield	5	-	2		H
	24	Coventry	3	-	1		A
	29	Belfast	2	-	4		A
	30	Belfast	1	-	3		A
FEB	6	Hull	9	-	1		H
	7	Coventry	3	-	5		A
	13	Sheffield	4	-	6		A
	14	Belfast	3	-	1		H
	17	Newcastle	4	-	5		H
	20	Coventry	7	-	2		H
	27	Cardiff	2	-	3	PS	H
MAR	6	Sheffield	4	-	3	PS	H
	7	Hull	7	-	6		A
	13	Coventry	8	-	3		H
	14	Cardiff	0	-	3		A
	17	Edinburgh	3	-	2		H
	20	Sheffield	2	-	6		A
	21	Newcastle	3	-	5		A

BL Play-Offs

Quarter Final

Mar	27	Edinburgh	4	-	4	A
	28	Edinburgh	5	-	0	H

semi Final

APR		Belfast	1	-	2	PS	at Nottingham

OTHERS

Charity Sheild

Sept	2	Sheffield	6	-	7	PS	H

Challenge Games

INTERNATIONAL CHALLENGE GAMES
HULL (P and O Ferries Cup)   at HULL

AUG	30	Tilburg Trappers (Netherla	11	-	3	
	31	Hull	2	-	3	

NB) Stanley Kegg Cup
Played as Nottingham Panthers. A selection of players and young whilst at camp in Canada.
Included some former and non Panthers
Also an all-day Hoktoberfest AT Sheffield involved all club teams on short games on a KO basis.

League games tied go into 5mins ot before possible ps for result (thus 1pt for 60 min drawn game)
Cup games only played to regulation time of 60 mins

20/20 fest   Play-Off games-
                at sheffield

Domestic season
Challenge Cup
Semi finals-aggregate score
Cardiff 5 Belfast 2, Belfast 5 Cardiff 3
Sheffield 2 Nottingham 4, Nottingham 3 Sheffield 1
Final-aggregate score
Cardiff 2 Nottingham 4, Nottingham 4 Cardiff 5

Nottingham win the Cup

*****

League Table
2009-10 Elite

	GP	RW	OW	PW	RL	OL	PL	GF	GA	GD	Pts
Coventry	56	33	4	1	18	0	0	228	174	+54	76
Belfast	56	34	0	1	16	2	3	212	137	+75	75
Nottingham	56	29	3	2	20	1	1	215	177	+38	70
Cardiff	56	25	4	2	22	1	2	193	158	+35	65
Sheffield	56	21	0	3	26	3	3	194	196	-02	54
Edinburgh	56	18	2	2	26	5	3	177	224	-47	52
Newcastle	56	17	1	3	31	1	3	165	236	-71	46
Hull	56	14	1	4	32	2	3	152	234	-82	43

Play offs

Quarter final
Coventry beat Hull 6-2 on aggregate
Belfast beat Newcastle 10-3 on aggregate
Nottingham beat Edinburgh 9-4 on aggregate
Cardiff beat Sheffield 9-5 on aggregate

Semi final
Coventry 3 Cardiff 6
Belfast 2 Nottingham 1

Final
Belfast 3 Cardiff 2

Player stats

Name	GP	GPi	Mins	Sts	GA	GAA	%sv	Pts	Pims	SO
Kenin St.Pierre	62	62	3712	1923	174	2.81	90.95	3	10	2
Geoff Woolhouse	7	5	294	144	18	3.67	87.50	1	0	0
Mark Hartley	67	6	110	59	5	2.73	91.52	0	0	0

Name…….	Games	Goals	Assists	Points	Penalties
Jade Galbraith	68	25	72	97	106
Sean McAslan	68	43	44	87	64
David Clarke	67	37	39	76	106
Cameron Mann	61	36	33	69	107
Corey Neilson	68	16	50	66	143
Bruce Richardson	63	18	46	64	132
Marty Gascon	66	16	49	65	26
Kevin Bergin	55	16	27	43	106
Dominic D'Amour	65	13	24	37	219
Marc Levers	68	16	19	35	131
Jay Henderson	21	5	9	14	60
Johan Molin	16	4	7	11	6
Danny Meyers	62	2	9	11	44
Stephen Lee	64	3	6	9	112
Ross Dalgleish	53	4	4	8	50
Marion Larocque	21	2	5	7	80
Nick Toneys	33	1	6	7	28
Robert Lachowicz	12	1	3	4	2
Tom Norton	58	0	2	2	4
Josh Ward	22	1	0	1	2
Tom Soar	3	0	1	1	0
James Ferrara	21	0	0	0	4
Tristan Harper	1	0	0	0	2
James Neil	6	0	0	0	0
Sam Bullas	6	0	0	0	0
Will Weldon	3	0	0	0	0
Callam Bowley	2	0	0	0	0
Joe Graham	1	0	0	0	0

Kevin Birgin
(photo:Geraldine Ellis)

2010-11

20/20 hockey fest in Nottingham
One International match

Challenge Cup winners
League placing 4th
Play off winners

Seasons Iron men: Clarke, Green, Lachowicz, Neilson, Ryan

Player's player of the year – Guillaume Lepine

Returnees: Bowley, D.Clarke, Galbraith, Lachowicz, Lee, M.Levers, Meyers, Neilson, Norton, St.Pierre, Soar, Ward, Weldon

LIONS CONTACT

- - - - - - - - - - - - -

Keep in touch with Nottingham prospects
http://nihc.co.uk
https://www.facebook.com/LionsENL/

- - - - - - - - - - - - -

Players IN	Players NOT returning
BEAUREGARD David	BERGIN Kevin
BELLAMY Rob	BULLAS Sam
GREEN Dan	DALGLIESH Ross
HEEREMA Jeff	D'AMOUR Dominic
KOWALSKI Craig n/m	FERRARA James
LEPINE Guillaume	GASCON Marty
LEVERS Alan n/m	HARPER Tristan
LISCAK Robert	HARTLEY Mark n/m
McDonald Ian	LAROCQUE Mario
MYERS Matthew	McASLAN Sean
NIKOLOV Angel	MANN Cameron
PENNER Alex	MOLIN Johan
RYAN Billy	NEIL James
SPROUT Dustin	RICHARDSON Bruce
TKACZUK Daniel	TONEYS Nick
ZION Jonathan	WOOLHOUSE Geoff n/m

(photo: Marclevers)

Marc Levers

2010-11

CHALLENGE CUP QUARTER

DATE	VERSUS	SCORE			HOME/AWAY	
SEPT	19 Coventry	3	-	3	A	
OCT	27 Sheffield	1	-	3	H	
	29 Sheffield	5	-	2	A	
NOV	2 Hull	5	-	0	H	also league
	13 Cardiff	2	-	2	H	also league
	20 Coventry	3	-	1	H	
	28 Hull	1	-	1	A	
JAN	19 Cardiff	3	-	3	A	

Semi-Final
JAN	26 Newcastle - 1st leg	3	-	4	A	
	30 Newcastle - 2nd leg	15	-	0	H	also league

Final
FEB	8 Belfast - 1st leg	3	-	1	H
	16 Belfast - 2nd leg	1	-	2	A

Nottingham win 4-3 on aggregate

BRITISH LEAGUE

DATE	VERSUS	SCORE				HOME/AWAY	
SEPT	4 Belfast	4	-	3	PS	H	
	5 Coventry	7	-	4		A	
	11 Cardiff	5	-	4		H	
	12 Dundee	9	-	4		A	
	18 Coventry	6	-	4		H	
	25 Braehead	3	-	4		H	
OCT	3 Belfast	3	-	5		A	
	9 Sheffield	1	-	4		H	
	13 Braehead	5	-	2		A	
	16 Dundee	12	-	2		H	
	17 Hull	3	-	2		A	
	23 Edinburgh	8	-	2		H	
	24 Dundee	7	-	4		A	
	31 Newcastle	6	-	2		A	
NOV	2 Hull	5	-	0		H	also Cup
	6 Braehead	6	-	3		A	
	7 Edinburgh	5	-	4		A	
	13 Cardiff	2	-	3	PS	H	also Cup
	14 Dundee	3	-	2		A	
	21 Newcastle	4	-	2		A	
	27 Edinburgh	7	-	1		H	
DEC	4 Coventry	1	-	2		A	
	5 Hull	4	-	5	PS	H	
	11 Edinburgh	4	-	5		A	
	12 Edinburgh	11	-	5		A	
	26 Sheffield	3	-	6		A	
	27 Sheffield	3	-	5		H	

	29	Braehead	2 - 3	PS	H	
JAN	2	Dundee	6 - 5	PS	H	
	3	Newcastle	11 - 4		A	
	7	Belfast	3 - 4	PS	H	
	8	Cardiff	5 - 6		H	
	9	Hull	3 - 0		A	
	14	Belfast	3 - 2	PS	A	
	15	Belfast	2 - 7		A	
	22	Hull	3 - 1		H	
	23	Braehead	3 - 6		A	
	30	Newcastle	15 - 0		H	also Cup
FEB	2	Cardiff	5 - 6	OT	A	
	5	Sheffield	1 - 6		A	
	6	Newcastle	5 - 6		A	
	8	Coventry	3 - 1		H	
	12	Sheffield	4 - 3	PS	A	
	13	Braehead	4 - 3	PS	H	
	18	Dundee	6 - 3		H	
	20	Coventry	5 - 1		A	
	23	Newcastle	4 - 1		H	
	26	Coventry	3 - 2		H	
	27	Cardiff	1 - 3		A	
MAR	4	Edinburgh	16 - 0		H	
	6	Sheffield	4 - 1		H	
	13	Cardiff	1 - 2	PS	A	
	19	Belfast	2 - 6		H	
	20	Hull	1 - 6		A	

BL Play-Offs

Quarter Final

MAR	25	Braehead	5 - 4	A
	26	Braehead	3 - 0	H

Semi-Final

APR	3	Sheffield	4 - 3	OT	at Nottingham

FINAL

APR	4	Cardiff	5 - 4	at Nottingham

OTHERS

Challenge Games

MAR 12 20/20 Tournament (Braehead,Coventry,Nottingham,Sheffield)
Nottm 1-3 Braehead, Nottm 5-2 Sheffield, Nottm 3-0 Coventry.
FINAL - Braehead 3-0 Nottm
20 mins straight with pims stoptime.

INTERNATIONAL CHALLENGE GAMES

SEPT	28	Tilburgh Trappers	7 - 5

OCT 2 Boston v Belfast select inc Panthers players Kowalski, Zion, Neilson, Beauregard and Galbraith

Domestic season
Challenge Cup
Semi-finals- aggregate score
Newcastle 4 Nottingham 3, Nottingham 15 Newcastle 0
Belfast 4 Cardiff 0, Cardiff 2 Belfast 1
Final-aggregate score
Nottingham 3 Belfast 1, Belfast 2 Nottingham 1

Nottingham win the Cup

∙∙∙

League Table
2010-11 Elite

	GP	RW	OW	PW	RL	OL	PL	GF	GA	GD	Pts
Sheffield	54	40	1	2	10	0	1	265	132	133	87
Cardiff	54	37	2	3	9	2	1	269	141	128	87
Belfast	54	37	2	2	9	2	2	239	130	109	86
Nottingham	54	28	0	5	15	1	5	260	179	81	72
Braehead	54	24	2	2	23	0	3	206	174	32	59
Coventry	54	21	1	1	27	2	2	198	185	13	50
Hull	54	20	1	2	28	3	0	178	202	-24	49
Dundee	54	15	0	4	32	0	3	178	235	-57	41
Newcastle	54	11	1	0	40	0	2	151	282	-131	26
Edinburgh	54	5	1	0	45	1	2	134	418	-284	15

∙∙∙

Play-Offs

Quarter final
Sheffield beat Dundee 8-4 on aggregate
Nottingham beat Braehead 8-4 on aggregate
Cardiff beat Hull 8-4 on aggregate
Belfast beat Coventry in shoot out after 3-3 aggregate score

Semi final
Sheffield 3 Nottingham 4
Cardiff 4 Belfast 1

Final
Nottingham 5 Cardiff 4

Player stats

Name	GP	GPi	Mins	shots	GA	GAA	%sv	Pts	Pims	SO
Craig Kowalski	61	59	3397	1806	150	2.65	91.7	1	18	5
Dan Green	67	13	376	205	30	4.79	85.4	0	2	0
Kevin St.Pierre	5	5	293	148	21	4.30	85.8	0	2	0
Alan Levers	1	0								

Name…….	Games	Goals	Assists	Points	Penalties
Jade Galbraith	60	28	69	97	99
David Clarke	67	46	39	85	61
Billy Ryan	67	31	48	79	64
Matthew Myers	64	25	46	71	115
David Beaurgard	66	34	35	69	68
Corey Neilson	67	11	52	63	120
Rob Bellamy	56	23	32	55	84
Jeff Heerema	35	22	20	42	38
Marc Levers	54	10	26	36	24
Jonathan Zion	39	9	24	33	22
Robert Lachowicz	67	12	18	30	6
Ian McDonald	34	12	17	29	16
Angel Nikolov	53	2	27	29	40
Danny Meyers	60	7	18	25	40
Stephen Lee	61	3	19	22	100
Dustin Sproat	17	6	12	18	33
Daniel Tkaczuk	12	2	11	13	18
Guillaume Lepine	62	4	8	12	245
Alex Penner	30	4	5	9	289
Jeremy Van Hoof	18	1	3	4	10
Josh Ward	39	0	4	4	6
Tom Norton	65	2	1	3	18
Will Weldon	2	1	0	1	0
Robert Liscak	4	0	1	1	6
Callum Bowley	1	0	0	0	0
Tom Soar	1	0	0	0	0

On the left, the late Andy Smith 'goal judge'

2011-12

Two UK change matches

Challenge Cup winners
League placing 3rd
Play off winners

Elite All Star chosen: Corey Neilson

Seasons Iron men: Beauregard, Fox, Francis, Lachowicz and Wilson

Player's player of the year – Jordon Fox

Returnees: Beauregard, Bowley, D.Clarke, Green, Heerema, Kowalski, Lachowicz, lee, Lepine, M.Levers, Meyers, Myers, Neilson, Norton, Soar, Ward

- - - - - - - - - - - - -
A forum for the fans
https://thecageforum.proboards.com/
- - - - - - - - - - - - -

Players IN	Players NOT returning
BENEDICT Brandon	BELLAMY Rob
BETTERIDGE Oliver	GALBRAITH Jade
CHAMPAGNE Scott	LEVERS Alan n/m
FOX Jordon	LISCAK Robert
FRANCIS Matt	McDONALD Ian
GORDON Rhett	NIKOLOV Angel
GOSPEL Sam n/m	PENNER Alex
McASLAN Sean	RYAN Billy
MAYNARD Marcus	St.PIERRE Kevin n/m
ROSE Danny	SPROUT Dustin
RYHANEN Sami	TKACZUK Daniel
WILSON Brock	VAN HOOF Jeremy
	WELDON Will
	ZION Jonathan

(photo:Geraldine Ellis)

Shaun McAslan

2011-12

CHALLENGE CUP QUARTER

DATE	VERSUS	SCORE			HOME/AWAY	
Sept	03 Cardiff Devils	6	-	1	H	also league
	04 Cardiff Devils	1	-	4	A	
	07 Coventry Blaze	10	-	1	H	
	21 Hull Stingrays	6	-	2	H	also league
Oct	02 Hull Stingrays	3	-	2	A	
	16 Sheffield Steelers	4	-	2	A	
	22 Sheffield Steelers	3	-	0	H	
Nov	27 Coventry Blaze	5	-	5	A	

Semi-Final

Jan	14 Braehead Clan	3	-	4	A	also league
	15 Braehead Clan	3	-	0	H	

Final

Mar	7 Belfast	5	-	1	A	
	13 Belfast	5	-	3	H	

BRITISH LEAGUE

DATE	VERSUS	SCORE			HOME/AWAY	
Sept	03 Cardiff Devils	6	-	1	H	also Cup
	11 Edinburgh	5	-	1	A	
	17 Fife Flyers	6	-	2	A	
	18 Edinburgh Capitals	8	-	0	A	
	21 Hull Stingrays	6	-	2	H	also Cup
	24 Belfast Giants	1	-	2	A	
	25 Dundee Stars	4	-	1	A	
Oct	01 Coventry Blaze	6	-	7	H	
	08 Edinburgh Capitals	7	-	3	H	
	09 Braehead Clan	3	-	0	H	
	15 Hull Stingrays	3	-	2	A	
	19 Braehead Clan	8	-	3	A	
	23 Coventry Blaze	3	-	4	A	
	26 Dundee Stars	6	-	0	H	
	29 Belfast Giants	2	-	3	H	
Nov	05 Cardiff Devils	1	-	3	A	
	06 Fife Flyers	3	-	2	H	
	12 Sheffield Steelers	1	-	0	H	
	13 Fife Flyers	8	-	1	A	
	20 Sheffield Steelers	2	-	3	A	
	26 Hull Stingrays	6	-	1	H	
	30 Cardiff Devils	4	-	3	A	
Dec	04 Dundee Capitals	5	-	4	H	
	08 Edinburgh Capitals	6	-	2	H	
	17 Coventry Blaze	3	-	4	H	
	20 Braehead Clan	3	-	1	H	

	23	Dundee Capitals	6	-	4	A	
	26	Sheffield Steelers	5	-	3	A	
	27	Sheffield Steelers	5	-	1	H	
	29	Hull Stingrays	9	-	3	A	
Jan	02	Hull Stingrays	5	-	0	H	
	03	Braehaed Clan	3	-	6	A	
	07	Cardiff Devils	2	-	4	H	
	08	Cardiff Devils	4	-	1	A	
	14	Braehaed Clan	3	-	4	A	also Cup
	21	Belfast Giants	3	-	2	A	
	22	Fife Flyers	4	-	1	H	
	28	Coventry Blaze	6	-	1	H	
	29	Coventry Blaze	6	-	1	A	
Feb	4	Dundee Stars	6	-	2	H	
	11	Belfast Giants	3	-	4	A	
	12	Belfast Giants	2	-	3	A	
	14	Sheffield Steelers	2	-	4	A	
	18	Sheffield Steelers	5	-	1	H	
	19	Edinburgh Capitals	9	-	0	A	
	25	Cardiff devils	6	-	3	H	
	26	Fife Flyers	4	-	3	A	
Mar	3	Fife Flyers	4	-	3	H	
	4	Coventry Blaze	3	-	5	A	
	8	Dundee Stars	3	-	8	A	
	10	Hull Stingrays	4	-	1	A	
	18	Braehead Clan	4	-	3	H	
	23	Edinburgh Capitals	7	-	0	H	
	24	Belfast Giants	3	-	4	A	

BL Play-Offs

Quarter Final

Mar	27	Braehead Clan	0	-	3	A
	31	Braehead Clan	5	-	1	H

Semi-Final

April	7	Hull Stingrays	10	-	3	at Nottingham

FINAL

April	8	Cardiff Devils	2	-	0	at Nottingham

OTHERS

Challenge Games

Aug	27	Belfast Giants	1	-	2	A
	28	Belfast Giants	4	-	2	A

Domestic season
Challenge Cup
Semi Finals-on aggregate
Braehead 3 Nottingham 2, Nottingham 3 Braehead 2
Cardiff 2 Belfast 1, Belfast 4 Cardiff 1
Final-aggregate score
Belfast 1 Nottingham 5, Nottingham 5 Belfast 3

Nottingham win the Cup

*****

League Table
2011-12 Elite

	GP	RW	OW	PW	RL	OL	PL	GF	GA	GD	Pts
Belfast	54	39	2	5	5	1	2	237	102	135	95
Sheffield	54	32	5	4	11	1	1	209	130	79	84
Nottingham	54	35	2	1	12	2	2	241	129	112	80
Cardiff	54	30	2	0	12	4	6	191	158	33	74
Coventry	54	26	3	3	20	1	1	203	159	44	66
Braehead	54	26	2	3	19	2	2	204	179	25	66
Hull	54	12	0	4	34	2	2	143	220	-77	36
Dundee	54	10	1	2	35	3	3	140	215	-75	32
Edinburgh	54	10	2	1	37	1	3	133	265	-132	30
Fife	54	5	0	3	40	3	3	110	254	-144	22

....

Play-Offs

Quarter Final
Nottingham beat Braehead 5-4 on aggregate
Belfast beat Dundee 14-0 on aggregate
Cardiff beat Coventry 7-4 on aggregate
Hull beat Sheffield 7-4 on aggregate

Semi final
Cardiff 4 Belfast 3 after shoot out
Nottingham 10 Hull 3

Final
Cardiff 0 Nottingham 2

Player stats

Name	GP	GPi	Mins	SOG	GA	GAA	%sv	Pts	Pims	SO
Craig Kowalski	66	64	3686	1579	120	1.95	92.4	3	4	10
Dan Green	67	19	356	190	31	5.22	83.7	0	0	0
Sam Gospel	1	0								

Name…….	Games	Goals	Assists	Points	Penalties
Jordan Fox	67	29	56	85	82
David Beauregard	67	44	36	80	72
David Clarke	63	43	32	75	60
Matt Francis	67	28	40	68	33
Brandon Benedict	66	23	40	63	50
Corey Neilson	66	13	48	61	119
Matthew Myers	64	20	40	60	50
Robert Lachowicz	67	23	33	56	14
Sami Ryhanen	33	9	28	37	22
Scott Champagne	29	9	28	37	22
Jeff Heerema	31	13	23	36	49
Brock Wilson	67	7	29	36	127
Marc Levers	66	11	20	31	57
Danny Myers	56	7	19	26	27
Guillaume Lepine	66	7	18	25	191
Stephen Lee	63	5	16	21	102
Rhett Gordon	23	4	17	21	12
Sean McAslan	4	1	1	2	2
Marcus Maynard	49	0	2	2	4
Tom Norton	12	0	2	2	4
Josh Ward	7	0	2	2	2
Danny Rose	6	0	0	0	0
Ollie Betteridge	5	0	0	0	0
Callum Bowley	2	0	0	0	0
Tom Soar	1	0	0	0	0

(photo:Geraldine Ellis)
Danny Meyers and Media man Chris Ellis

2012-13

Two International matches

Challenge Cup winners
League Winners
Play off winners

Elite All Star chosen: Graham, Kowalski, Ling, Werner

Seasons Iron men: Francis, Lachowicz, Ling, M.Levers, Myers and Werner

Player's player of the year – David Ling

And Elites top points - David Ling
Elites Top % net minder – Craig Kowalski

Returnees: Beauregard, Benedict, Betteridge, Clarke, Fox, Francis, Gospel, Green, Kowalski, Lachowicz, Lee, Lepine, M.Levers, Myers, Neilson, Norton, Ward

(And, Lions are the National League winners)

Players IN	Players NOT returning
BECKETT Jason	BOWLEY Callum
BOWLEY Callum	CHAMPAYNE Scott
FERRARA Luke	GORDON Rhett
GALLIVAN Pat	HEEREMA Jeff
GRAHAM Bruce	McASLAN Sean
HOOK Lewis	MAYNARD Marcus
HOVEL Tom n/m	MEYERS Danny
LING David	ROSE Danny
STEWART Anthony	RYHANEN Sami
TUMA Martin	SOAR Thomas
WEAVER Johnathan	WILSON Brock
WERNER Eric	
WILSON Kelsey	

(photo: D.Beauregard)

David Beauregard

2012-13

CHALLENGE CUP - first round

DATE	VERSUS	SCORE		HOME/AWAY	
Sept	08 Hull	4 - 2		A	
	23 Cardiff	5 - 6	OT	A	
Oct	02 Cardiff	4 - 2		H	also L
	13 Hull	6 - 0		H	also L
	14 Coventry	1 - 3		A	
Nov	04 Sheffield	3 - 4	OT	A	
	16 Sheffield	3 - 2		H	
Dec	05 Coventry	4 - 3		H	also L

Q-Final

Jan	22 Fife - 1st leg	3 - 2	A
	30 Fife - 2nd leg	5 - 2	H
	Nottingham win 8-4 on aggregate		

S-Final

Feb	13 Belfast - 1st leg	5 - 1	H
	26 Belfast - 2nd leg	4 - 3	A
	Nottingham win 9-4 on aggregate		

Final

Mar	20 Sheffield - 1st leg	4 - 1	A
Apr	02 Sheffield - 2nd leg	1 - 2	H
	Nottingham win 5-3 on aggregate		

BRITISH LEAGUE

DATE	VERSUS	SCORE		HOME/AWAY	
Sept	08 Dundee	5 - 1		H	
	15 Belfast	3 - 5		H	
	16 Belfast	3 - 2	PS	H	
	22 Sheffield	2 - 3		H	
	29 Sheffield	2 - 1	PS	A	
Oct	02 Cardiff	4 - 2		H	also C
	05 Coventry	4 - 2		H	
	06 Belfast	2 - 3	PS	A	
	13 Hull	6 - 0		H	also C
	21 Cardiff	1 - 2		A	
	26 Braehead	5 - 1		A	
	27 Edinburgh	5 - 0		A	
	28 Fife	5 - 3		A	
	30 Edinburgh	10 - 0		H	
Nov	02 Braehead	5 - 4	OT	H	
	18 Coventry	2 - 5		A	
	24 Cardiff	5 - 0		H	
	30 Belfast	3 - 2	PS	A	

Dec	02	Dundee	5	-	1		A
	05	Coventry	4	-	3		H	also C
	08	Cardiff	3	-	2	PS	A
	08	Hull	8	-	4		H
	12	Edinburgh	1	-	2		H
	15	Hull	3	-	1		A
	16	Belfast	6	-	1		H
	22	Fife	7	-	1		H
	23	Coventry	8	-	0		A
	26	Sheffield	3	-	2	PS	H
	27	Sheffield	4	-	9		A
	29	Dundee	8	-	1		H
Jan	05	Coventry	1	-	0		H
	06	Coventry	4	-	1		A
	12	Cardiff	4	-	1		H
	19	Belfast	4	-	5		H
	20	Sheffield	4	-	2		A
	26	Coventry	8	-	3		H
	27	Cardiff	4	-	2		A
Feb	02	Coventry	6	-	2		A
	03	Sheffield	2	-	5		A
	16	Braehead	7	-	3		H
	17	Fife	5	-	3		H
	22	Sheffield	4	-	2		H
	23	Braehead	5	-	0		A
Mar	01	Dundee	4	-	1		A
	02	Fife	10	-	2		A
	03	Edinburgh	6	-	1		A
	08	Sheffield	2	-	0		H
	10	Hull	3	-	1		A
	15	Belfast	5	-	3		A
	16	Belfast	2	-	5		A
	22	Cardiff	4	-	3	PS	H
	24	Cardiff	6	-	3		A

BL Play-Offs

Quarter Final

Mar	30	Fife - 1st leg	2	-	4	A
	31	Fife - 2nd leg	3	-	0	H
		Nottingham win 5-4 on aggregate				

Semi-Final

Apr	06	Cardiff	6	-	3	at Nottingham

FINAL

Apr	07	Belfast	3	-	2	OT	at Nottingham

International Challenge Games

Sept	01	Asiago (Italy)	6	-	3	H
	02	Asiago (Italy)	5	-	6	H
		For the Alladin Cup over a series of 2 games				
		(0-1, 20min mini 3rd game resulted in Asiago win)				

Domestic season
Challenge Cup
Quarter finals-aggregate score
Hull 1 Belfast 3, Belfast 5 Hull 4
Coventry 2 Braehead 2, Braehead 4 Coventry 3
Fife 2 Nottingham 3, Nottingham 5 Fife 2
Dundee 4 Sheffield 2, Sheffield 7 Dundee 0
Semi finals-aggregate score
Nottingham 5 Belfast 1, Belfast 3 Nottingham 4
Braehead 2 Sheffield 4, Sheffield 4 Braehead 2
Finals-aggregate score
Sheffield 1 Nottingham 4, Nottingham 1 Sheffield 2
Nottingham win the Cup

League table
2012-13 Elite

	GP	RW	OW	PW	RL	OL	PL	GF	GA	GD	Pts
Nottingham	52	35	1	6	9	0	1	232	111	121	85
Belfast	52	33	1	3	10	2	3	191	132	59	79
Sheffield	52	28	5	2	14	0	3	184	133	51	73
Coventry	52	18	3	3	22	4	2	157	181	-24	54
Cardiff	52	16	4	1	23	2	6	160	168	-8	50
Edinburgh	52	18	1	3	26	3	1	149	184	-35	48
Fife	52	17	2	4	27	1	1	154	176	-22	48
Braehead	52	16	0	4	26	6	0	163	200	-37	46
Dundee	52	14	3	2	27	2	4	138	194	-56	44
Hull	52	15	2	0	26	2	7	137	186	-49	43

Play offs

Quarter Final
Belfast beat Edinburgh 7-4 on aggregate
Cardiff beat Braehead 12-9 on aggregate
Nottingham beat Fife 5-4 on aggregate
Coventry beat Sheffield 6-5 on aggregate

Semi final
Nottingham 6 Cardiff 3
Belfast 5 Coventry 1

Final – Nottingham 3 Belfast 2

Player stats

Name	GP	Gpi	Mins	Shots	GA	GAA	%sv	Pts	Pims	SO
Craig Kowalski	64	64	3721	1583	128	2.06	91.9	1	18	8
Dan Green	67	17	342	157	17	2.98	89.2	0	0	0
Sam Gospel	5	1	4	5	0	0.00	100	0	0	0
Tom Hoval	1	0								

Name…….	Games	Goals	Assists	Points	Penalties
David Ling	67	38	70	108	160
Bruce Graham	66	42	37	79	59
Matt Francis	67	26	41	67	61
Matt Fox	63	16	51	67	47
David Clarke	61	27	38	65	65
Pat Galivan	62	24	35	59	31
Brandon Benedict	65	19	37	56	42
Robert Lachowicz	67	20	31	51	8
Matthew Myers	67	19	29	48	74
Jonathan Weaver	55	10	35	45	27
Eric Werner	67	7	33	40	28
Guillaume Lepine	60	4	17	21	165
Kelsey Wilson	34	10	9	19	112
Jason Beckett	66	5	12	17	192
Stephen Lee	58	2	11	13	45
Anthony Stewart	19	6	5	11	14
David Beaurgard	8	1	6	7	2
Marc Levers	67	0	7	7	16
Corey Neilson	9	0	6	6	18
Josh Ward	61	2	3	5	2
Martin Tuma	12	0	1	1	43
Tom Norton	3	0	0	0	0
Ollie Betteridge	2	0	0	0	0

Callum Bowley, Lewis Hook and Luke Ferrara only challenge games

Away travel to Blackpool by TRAIN

2013-14

Two International Tournaments
The European Continental Cup

Challenge Cup winners
League placing 4th
Play off quarter final
Continental Cup 3rd round

Seasons Iron men: Norton, Weaver

Player's player of the year – Matt Francis

Returnees: Benedict, Betteridge, Clarke, Francis, Green, Kowalski, Lachowicz, Lee, Neilson, Norton, Weaver, Werner

(Also Lions runners up in National play offs)

Players IN	Players NOT returning
ANDERSON Nic	BEAUGUARD David
BOXHILL Jonathan	BECKETT Jason
CAPRARO Chris	BOWLEY Callum
CONWAY Neil n/m	FERRARA Luke
FARMER Robert	FOX Jordon
GRIMALDI Joe	GALLIVAN Pat
HENLEY Brent	GOSPEL Sam n/m
JACINA Greg	GRAHAN Bruce
JENSON Joe	HOOK Lewis
KALUS Petr	HOVEL Tom n/m
LYONS Lynn	LING David
MAKELA Tuuka	MYERS Matthew
MURRAY Chris	STEWART Anthony
ORESKOVIC Phil	TUMA Martin
RYAN Matt	WARD Josh
SAARI Joonas	WILSON Kelsey
SALTERS Leigh	
WREN Bob	

Petr Kalus played this season then returned to help out three seasons later for our Continental Cup endeavour and came back with a winner's medal.

Stats from matches
13/14 -- 47games, 18 goals, 22 assists, 63 penalty minutes
16/17 -- 13 games, 3 goals, 5 assists, 13 penalty minutes
(16/17 -- Continental Cup – 6 games, 3 goals, 4 assists, 8 penalty minutes)

2013-14

CHALLENGE CUP - first round

DATE		VERSUS	SCORE			HOME/AWAY	
Sept	7	Hull	9	-	3	H	also L
	8	Sheffield	4	-	1	A	
	21	Sheffield	7	-	3	H	
	22	Cardiff	5	-	3	A	
Oct	6	Coventry	6	-	1	A	
	12	Coventry	5	-	3	H	
	13	Hull	6	-	4	A	
Dec	1	Cardiff	3	-	2	H	also L

Q-Final

Dec	15	Braehead - 1st leg	8	-	0	H	also L
Jan	8	Braehead - 2nd leg	2	-	7	A	
		Nottingham won 10-7 on aggregate					

Semi-Final

Feb	12	Sheffield - 1st leg	5	-	3	A	
	18	Sheffield - 2nd leg	6	-	4	H	
		Nottingham won 11-7 on aggregate					

FINAL

Mar	21	Belfast - 1st leg	2	-	5	A	
	25	Belfast - 2nd leg	5	-	1	H	PS
		Nottingham won 7-6 on aggregate					

BRITISH LEAGUE

DATE		VERSUS	SCORE				HOME/AWAY	
Sept	7	Hull	9	-	3		H	also cup
	13	Dundee	2	-	5		A	
	14	Fife	5	-	4	PS	A	
	15	Edinburgh	4	-	2		A	
	28	Belfast	3	-	2		A	
Oct	5	Braehead	4	-	2		H	
	25	Belfast	3	-	4		A	
	26	Coventry	4	-	5	PS	H	
Nov	1	Dundee	4	-	3	OT	H	
	3	Fife	7	-	1		H	
	9	Fife	2	-	4		A	
	10	Edinburgh	6	-	7	OT	A	
	16	Sheffield	3	-	5		A	
	17	Sheffield	6	-	1		H	
	27	Edinburgh	4	-	1		H	
	30	Cardiff	0	-	5		A	
Dec	1	Cardiff	3	-	2		H	also cup
	3	Belfast	8	-	3		H	
	6	Braehead	5	-	4	OT	A	
	14	Cardiff	2	-	4		A	
	15	Braehead	8	-	0		H	also cup qf 1st leg
	21	Hull	5	-	7		A	
	26	Sheffield	0	-	2		A	

	28	Sheffield	2	-	3	OT	H
	29	Coventry	3	-	2		A
	31	Coventry	5	-	3		H
Jan	2	Belfast	3	-	4		A
	4	Cardiff	9	-	2		H
	11	Edinburgh	5	-	2		H
	12	Coventry	5	-	3		A
	16	Cardiff	4	-	8		A
	18	Coventry	2	-	3	OT	H
	25	Sheffield	2	-	5		A
	26	Hull	6	-	4		H
	30	Cardiff	3	-	4	OT	A
Feb	1	Cardiff	1	-	2		H
	2	Coventry	1	-	3		A
	8	Sheffield	5	-	2		H
	9	Hull	3	-	4	PS	A
	15	Belfast	1	-	3		H
	16	Belfast	1	-	3		H
	22	Dundee	2	-	0		H
	23	Sheffield	3	-	1		A
	26	Coventry	7	-	2		H
Mar	1	Sheffield	2	-	3	PS	H
	2	Dundee	2	-	0		A
	4	Cardiff	1	-	0		H
	8	Braehead	2	-	8		A
	9	Fife	5	-	2		H
	12	Belfast	1	-	4		A
	16	Coventry	3	-	4		A
	22	Belfast	3	-	5		A

BL Play-Offs
Quarter Final

Mar	27	Braehead - 1st leg	0	-	4	H
	29	Braehead - 2nd leg	1	-	5	A
		Braehead win 9-1 on aggregate				

Challenge Games

Aladdin Cup

Aug	30	Amiens (France)	7	-	3		H
Sep	1	Braehead	4	-	5	PS	A

International Challenge Games

Aug	24	Cologne (Ger) - Rotterdam	0	-	4	Holland
	25	Geneva (Swit) - Rotterdam	3	-	8	Holland

EUROPEAN CONTINENTAL CUP
Third Round - RR

Oct	18	Vitoria-gasteiz	5	-	3	H
	19	The Hague	7	-	3	H
	20	Dinamo juniors	3	-	1	H
		Nottingham won group				

Fourth Round - semi-final stage — Italy

Nov	22	Toros Neftekamsk	3	-	4
	23	Yertis Pavlodar	2	-	1
	24	Asiago	2	-	3

Domestic season
Challenge Cup
Quarter finals-aggregate score
Nottingham 8 Braehead 0, Braehead 7 Nottingham 2
Belfast 6 Hull 1 (this was a one off game)
Sheffield 4 Dundee 0, Dundee 5 Sheffield 6
Cardiff 7 fife 3, Fife 2 Cardiff 3
Semi finals-aggregate score
Sheffield 3 Nottingham 5, Nottingham 6 Sheffield 4
Belfast 7 Cardiff 1, Cardiff 3 Belfast 3
Finals-aggregate score
Belfast 5 Nottingham 2, Nottingham 5 Belfast 1

Nottingham win the Cup

*****

League table
2013-14 Elite

	GP	RW	OW	PW	RL	OL	PL	GF	GA	GD	Pts
Belfast	52	38	4	1	6	1	2	210	127	83	89
Sheffield	52	27	2	2	17	1	3	172	141	31	66
Dundee	52	25	2	1	20	1	3	150	146	4	60
Nottingham	52	22	2	1	20	4	3	188	169	19	57
Braehead	52	20	1	3	20	5	3	180	171	9	56
Coventry	52	18	3	3	22	4	2	168	167	1	54
Fife	52	17	2	5	23	3	2	170	186	-16	53
Hull	52	19	1	4	24	1	3	168	186	-22	52
Cardiff	52	17	2	5	24	2	2	162	182	-20	52
Edinburgh	52	9	3	1	36	0	3	134	227	-93	29

Play offs

Quarter final
Belfast beat Hull 7-3 on aggregate
Fife beat Dundee 8-4 on aggregate
Sheffield beat Coventry 9-3 on aggregate
Braehead beat Nottingham 9-1 on aggregate

Semi final
Belfast 1 Fife 0
Braehead 2 Sheffield 3

Final – Belfast 2 Sheffield 3 after over time

Player stats

Name	GP	GPi	Mins	Shots	GA	GAA	%sv	Pts	Pims	SO
Craig Kowalski	43	41	2374	1248	113	2.86	90.94	5	12	2
Neil Conway	28	28	1615.36	815	84	3.12	89.69	0	6	1
Dan Green	71	18	296	147	22	4.46	85.03	0	0	0

Sam Gospel listed but not played

Name…….	Games	Goals	Assists	Points	Penalties
David Clarke	69	39	34	73	126
Matt Francis	67	31	42	73	115
Matt Ryan	68	19	45	64	83
Robert Lachowicz	69	21	42	63	38
Leigh Salters	65	28	34	62	148
Jonathan Weaver	71	9	39	48	56
Brandon Benedict	52	13	33	46	36
Chris Murray	45	9	35	44	152
Petr Kalus	47	18	22	40	63
Lynn Loyns	52	15	18	33	16
Robert Farmer	35	11	15	26	70
Chris Capraro	28	10	16	26	18
Bob Wren	20	7	15	22	39
Greg Jacina	30	5	15	20	61
Stephen Lee	51	4	15	19	71
Jonathan Boxhill	65	8	8	16	37
Joe Jensen	19	4	13	17	50
Eric Werner	38	4	7	11	18
Tom Norton	71	3	8	11	31
Joe Gromaldi	7	2	6	8	110
Nic Anderson	15	2	4	6	20
Brent Henley	42	0	4	4	294
Joonas Saari	54	0	4	4	13
Phil Oreskovic	26	0	3	3	31
Tuuka Makela	7	0	1	1	38
Ollie Betteridge	3	0	0	0	0

Brandon Benedict
Here with family, photo supplied by Brandon after the usual 'chat' on facebook messenger. He's one of my friends on there I let you know, Hee hee

2014-15

Two International matches
An International tournament
The European Champions Hockey league

Challenge Cup semi-final
League placing 4th
Play off quarter final
Champions Hockey League – bottom of group

Seasons Iron men: Boxhill, Lachowicz, Schmidt

Player's player of the year – Brandon Benedict

Returnees: Benedict, Betteridge, Boxhill, Clarke, Farmer, Gospel, Green, Jacina, Kowalski, Lachowicz, Lee, Neilson.

Players IN	Players NOT returning
BERUBE Mike	ANDERSON Nic
COHEN Colby	CAPRARO Chris
COWNIE Jordon	CONWAY Neil n/m
DOUCET Guillaume	GRIMALDI Joe
GOSPEL Sam n/m	HENLEY Brent
GRAHAM Bruce	JENSON Joe
HIGGINS Chris	KALLUS Petr
HOOK Lewis	LYONS Lynn
HOVEL Tom n/m	MAKELA Tuuka
LANDRY Charles	MURRAY Chris
LANGELIER-PARENT Maxime	ORESKOVIC Phil
LAWRENCE Chris	RYAN Matt
LEE Mark	SAARI Joonas
MODIG Mattias n/m	SALTERS Leigh
MOSEY Evan	WREN Bob
OAKFORD Sam	
PODLESAK Martin	
RAITUMS Martins n/m	
ROBINSON Nathan	
SCHMIDT Bryan	
WILD Cody	

Not seen a score like this for a while

2014-15

CHALLENGE CUP - first round

DATE	VERSUS	SCORE			HOME/AWAY	
Sept	13 Cardiff	3	-	1	H	also L
	20 Sheffield	2	-	1	H	
	21 Coventry	3	-	4	A	
	27 Hull	1	-	6	H	also L
	28 Cardiff	2	-	5	A	
Oct	3 Coventry	2	-	1	H	
	4 Sheffield	2	-	4	A	
	19 Hull	3	-	2 ot	A	

Q-Final

| Dec | 9 Fife | 7 | - | 2 | A |
| Jan | 7 Fife | 4 | - | 6 | H |

Semi-Final

| Feb | 19 Sheffield | 3 | - | 1 | A |
| | 24 Sheffield | 4 | - | 7 ps | H |

BRITISH LEAGUE

DATE	VERSUS	SCORE			HOME/AWAY	
Sept	13 Cardiff	3	-	1	H	also Cup
	27 Hull	1	-	6	H	also Cup
Oct	11 Fife	3	-	4 ps	H	
	12 Fife	2	-	1	A	
	15 Braehead	3	-	4 ot	A	
	18 Dundee	5	-	1	H	
	21 Edinburgh	5	-	2	H	
	25 Belfast	4	-	3 ot	H	
	26 Dundee	4	-	3 ot	A	
Nov	1 Coventry	3	-	1	H	
	2 Cardiff	3	-	1	A	
	8 Sheffield	7	-	2	H	
	9 Edinburgh	3	-	5	A	
	15 Cardiff	2	-	3 ps	H	
	16 Belfast	1	-	2	A	
	22 Fife	5	-	3	A	
	23 Dundee	3	-	4 ot	H	
	29 Hull	4	-	0	A	
	30 Coventry	3	-	1	H	
Dec	6 Sheffield	2	-	3	A	
	7 Coventry	4	-	3	A	
	14 Belfast	3	-	6	H	
	20 Fife	1	-	5	H	
	21 Cardiff	2	-	5	A	
	26 Sheffield	4	-	0	A	
	27 Sheffield	3	-	2 ot	H	
	31 Coventry	3	-	2	H	
Jan	3 Edinburgh	6	-	1	H	
	4 Coventry	1	-	2 ps	A	
	10 Sheffield	4	-	1	A	
	11 Cardiff	4	-	3 ot	H	

	16	Coventry	5	-	0	H
	17	Cardiff	2	-	7	A
	23	Belfast	4	-	0	A
	25	Braehead	6	-	3	H
	28	Coventry	3	-	4 ps	A
	31	Belfast	4	-	3 ps	H
Feb	1	Belfast	1	-	0	H
	7	Sheffield	2	-	4	A
	8	Hull	2	-	5	A
	14	Sheffield	2	-	3	H
	21	Cardiff	2	-	3	H
	22	Coventry	1	-	2	A
	27	Braehead	2	-	4	A
	28	Dundee	2	-	3	A
Mar	1	Edinburgh	5	-	3	A
	4	Hull	4	-	3	H
	7	Braehead	6	-	0	H
	14	Belfast	3	-	2 ps	A
	15	Belfast	5	-	1	A
	20	Sheffield		-		
	22	Cardiff		-		

BL Play-Offs

Quarter Final

Mar	28	Coventry	3	-	3	H
		Coventry	1	-	2	A

International Challenge games

Aug	17	Ljubiana	1	-	3	A
	18	Ljubiana	3	-	4	A

International Tournament

Aug	29	Amiens - France	4	-	3	A
	30	Rouen - France	3	-	1	A
	31	UQTR - Cnada	5	-	6 PS	A

European Champions Hockey league (CHL)
Group...

AUG	22	Lukko - Finland	2	-	4	H
	24	Lulea - Sweden	1	-	10	H
Sept	5	Lukko	2	-	6	A
	7	Lulea	1	-	9	A
	23	Hamburg - Germany	3	-	1	H
Oct	7	Hamburg	0	-	6	A

Domestic season
Challenge Cup
Quarter finals
Coventry 3 Braehead 1, Coventry 4 Braehead 1 ot
Fife 2 Nottingham 7, Nottingham 4 Fife 6
Belfast 3 Cardiff 4, Cardiff 2 Belfast 4
Dundee 0 Sheffield 3, Sheffield 11 Dundee 1
Semi finals
Sheffield 1 Nottingham 3, Nottingham 4 Sheffield 6 (Sheffield win on shoot out)
Cardiff 4 Coventry 1, Coventry 3 Cardiff 5
Final
Sheffield 1 Cardiff 2

*****

League Table
2014-15 Elite

	GP	RW	OW	PW	RL	OL	PL	GF	GA	GD	Pts
Sheffield	52	30	4	1	13	1	3	193	134	59	74
Braehead	52	33	1	1	14	2	1	190	136	54	73
Cardiff	52	29	4	1	14	2	2	210	151	59	72
Nottingham	52	23	4	2	16	3	4	166	141	25	65
Belfast	52	25	1	1	19	2	4	177	148	29	60
Coventry	52	17	2	5	25	2	1	127	145	-18	51
Hull	52	16	1	3	23	3	6	154	192	-38	49
Fife	52	18	0	4	27	1	2	170	180	-10	47
Edinburgh	52	13	2	5	26	1	5	135	215	-80	46
Dundee	52	6	2	6	33	2	3	123	203	-80	33

Play offs

Quarter final
Belfast beat Cardiff 8-3 on aggregate
Sheffield beat Fife 6-5 on aggreagate
Hull beat Braehead 5-4 on aggreagate
Coventry beat Nottingham 5-4 on aggregate

Semi final
Sheffield 3 Hull 2
Belfast 2 Coventry 3 after shoot out

Final
Sheffield 2 Coventry 4

Player stats

Name……….	GP	GPi	Mins	Sts	GA	GAA	%sv	Pts	Pims	SO
Craig Kowlaski	37	35	1960.16	983	95	2.91	90.34	0	12	4
Mattias Modig	38	34	1897	962	86	2.72	91.06	0	14	2
Dan Green	61	11	342	137	17	2.98	87.59	0	0	0
Martins Raitums	2	1	37.44	29	6	9.68	79.31	0	0	0
Sam Gospel	1	0								
Tom Hovel	1	0								

Name…….	Games	Goals	Assists	Points	Penalties
Chris Lawrence	67	25	39	64	151
Robert Lachowicz	70	15	31	46	18
Robert Farmer	59	16	29	45	178
Cody Wild	52	13	30	43	18
Bruce Graham	55	16	25	41	70
Greg Jacina	64	14	24	38	133
Brandon Benedict	61	12	25	37	40
Jonathan Boxhill	70	7	26	33	74
Chris Higgins	38	11	22	33	30
Evan Mosey	68	13	17	30	38
Guillame Doucet	27	19	10	29	34
David Clarke	25	11	14	25	16
Max Parent	51	11	12	23	81
Nathan Robinson	24	6	15	21	40
Stephen Lee	47	5	15	20	33
Chris Landry	66	6	11	17	60
Mike Berube	67	2	14	16	36
Bryan Schmidt	70	2	8	10	75
Colby Cohen	18	2	6	8	37
Sam Oakford	60	2	5	7	14
Jordan Cownie	4	1	0	1	2
Lewis Hook	3	0	0	0	2
Ollie Betteridge	11	0	0	0	2
Martin Podlesak	2	0	0	0	0
Mark Lee	1	0	0	0	0

****

AD

https://www.facebook.com/JkMuddimanArt

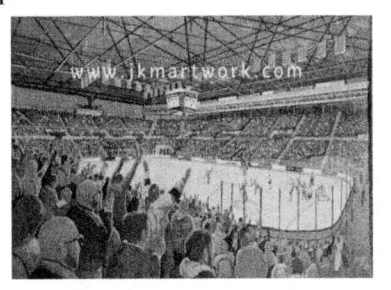

Check the site out for sports paintings of your club

2015-16

Three UK challenge matches

Challenge Cup winners
League placing 5th
Play off winners

Elite All Star chosen: Juraj Kolnik

Seasons Iron men: Mosey, Myers, Oakford, Schmidt

Player's player of the year – Evan Mosey

Returnees: Betteridge, Clarke, Farmer, Green, Hovell, Lachowicz, Lawrence, Lee, Mosey, Neilson, Oakford, Schmidt,

Players IN	Players NOT returning
BOHMBACH Andy	BENEDICT Brendon
DIMMEN Jeff	BERUBE Mike
GLOSSOP Connor	BOXHILL Jonathan
HARDY Kyle	COHEN Colby
HOVELL Tom n/m	COWNIE Jordon
JANSSEN Cam	DOUCET Guillaume
JOHNSTON Kyle n/m	GOSPEL Sam n/m
KOLNIK Juraj	GRAHAM Bruce
LING David	HIGGINS Chris
McDONALD Franklin	HOOK Lewis
McMILAN Logan	JACINA Greg
MADOLORA Shane n/m	KOWALSKI Craig n/m
MORAN Brad	LANDRY Charles
MYERS Matthew	LANGELIER-PARENT Maxime
PRECENICKS Stanislaus	LEE Mark
QUICK Kevin	MODIG Mattias
RAYNOR Kieran	PODLESAK Martin
SCHULTZ Stephen	RAITUMS Martin n/m
SWINDLEHURST Paul	ROBINSON Nathan
WAUGH Geoff	WILD Cody
WIEDERGUT Andreas	
WILKMAN Wiika n/m	

Cam Janssen (photo:Lisa Atkin)

2015-16

CHALLENGE CUP - first round

DATE		VERSUS	SCORE				HOME/AWAY	
Sept	12	Cardiff	1	-	2	OT	A	
	19	Manchester	7	-	2		H	also L
	20	Coventry	0	-	1		A	
	26	Cardiff	3	-	1		H	also L
Oct	3	Coventry	6	-	2		H	
	4	Manchester	4	-	2		A	
	10	Sheffield	1	-	2		A	
	17	Sheffield	2	-	3		H	

Q-Final

Jan	10	Braehead	5	-	4		H	
	17	Braehead	5	-	3		A	

Nottingham win 10-7 on aggregate

Semi-Final

Feb	23	Sheffield	8	-	0		A	
	24	Sheffield	2	-	0		H	

Nottingham win 10-0 on aggregate

FINAL

March   06

BRITISH LEAGUE

DATE		VERSUS	SCORE				HOME/AWAY	
Sept	5	Dundee	3	-	2	PS	H	
	13	Belfast	1	-	2	OT	H	
	19	Manchester	7	-	2		H	also C
	26	Cardiff	3	-	1		H	also C
	27	Braehead	4	-	1		H	
Oct	11	Fife	5	-	2		H	
	18	Coventry	3	-	4		A	
	24	Dundee	7	-	1		H	
	25	Cardiff	1	-	2	PS	A	
	28	Edinburgh	4	-	3	OT	H	
	31	Sheffield	7	-	4		H	
Nov	07	Belfast	4	-	3		H	
	14	Coventry	4	-	0		H	
	15	Sheffield	4	-	1		A	
	20	Edinburgh	3	-	2		A	
	21	Edinburgh	2	-	5		A	
	28	Cardiff	7	-	3		A	
	29	Sheffield	4	-	6		H	
Dec	04	Belfast	3	-	4		A	
	05	Belfast	3	-	2		A	
	11	Dundee	2	-	5		A	

	12	Braehead	4	-	3	PS	A
	13	Fife	2	-	5		A
	19	Cardiff	3	-	5		H
	20	Manchester	5	-	2		A
	26	Sheffield	1	-	2		A
	27	Sheffield	5	-	3		H
	29	Coventry	3	-	5		A
	31	Coventry	3	-	5		H
Jan	02	Edinburgh	8	-	2		H
	09	Cardiff	1	-	3		A
	10	Fife	3	-	2	PS	H
	15	Belfast	4	-	2		H
	16	Sheffield	4	-	5		A
	23	Manchester	4	-	0		H
	24	Manchester	4	-	2		A
	30	Cardiff	0	-	3		H
	31	Belfast	5	-	4	PS	A
Feb	06	Braehead	5	-	3		H
	07	Dundee	6	-	3		A
	17	Coventry	2	-	1		A
	19	Belfast	2	-	6		A
	21	Coventry	4	-	2		H
	26	Belfast	1	-	5		H
	28	Braehead	2	-	4		A
Mar	04	Cardiff	6	-	1		H
	09	Coventry	1	-	6		A
	12	Sheffield	2	-	4		H
	13	Fife	2	-	1	OT	A
	16	Coventry	5	-	0		H
	19	Sheffield	3	-	4		A
	20	Cardiff	3	-	4		A

BL Play-Offs

Quarter Final

Mar	26	Belfast	4	-	3	H
	28	Belfast	3	-	1	A

(Nottingham won on aggregate 7-4)

Semi Final

Apr	02	Fife	4	-	1	Nottingham

Final

Apr	03	Coventry	2	-	0	Nottingham

Challenge Games

Aug	26	Coventry	3	-	2		A
	29	Manchester Storm	4	-	5	PS	A
	30	Braehead - ? Alladin Cup	0	-	1		H

Testimonial

Oct	21	Corey Neilson All Stars v N	10	-	8	Nottingham

Domestic season
Challenge cup
Quarter finals-aggregate score
Dundee 0 Cardiff 3, Cardiff 7 Dundee 6
Fife 2 Sheffield 4, Sheffield 2 Fife 3,
Belfast 5 Manchester 2, Manchester 2 Belfast 6
Nottingham 5 Braehead 4, Braehead 3 Nottingham 5
Semi finals-aggregate score
Sheffield 0 Nottingham 8, Nottingham 2 Sheffield 0
Cardiff 5 Belfast 3, Belfast 1 Cardiff 3
Final
Nottingham 1 Cardiff 0 in sudden death over time

*****

League Table
2015-16 Elite

	GP	RW	OW	PW	RL	OL	PL	GF	GA	GD	Pts
Sheffield	52	28	5	1	14	0	4	190	161	29	72
Cardiff	52	27	4	2	15	3	1	179	139	40	70
Braehead	52	28	2	0	15	4	3	185	145	40	67
Belfast	52	24	4	3	17	2	2	184	148	36	66
Nottingham	52	24	2	4	20	1	1	185	152	33	62
Fife	52	21	2	3	23	2	1	171	164	7	55
Dundee	52	19	1	2	19	7	4	200	196	4	55
Coventry	52	18	2	4	25	2	1	160	177	-17	51
Manchester	52	19	0	1	28	1	3	189	227	-38	44
Edinburgh	52	6	2	2	37	3	2	153	289	-136	25

Play offs

Quarter final
Cardiff beat Dundee 6-5 on aggregate
Coventry beat Sheffield 8-6 on aggregate
Fife beat Braehead 4-3 on aggregate
Nottingham beat Belfast 7-4 on aggregate

Semi final
Cardiff 2 Coventry 6
Fife 1 Nottingham 4

Final
Coventry 0 Nottingham 2

Player Stats

Name……….	GP	GPi	Mins	Sts	GA	GAA	%sv	Pts	Pims	SO
Miika Wilkman	50	47	2698	1248	110	2.45	91.2	0	4	4
Dan Green	60	12	437	196	20	2.75	89.8	0	0	0
Shane Madolora	20	15	907	454	38	2.52	91.6	0	2	3
Tom Hovel	3	0								
Kyle Johnston	1	0								

Name…….	Games	Goals	Assists	Points	Penalties
Juraj Kolnik	65	33	40	73	44
Brad Moran	60	19	35	54	18
Evan Mosey	67	19	33	52	34
Andy Bohmbach	66	23	27	50	49
David Clarke	63	21	29	50	75
David Ling	34	14	32	46	83
Stepehn Schultz	47	19	21	40	34
Matthew Myers	67	15	20	35	55
Stephen Lee	62	5	23	28	42
Logan McMillan	60	12	15	27	36
Chris Lawrence	40	6	18	24	42
Robert Farmer	55	9	14	23	100
Geogg Waugh	54	7	16	23	59
Bryan Schmidt	67	5	15	20	55
Robert Lachowicz	64	5	14	19	8
Paul Swindlehurst	48	3	13	16	36
Jeff Dimmen	36	2	12	14	40
Can Janssen	66	5	6	11	122
Kevin Quick	18	2	6	8	8
Ollie Betteridge	61	3	2	5	13
Franklin McDonald	18	1	3	4	6
Sam Oakford	67	1	3	4	16
Kyle Hardy	10	0	4	4	10
Andreas Wiedergut	2	0	0	0	0

Miika Wiikman (photo:Lisa Atkin)

2016-17

Two UK challenge matches
An International Tournament
The European Continental Cup

Challenge Cup semi final
League placing 4th
Play-offs quarter final
Continental Cup Gold Medal winners

Seasons Iron men: Beteridge, Lachowicz and Lindhagen

Player's player of the year – Brad Moran

Returnees: Betteridge, Clarke, Dimmen, Farmer, Green, Lachowicz, Lawrence, Lee, McMillan, B.Moran, Neilson, Oakford, Schultz, Waugh, Wiikman

Players IN	Players NOT returning
BROWN Jeff	BOHMBACH Andy
CARTER Matthew	GLOSSOP Connor
KALUS Petr	HARDY Kyle
KUDROC Kristian	HOVELL Tom n/m
LINDHAGEN Eric	JANSSEN Cam
NIKIFORUK Alex	JOHNSTON Kyle n/m
McGRATTON Brian	KOLNIK Juraj
PACL Jindrich n/m	LING David
SARKANIS Deivids	McDONALD Franklin
SETICH Andy	MADOLORA Shane n/m
SPANG Dan	MOSEY Evan
WILLIAMS Jason	MYERS Matt
	PRECENIUKS Stanislaus
	QUICK Kevin
	RAYNOR Kevin
	SCHMIDT Bryan
	SWINDLEHURST Paul
	WIEDERGUT Andreas

Celebrations after the Continental Cup success
And to think we nearly did it the following 2020 event that we entered

2016-17

CHALLENGE CUP - first round

DATE	VERSUS	SCORE			HOME/AWAY	
Sept	04 Coventry	1	-	3	A	
	17 Cardiff	2	-	0	H	also L
	18 Sheffield	5	-	7	A	
	24 Sheffield	4	-	3	H	
Oct	01 Manchester	8	-	5	H	also L
	02 Cardiff	3	-	1	A	
	08 Manchester	3	-	2 PS	A	
NOV	11 Coventry	2	-	1	H	
Q-Final						
DEC	08 Braehead	3	-	3	A	
	14 Braehead	3	-	1	H	
semi-final						
JAN	25 Sheffield	1	-	2	H	
FEB	14 Sheffield	0	-	3	A	

BRITISH LEAGUE

DATE	VERSUS	SCORE			HOME/AWAY	
Sept	08 Dundee	3	-	1	A	
	10 Braehead	4	-	1	A	
	11 Fife	1	-	4	A	
	17 Cardiff	2	-	0	H	also Cup
	25 Coventry	5	-	3	A	
Oct	01 Manchester	8	-	5	H	also Cup
	08 Dundee	2	-	1	H	
	16 Belfast	1	-	2 OT	H	
	29 Edinburgh	2	-	4	H	
	30 Braehead	2	-	5	A	
Nov	05 Manchester	3	-	4	A	
	06 Belfast	2	-	4	H	
	12 Sheffield	1	-	8	A	
	25 Belfast	3	-	2 PS	H	
	27 Fife	3	-	2	H	
	30 Cardiff	1	-	3	A	
Dec	03 Sheffield	4	-	5	H	
	04 Sheffield	1	-	6	A	
	10 Cardiff	8	-	0	A	
	11 Coventry	6	-	5 PS	H	
	17 Belfast	4	-	7	A	
	18 Cardiff	5	-	2	H	
	23 Dundee	4	-	2	H	
	26 Sheffield	3	-	2	A	
	27 Sheffield	3	-	2	H	
	29 Coventry	4	-	2	A	
	31 Coventry	5	-	6 OT	A	

Jan	02	Edinburgh	4	-	2		H
	07	Braehead	4	-	3	OT	H
	08	Coventry	2	-	3	PS	A
	20	Belfast	4	-	5		A
	22	Fife	2	-	3	PS	H
	25	Sheffield	1	-	2		H
	28	Cardiff	0	-	5		A
	29	Coventry	8	-	3		H
Feb	04	Cardiff	3	-	4	OT	H
	05	Fife	3	-	4	OT	A
	11	Sheffield	5	-	4		H
	12	Cardiff	0	-	3		A
	18	Coventry	4	-	1		H
	19	Coventry	1	-	5		A
	21	Cardiff	7	-	4		H
	25	Sheffield	2	-	4		A
	26	Belfast	3	-	4		H
Mar	03	Braehead	5	-	4		H
	10	Belfast	3	-	7		H
	12	Belfast	2	-	5		H
	17	Dundee	4	-	1		A
	18	Edinburgh	3	-	2		A
	19	Edinburgh	4	-	3		A
	22	Manchester	1	-	3		H
	24	Sheffield	2	-	3		H
	26	Manchester	3	-	2	ps	A

BL Play-Offs
Quarter Final

Apr	01	Sheffield	5	-	2		H
	02	Sheffield	1	-	5	ot	A

Challenge Games

Aug	20	Braehead	2	-	5		H
	24	Coventry	5	-	6		A

Int.Tour
Amiens/Fra

Aug	21	Kassel Huskies (Germany)	3	-	0	
	22	Amiens (France)	5	-	3	
	23	UQTR (Canada)	3	-	7	

Continental Cup
Jaca/Spain
Grioup C

Oct	21	Club hielo Jaca (Spain)	13	-	2	
	22	Zeytinburnu Istanbul (Turkey)	12	-	1	
	23	HK Liepaja (latvia)	3	-	1	

Odense/Den
Group D

Nov	18	Odense Bulldogs (Denmar	5	-	4	
	19	Ducs D'Angers (France)	4	-	3	
	20	HC Donbass (Ukraine)	1	-	3	

Ritten/Ita	Jan	13	Odense	2	-	0	
Super-final		14	Beibarys Atyrau	3	-	2	ps
		15	Ritten Sport	4	-	1	Nottingham Champion 2017

Domestic season
Challenge Cup
Quarter finals-aggregate score
Edinburgh 2 Sheffield 2, Sheffield 7 Edinburgh 1
Dundee 1 Cardiff 4, Cardiff 4 Dundee 2
Braehead 3 Nottingham 3, Nottingham 3 Braehead 1
Manchester 3 Belfast 3, Belfast 4 Manchester 3 after over time
Semi finals-aggregate score
Belfast 5 Cardiff 4, Cardiff 5 Belfast 1
Sheffield 2 Nottingham 1, Nottingham 0 Sheffield 3
Final
Cardiff 3 Sheffield 2

*****

League Table
2016-17 Elite

	GP	RW	OW	PW	RL	OL	PL	GF	GA	GD	Pts
Cardiff	52	32	4	3	10	3	0	200	136	64	
Belfast	52	30	4	1	13	2	2	194	147	47	
Sheffield	52	31	2	2	14	2	1	196	133	63	
Nottingham	52	22	2	2	20	4	2	170	175	-5	
Braehead	52	24	2	1	22	1	2	191	174	17	
Fife	52	20	4	1	24	2	1	174	186	-12	
Dundee	52	16	2	2	26	1	5	161	182	-21	
Manchester	52	17	0	1	26	4	4	138	163	-25	
Coventry	52	13	4	2	28	4	1	147	198	-51	
Edinburgh	52	11	2	3	33	1	2	156	233	-77	

....

Play offs

Quarter final
Cardiff beat Manchester 6-3 on aggregate
Dundee beat Braehead 6-1 on aggregate
Belfast beat Fife 8-3 on aggregate
Sheffield beat Nottingham 7-6 on aggregate

Semi final
Belfast 0 Sheffield 2
Cardiff 4 Dundee 2

Final
Cardiff 5 Sheffield 6

Player stats

Name	GP	GPi	Mins	Shots	GA	GAA	%sv	Pts	Pims	SO
Miika Wiikman	60	55	3007.22	1538	137	2.73	91.09	2	2	4
Dan Green	30	3	87	34	9	6.21	73.53	0	0	
Jindrich Pacl	56	27	1303.3	641	68	3.13	89.39	0	4	

Name…….	Games	Goals	Assists	Points	Penalties
Stephen Schultz	46	15	35	50	32
Brad Moran	72	22	38	60	40
Chris Lawrence	56	22	24	46	72
Alex Nikiforuk	70	22	32	54	77
Robert Farmer	67	19	28	47	90
Jeff Brown	72	17	26	33	128
Dan Spang	72	9	26	35	24
Matt Carter	67	22	17	39	20
Andy Sertich	72	5	28	33	22
Erik Lindhagen	73	8	25	33	44
David Clarke	39	18	14	32	21
Robert Lachowicz	75	5	23	28	14
Jeff Dimmen	49	9	19	28	38
Brian McGrattan	66	19	8	27	149
Stephen Lee	64	3	21	24	45
Logan McMillan	66	3	17	20	8
Jason Williams	17	6	13	19	0
Ollie Beteridge	73	7	13	20	32
Geoff Waugh	43	3	6	9	24
Deivids Sarkanis	13	2	4	6	2
Kristian Kudroc	12	1	5	6	12
Petr Kalus	13	3	5	8	13
Sam Oakford	8	0	0	0	7

(photo:Lisa Atkin)
Jeff Brown

Merv Magus Cartoons

2017-18

One International challenge match
Three UK challenge matches
The European Champions Hockey league

Challenge Cup semi final
League placing 4th
Play-offs semi final
Champions Hockey league last 16

Seasons Iron men: Betteridge, Billingsley, Brown, Lachowicz, Lindhagen, Mokshantsev, Phillips

Player's player of the year – Mark Delargo

Returnees: Betteridge, Brown, D.Clarke, Farmer, Lachowicz, Lee, Lindhagen, Neilson, Spang

Players IN	Players NOT returning
BILLINSLEY Tim	CARTER Matthew
BRISEBOIS Mathieu	DIMMEN Jeff
BUSSIERIES Rapheal	GREEN Dan n/m
DERLAGO Mark	KALUS Petr
GAGNON Mathieu	KUDROC Kristian
GALBRAITH Patrick n/m	LAWRENCE Chris
GARNETT Mike n/m	LEVERS Marc
GOSPEL Sam n/m	McGRATTAN Brian
HAZLEDINE Joeseph	McMILAN Logan
KELSALL Jordon	MORAN Brad
MOKSHANSTEV Alex	NIKIFORUK Alex
MOSEY Evan	NORTON Tom
PERLINI Brett	OAKFORD Sam
PHILLIPS Zack	PACL Jindrich n/m
PITHER Luke	SARKANIS Deivids
SAUVE Yann	SCHULTZ Stephen
SHALLA Josh	SERTICH Andy
TETLOW Josh	WAUGH Geoff
VASKIUVO Mike	WIIKMAN Miika n/m
	WILLIAMS Jason

41, Brantford Ave
Clifton Estate
Nottingham
NG11 8LR

Dear Mick,
Thanks for your support and sponsorship and I hope everything on Saturday went as you would have hoped.
Sadly we could not win the match let alone the tie, but I am sure this didn't detract from what was, for you and your family a unique occasion.
Once again many thanks for your support.

Yours
sincerely

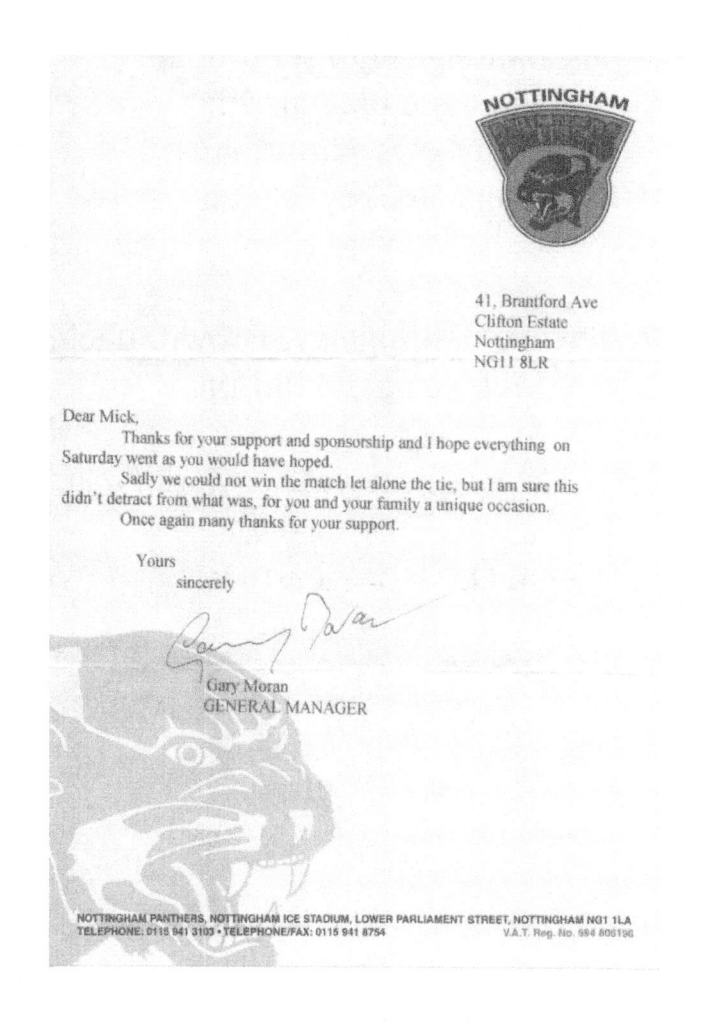

Gary Moran
GENERAL MANAGER

2017-18

CHALLENGE CUP - first round

	DATE		VERSUS	SCORE			HOME/AWAY
	Sept	10	Sheffield	5	-	6	A
		30	Manchester	3	-	2	H
	Oct	07	Sheffield	2	-	3	H
		18	Braehead	5	-	3	A
	Nov	11	Braehead	5	-	1	H
		25	Manchester	3	-	5	A
Q-Final	Dec	22	Milton Keynes	1	-	2	A
	Jan	03	Milton Keynes	6	-	2	H
Semi-Final	Jan	31	Belfast	1	-	5	A
	Feb	07	Belfast	6	-	7	H

BRITISH LEAGUE

DATE		VERSUS	SCORE				HOME/AWAY
Sept	09	Coventry	4	-	3		H
	16	Guildford	3	-	2	ot	H
	17	Cardiff	1	-	4		A
	23	Braehead	3	-	5		H
	24	Guilford	3	-	2	ps	A
	27	Belfast	5	-	4		H
Oct	14	Sheffield	4	-	3	ps	A
	15	Belfast	4	-	3		H
	21	Edinburgh	4	-	2		H
	22	Cardiff	4	-	2		A
	28	Milton Keynes	4	-	3	ot	H
	29	Coventry	4	-	2		A
Nov	03	Guildford	2	-	1	ot	H
	04	Milton Keynes	5	-	3		A
	15	Belfast	5	-	4	ot	A
	19	Cardiff	7	-	4		H
	26	Fife	4	-	5	ot	H
Dec	02	Sheffield	4	-	1		H
	03	Braehead	3	-	0		A
	09	Cardiff	1	-	2		H
	10	Guildford	2	-	5		A
	16	Manchester	1	-	2	ot	A
	17	Belfast	2	-	6		H
	23	Manchester	1	-	2	ps	H
	26	Sheffield	0	-	4		A
	27	Sheffield	0	-	5		H
		Coventry	4	-	3		H
Jan	01	Coventry	2	-	1		A
	06	Manchester	4	-	3	ot	H

		07 Cardiff	2	-	5		A
		12 Belfast	2	-	5		A
		13 Belfast	4	-	6		A
		20 Cardiff	6	-	4		H
		21 Milton keynes	6	-	3		A
		27 Belfast	4	-	2		H
		28 Fife	2	-	3		A
	Feb	04 Dundee	3	-	0		H
		09 Sheffield	0	-	4		H
		10 Cardiff	3	-	7		A
		17 Cardiff	7	-	2		H
		18 Braehead	4	-	3	ot	A
		23 Dundee	3	-	1		A
		24 Fife	4	-	5	ps	A
		25 Edinburgh	10	-	1		A
	Mar	04 Dundee	3	-	4		H
		05 Milton Keynes	5	-	1		H
		10 Sheffield	2	-	3		H
		11 Belfast	4	-	6		A
		13 Edinburgh	12	-	1		H
		17 Sheffield	3	-	2		A
		18 Manchester	3	-	4	ps	A
		20 Fife	2	-	1		H
		23 Braehead	6	-	3		A
		24 Dundee	4	-	3		A
		25 Edinburgh	4	-	3		A

BL Play-Offs

Quarter Final

	Mar	30 Belfast	3	-	4	A
	Apr	01 Belfast	5	-	3	A

Semi-Final

	Apr	07 Sheffield	4	-	5	Nottm

Challenge Games

	Aug	12 Cardiff (Aladin Cup)	1	-	3	H
		13 Cardiff	2	-	3	A
		19 Krefeld Pinguine	3	-	2	H
		20 Braehead (Aladin Cup)	4	-	2	H

CHL

Group	Aug	24 SC Bern	2	-	5	A
		26 Mountfield HK	4	-	2	A
		31 Mountfield HK	4	-	3	H
	Sept	02 SC Bern	4	-	2	H
	Oct	03 TPS Turku	2	-	0	H
		10 TPS Turku	2	-	5	A
Play-Offs	Oct	31 Zurich	1	-	3	A
	Nov	07 Zurich	0	-	3	H

Domestic season
Quarter finals
Dundee 2 Sheffield 7, Sheffield 6 Dundee 1
Milton Keynes 2 Nottingham 1, Nottingham 6 Milton Keynes 2
Fife 3 Belfast 3, Belfast 7 Fife 0
Guildford 3 Cardiff 3, Cardiff 6 Guildford 2
Semi finals
Nottingham 1 Belfast 5, Belfast 7 Nottingham 6
Sheffield 6 Cardiff 2, Cardiff 7 Sheffield 1
Final
Belfast 6 Cardiff 3

*****

League Table
2017-18 Elite

	GP	RW	OW	PW	RL	OL	PL	GF	GA	GD	Pts
Cardiff	56	37	3	1	12	1	2	234	149	85	85
Manchester	56	28	3	4	16	3	2	216	169	47	75
Sheffield	56	32	1	1	19	2	1	217	140	77	71
Nottingham	56	25	6	2	18	2	3	203	177	26	71
Belfast	56	30	2	2	20	2	0	227	200	27	70
Guildford	56	27	2	1	17	5	4	215	173	42	69
Fife	56	27	5	1	21	1	1	218	172	46	68
Coventry	56	22	3	0	26	4	1	189	186	3	55
Braehead	56	24	0	0	26	5	1	161	186	-25	54
Dundee	56	16	2	4	30	3	1	167	233	-66	48
Milton Keynes	56	16	2	2	34	1	1	180	229	-49	42
Edinburgh	56	5	0	0	50	0	1	118	331	-215	11

Play offs

Quarter final
Belfast 4 Nottingham 3, Nottingham 5 Belfast 3 after over time
Coventry 2 Cardiff 4, Cardiff 4 Coventry 3
Fife 1 Manchester 4, Manchester 1 Fife 5
Sheffield 5 Guildford 2, Guildford 5 Sheffield 4

Semi final
Cardiff 4 Fife 0
Sheffield 5 Nottingham 4 after over time

Final
Cardiff 3 Sheffield 1

Player stats

Name	GP	GPi	Mins	Shots	GA	GAA	%sv	Pts	Pims	SO
Patrick Galbraith	48	35	1932.3	1092	92	2.86	91.55	0	0	2
Mike Garnett	61	44	2481.26	1289	129	3.12	89.99	0	2	1
Sam Gospel	45	6	235.43	123	15	3.83	87.80	0	0	0

Name…….	Games	Goals	Assists	Points	Penalties
Mark Derlago	73	27	42	69	49
Bret Perlini	76	23	46	69	22
Zack Phillips	77	18	39	57	20
Alex. Mokshantsev	77	28	27	55	57
Yann Sauve	74	17	33	50	110
Jeff Brown	77	19	29	48	88
Evan Mosey	63	23	23	46	52
Luke Pither	27	12	23	35	18
Robert Farmer	68	12	24	36	97
David Clarke	71	12	22	34	36
Tim Billingsley	77	10	24	34	66
Dan Spang	68	10	22	32	61
Raphael Bussieres	70	7	22	29	57
Robert Lachowicz	77	10	16	26	10
Erik Linahagen	77	7	17	24	40
Mike Vaskivuo	20	9	9	18	10
Stephen Lee	75	1	15	16	73
Josh Shalla	40	10	12	22	17
Ollie Beteridge	77	6	9	15	26
Mathieu Brisbois	37	3	9	12	43
Mathieu Gagnon	75	2	11	13	142
Josh Tetlow	41	1	2	3	6
Jordan Kelsall	12	2	0	2	0
Josepth Hazledine	8	0	0	0	0

Dan Spang   (photo:Lisa Atkin)

2018-19

Four International matches
Two UK challenge matches

Challenge Cup semi final
League placing 3rd
Play offs semi final

Seasons Iron men: Betteridge, Hurtubise, Pither, Tetlow

Player's player of the year – Kevin Henderson

Returnees: Betteridge, Billingsley, Farmer, Garnett, Gospel, J.Hazledine, Kelsall, Lachowicz, Lee, Perlini, Pither, Tetlow

Players IN	Players NOT returning
BIGGS Tyler	BROWN Jeff
BOLDUC Alexandre	BUSSIERIES Raphael
CHERNOMAZ Rich – coach	CLARKE David
DOTY Jacob	DERLAGO Mark
GUPTIL Alex	GAGNON Mathieu
HENDERSON Kevin	GALBRAITH Patrick n/m
HUGHES Tommy	LINDHARGEN Eric
HURTUBISE Mark	MOKSHANTSEV Alex
KOVACS Justin	MOSEY Evan
LEPINE Guillaume	PHILLIPS Zack
MUNSON Patrick n/m	SAUVE Yann
OLSEN Dylan	SPANG Dan
RHEAULT Jon	VASKIVUO Mike
RICHARD Dylan	
RISSLING Jaynen	
STEWART Chris	
TYRDON Marek	
VANKLEEF Tyler	

One of the 'homegrown' as they say
Oliver Betteridge

2018-19

CHALLENGE CUP - first round

DATE		VERSUS	SCORE			HOME/AWAY	
	Sept	01 Sheffield	5	-	2	H	
		29 Sheffield	2	-	3	A	
	Oct	03 Manchester	3	-	3	A	ot
	Nov	02 Manchester	3	-	0	A	

Q-Final
| | Dec | 04 Manchester | 6 | - | 1 | A | |
| | | 11 Manchester | 2 | - | 4 | H | |

Semi-Final
| | Jan | 25 Guildford | 2 | - | 5 | A | |
| | Feb | 14 Guildford | 1 | - | 3 | H | |

BRITISH LEAGUE

DATE		VERSUS	SCORE			HOME/AWAY	
	Sept	08 Manchester	2	-	1	H	
		09 Manchester	4	-	1	A	
		15 Cardiff	2	-	3	A	
		16 Coventry	5	-	4	A	ps
		19 Belfast	6	-	3	A	
		22 Glasgow	2	-	5	H	
		26 Cardiff	4	-	3	H	
		30 Guildford	3	-	2	A	
	Oct	06 Coventry	3	-	0	H	
		07 Milton keynes	1	-	5	A	
		13 Sheffield	5	-	2	H	
		14 Belfast	1	-	6	A	
		19 Glasgow	3	-	6	A	
		20 Fife	5	-	7	A	
		21 Dundee	2	-	1	A	ot
		27 Sheffield	1	-	2	A	ot
		28 Belfast	2	-	3	H	ot
	Nov	04 Cardiff	3	-	2	H	
		10 Belfast	0	-	4	H	
		11 Guildford	4	-	1	A	
		17 Cardiff	2	-	3	A	ot
		18 Fife	3	-	2	H	ps
		24 Milton Keynes	3	-	1	A	
		28 Milton Keynes	4	-	1	H	
	Dec	01 Guildord	8	-	3	A	
		02 Glasgow	7	-	2	H	
		08 Manchester	2	-	3	A	ot
		09 Coventry	3	-	4	A	ot
		14 Dundee	3	-	4	H	ot
		16 Guildord	2	-	6	H	

		22	Milton Keynes	6	-	2	H	
		23	Dundee	3	-	0	A	
		26	Sheffield	2	-	3	H	ps
		27	Sheffield	3	-	5	A	
		29	Coventry	4	-	5	A	
		31	Coventry	5	-	3	H	
	Jan	02	Guildford	3	-	1	H	
		05	Fife	2	-	6	H	
		06	Manchester	3	-	4	A	ot
		12	Manchester	0	-	3	H	
		13	Cardiff	4	-	5	A	ot
		18	Dundee	3	-	4	A	
		19	Glasgow	1	-	4	A	
		20	Fife	3	-	2	A	ps
		26	Cardiff	2	-	1	H	
	Feb	02	Milton Keynes	2	-	1	H	
		03	Belfast	5	-	8	A	
		09	Sheffield	1	-	3	A	
		10	Belfast	3	-	2	H	ot
		16	Sheffield	2	-	5	H	
		20	Coventry	1	-	3	H	
		23	Glasgow	6	-	3	H	
	Mar	02	Milton Keynes	3	-	4	A	ps
		03	Fife	4	-	3	H	ot
		09	Dundee	4	-	1	H	
		16	Manchester	5	-	2	H	
		17	Dundee	1	-	2	H	ot
		23	Glasgow	4	-	0	A	
		24	Fife	3	-	4	A	ot
		30	Guildford	0	-	2	H	ot

BL Play-Offs

Quarter Final

	Apr	06	Fife	3	-	3	A
		07	Fife	3	-	0	H

Semi-Final

	Apr	13	Cardiff	4	-	9	Nottm

Challenge Games

	Aug	11	Cardiff	5	-	5	H
		12	Cardiff	3	-	6	A
		18	Dresden Eislowen	7	-	5	H
		19	Fishtown Pinguins	2	-	1	H
		25	Stavanger Oilers -Norway	5	-	3	H
		26	MAC Budepest	4	-	2	H

Domestic season
Challenge Cup
Quarter final
Dundee 0 Belfast 8, Belfast 4 Dundee 2
Glasgow 3 Cardiff 4, Cardiff 4 Glasgow 6 after over time
Manchester 1 Nottingham 6, Nottingham 2 Manchester 4
Sheffield 4 Guildford 4, Guildford 5 Sheffield 4
Semi finals
Belfast 1 Glasgow 2, Glasgow 3 Belfast 6
Guildford 5 Nottingham 2, Nottingham 1 Guildford 3
Final
Belfast 2 Guildford 1

*****

League Table
2018-19 Elite

	GP	RW	OW	PW	RL	OL	PL	GF	GA	GD	Pts
Belfast	60	39	5	1	13	1	1	238	147	91	
Cardiff	60	38	5	0	11	3	3	235	146	89	
Nottingham	60	23	3	3	19	10	2	183	181	2	
Glasgow	60	28	2	1	24	4	1	202	186	16	
Guildford	60	22	6	2	23	5	2	189	180	9	
Fife	60	21	8	1	24	2	4	188	204	-16	
Sheffield	60	23	5	2	26	3	1	183	203	-20	
Coventry	60	19	4	4	25	5	3	209	221	-12	
Manchester	60	21	4	2	28	4	1	179	208	-29	
Dundee	60	16	4	3	25	8	4	169	201	-32	
Milton Keynes	60	9	3	3	41	4	0	148	246	-98	

Play offs

Quarter final
Cardiff beat Sheffield 11-8 on aggregate
Belfast beat Coventry 12-2 on aggregate
Guildford beat Glasgow 7-3 on aggregate
Nottingham beat Fife 6-3 on aggregate

Semi final
Cardiff 9 Nottingham 4
Belfast 2 Guildford 1

Final
Belfast 1 Cardiff 2

Player stats

Name	GP	GPI	Mins	Shots	GA	GAA	%sv	Pts	Pims	SO
Mike Garnett	61	53	3147.28	1672	150	2.85	91.03	1	2	3
Patrick Munson	31	17	983.47	518	42	2.56	91.89	0	0	2
Sam Gospel	50	4	162.13	73	12	4.44	83.56	0	0	0

Name…….	Games	Goals	Assists	Points	Penalties
Guptill	67	39	26	65	72
Hurtubise	71	16	39	55	54
Luke Pither	71	22	31	53	60
Kovacs	60	15	32	47	14
Robert Farmer	64	13	28	41	69
Brett Perlini	70	18	22	40	39
Bolduc	48	9	17	26	70
Olsen	56	9	15	24	49
Hughes	65	6	18	24	62
Rissling	62	4	20	24	124
Richard	43	10	13	23	4
Henderson	50	5	17	22	18
Ollie Betteridge	71	10	12	22	22
Billingsley	64	4	17	21	49
Rheault	36	6	12	18	28
Stewart	27	7	9	16	27
Stephen Lee	67	1	11	12	36
Robert Lachowicz	68	3	9	12	8
Biggs	27	4	7	11	61
Tvrdon	16	4	6	10	8
Guillaume lepine	65	2	8	10	131
Josh Tetlow	71	0	6	6	43
Doty	23	2	1	3	43
Vankleef	19	1	1	2	4
Hazledine	24	0	0	0	0

Kelsall played challenge games only

Another award from the fans to Coach driver 'John' who like driver 'Henry' looked after us all. We got away with a few things but these drivers were no mugs as they could put us in our places too, great times.

2019-20

> Four UK challenge matches
> The European Continental Cup

Challenge Cup semi final
League void
No play offs played (covid)
Continental Cup super final Silver Medal

Elite All Star chosen: Herr, Matheson

Seasons Iron men: Betteridge, Connelly, Herr, Kelsall, Lachowicz, Matheson, Whistle

Player's player of the year – Sam Herr

Returnees: Betteridge, Gospel, J.Hazledine, Kelsall, Lachowicz, Lepine, Perlini, Rheault, Tetlow

Players IN	Players NOT returning
BINKLEY Jason	BIGGS Tyler
BULMER Brett	BOLDUC Alexandre
CARR Kevin n/m	CHERNOMAZ Rich – Coach
CONNELLY Brian	DOTY Jacob
DeSANTIS Jason	GOSPEL Sam n/m
DOUCET Guillaume – Dir. Of Hoc	GUPTIL Alex
DUETSCH Adam	HENDERSON Kevin
FICK Danny	HUGHES Tommy
GOLOVKOVS Georgs	HURTUBISE Mark
HANSEN Jacob	KOVACS Justin
HERR Sam	LEE Stephen
HORVAT Ryan	MUNSON Patrick n/m
HOVEL Tom n/m	OLSEN Dylan
JAKOBS Jens	PITHER Luke
LOISEAU Alex	RICHARD Dylan
MALMQUIST Dylan	RISSLING Jaynen
MATHESON Mark	STEWART Chris
QUIST Willaim	TYRDON Marek
RUSSELL John n/m	VANKLEEF Tyler
TALBOT Julian	
TOUSIGNANT Mathieu	
WALLACE Tim – Coach	
WHISTLE Jackson n/m	

Long standing goal judge (stage end) Fraser 'BAZ' Shaw

2019-20

CHALLENGE CUP - first round

DATE		VERSUS	SCORE	HOME/AWAY	
Aug	31	Sheffield	4-6	A	
Sept	01	Sheffield	5-1	H	
	21	Manchester	2-1	A	
Oct	05	Sheffield	1-3	H	
	06	Sheffield	3-4	A	ps
	23	Manchester	3-4	H	ot
Nov	02	Manchester	4-1	H	
	03	Manchester	3-1	A	

Q-Final

Dec	11	Guildford	5-1	H	
	18	Guildford	3-5	A	

Semi-Final

Jan	22	Cardiff	5-5	H	
	29	Cardiff	3-4	A	

BRITISH LEAGUE

DATE		VERSUS	SCORE	HOME/AWAY	
Sept	07	Guildford	3-1	A	
	14	Dundee	5-1	A	
	15	Fife	2-4	A	
	22	Belfast	0-3	A	
	28	Glasgow	2-4	H	
	29	Glasgow	2-3	H	ps
Oct	12	Guildford	2-6	A	
	13	Fife	1-4	A	
	19	Cardiff	2-1	A	
	20	Cardiff	3-5	H	
	26	Fife	4-3	H	
	27	Coventry	3-4	A	
	30	Dundee	5-2	H	
Nov	09	Belfast	4-1	H	
	10	Belfast	2-0	H	
	23	Sheffield	4-5	A	ot
	24	Manchester	5-4	A	
	29	Glasgow	3-0	A	
Dec	01	Sheffield	1-3	H	
	04	Manchester	5-1	H	
	07	Coventry	6-3	A	
	08	Guildford	2-3	H	
	14	Cardiff	3-2	A	ot
	15	Manchester	2-3	H	

123

	21	Dundee	6-1	H	
	22	Dundee	3-2	A	
	26	Coventry	5-4	H	ot
	28	Coventry	4-3	A	ot
	31	Sheffield	2-3	H	
Jan	01	Sheffield	3-2	A	ot
	04	Dundee	5-4	H	ps
	05	Manchester	3-0	A	
	16	Glasgow	3-2	H	ot
	19	Fife	3-2	A	
	25	Guildford	3-5	H	
	26	Cardiff	2-4	A	
Feb	01	Sheffield	5-1	A	
	02	Fife	2-0	H	
	12	Manchester	3-4	A	ps
	14	Fife	3-2	H	
	16	Belfast	4-0	H	
	19	Glasgow	4-2	A	
	22	Sheffield	2-6	H	
	23	Guildford	1-4	A	
	29	Cardiff	7-3	H	
Mar	01	Coventry	3-4	H	ps

The remaining fixtures cancelled due to coronavirus

BL Play-Offs   No Play-Offs this season

Challenge Games

Aug	17 Cardiff	3-2	H	
	18 Cardiff	0-2	A	
	24 Coventry	4-2	H	
	25 Coventry	3-1	A	

Continental Cup

3rd round Nov Group E	15 Amiens Gothiques (France)	4-2	in Denmark	
	16 Ferencvarosi (Hungary)	2-3		
	17 SonderjyskE Vojens	4-2		
Final Round Jan	10 SonderjyskE Vojens (Denmark)	1-2	"	ps
	11 Cracovia Krakow (Poland)	4-3		
	12 Neman Grodno (Belarus)	4-3		

Domestic season
Quarter finals-aggregate score
Dundee 1 Glasgow 1, Glasgow 4 Dundee 1
Sheffield 5 Manchester 2, Manchester 3 Sheffield 3
Belfast 0 Cardiff 1, Cardiff 4 Belfast 0
Nottingham 5 Guildford 1, Guildford 5 Nottingham 3
Semi finals-aggregate score
Cardiff 5 Nottingham 5, Nottingham 3 Cardiff 4
Glasgow 1 Sheffield 5, Sheffield4 Glasgow 0
Final
Sheffield 4 Cardiff 3

*****

League Table
2019-20 Elite-incomplete (season void due to Covid:19 pandemic)

	GP	RW	OW	PW	RL	OL	PL	GF	GA	GD	Pts
Cardiff	46	28	1	2	13	2	0	162	138	24	64
Sheffield	49	28	3	0	17	1	0	211	154	57	63
Coventry	48	25	1	1	14	5	2	180	158	22	61
Belfast	48	26	1	1	16	2	2	149	125	24	60
Nottingham	46	21	5	1	15	1	3	147	124	23	58
Guildford	47	19	5	1	19	1	2	146	146	-	53
Glasgow	48	14	3	2	26	2	1	141	181	-40	41
Manchester	49	12	1	5	26	4	1	119	151	-32	41
Dundee	48	16	0	2	27	2	1	146	179	-33	39
Fife	49	14	1	0	30	1	3	124	169	-45	34

Play Offs
Not played due to the Covid:19 pandemic

****

AD
Merv Magus Cartoons
http://www.hockeycartoons.ca/index.html

Player stats

Name	GP	GPi	Mins	Shots	GA	GAA	%sv	Pts	Pims	SO
Kevin Carr	62	49	2965.23	1531	127	2.57	91.70	2	14	4
Jackson Whistle	64	15	897.49	417	38	2.54	90.89	0	0	1
Sam Gospel	0	0								
Tom Hovell	1	0								

John Russell only listed

Name…….	Games	Goals	Assists	Points	Penalties
Herr	64	41	44	85	56
Hansen	51	22	38	60	45
Matheson	64	11	45	56	30
Brett Perlini	55	23	19	42	14
Talbot	45	18	19	37	38
Connelly	64	7	29	36	42
Malmquist	63	9	25	34	8
Golovkovs	51	9	23	32	20
Bulmer	46	13	17	30	20
Ollie Betteridge	64	13	9	22	28
Deutsch	47	9	13	22	49
Horvat	34	5	13	18	41
DeSantis	47	4	12	16	27
Rheault	50	6	9	15	14
Guillaume Lepine	62	1	14	15	82
Robert Lachowicz	64	4	11	15	10
Fick	62	0	11	11	99
Quist	30	6	2	8	10
Josh Tetlow	60	0	6	6	15
Tousignant	10	3	1	4	17
Loiseau	5	1	1	2	2
Kelsall	64	1	1	2	6
Jakobs	11	1	0	1	13
Binkley	6	0	1	1	6
Hazledine	41	0	1	1	2

Station Hotel in Kirkcaldy for away supporters

2020-21

Elite 'Series' - No programme

One UK challenge match

Elite 'series' Cup winners

Elite All Star chosen: Matheson, Whistle

Seasons Iron men: 13 players

Player's player of the year – (unknown)

Returnees: Betteridge, Kelsall, Lachowicz, Matheson, Perlini, Tetlow, Wallace, Whistle

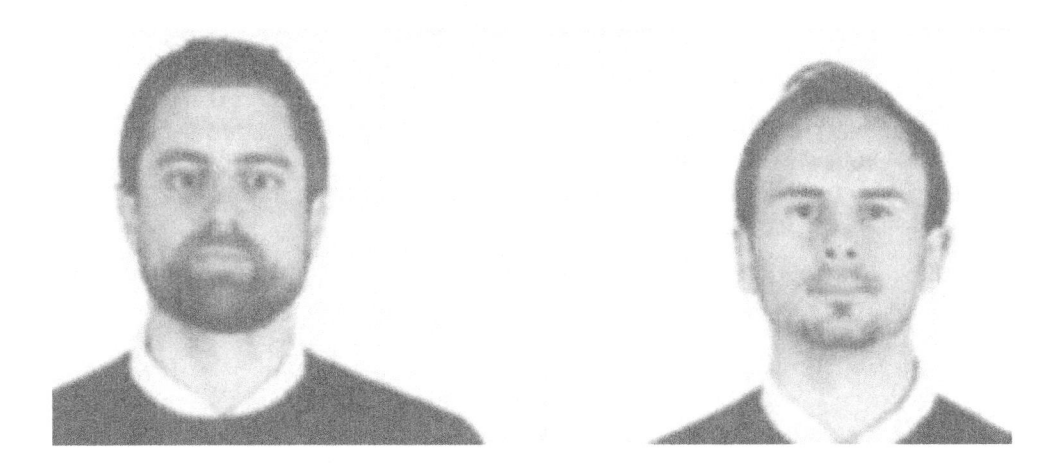

Success for the duo of Doucet and Wallace 'behind closed doors' as it were

Players IN	Players NOT returning
BOIVIN Christophe	BINKLY Jason
BOWNS Ben n/m	BULMER Brett
CANGELOSI Austin	CARR Kevin n/m
CHAMBERLAIN Bobby	CONNELLY Brian
CLARKE-PIZZO Morgan	DeSANTIS Jason
DINEEN Nick	DEUTSCH Adam
DOMINGUE Kevin	FICK Danny
ELLIS Brendan	GOLOVKOVS Georges
GARRIGAN Craig	GOSPEL Sam n/m
GARSIDE Mark	HANSEN Jake
GRIFFITHS Owen	HAZLEDINE Joesph
HOOK Lewis	HERR Sam
KERLIN Will n/m	HOVELL Tom n/m
MAY Johno	HORVAT Ryan
STENTON Liam	JAKOBS Jens
TALBOT-TASSI Dominic	LOIEAU Alexis
	LEPINE Guillaume
	MALMQUIST Dylan
	QUIST Willaim
	RHEAULT Jon
	RUSSELL John n/m
	TALBOT Julian
	TOUSIGNANT Mathieu

Another British player (Brett Perlini) whose father Fred had played for us

Domestic season and fixtures

The Covid situation claimed the end of the 2020 season, ruling it void but with government funding through a loan/grant, the sport was able to play a short 2021 season in the form of a CUP competition called the Elite 'Series'. A round robin of 24 games for four English teams (Guildford declined when the application for funding was put in) was played before a knock out play-offs.

An aggregate semi-final was followed by an arranged three game final series. The table finished like this.

2020-21 Elite 'Series' Trophy

Place	Team	Pld	RW	OW	RL	OL	Goals	GD	Pts
1	Sheffield	12	8	(0/0)	3	(1/0)	60-44	+16	17
2	Coventry	12	4	(1/0)	4	(3/0)	43-48	-5	13
3	Nottingham	12	3	(3/0)	5	(1/0)	37-42	-5	13
4	Manchester	12	3	(2/0)	6	(1/0)	40-46	-6	11

Fixtures and results

Date	Home Team	Score	Away Team	Score	
April 3rd	Manchester	3	Coventry	2	OT
April 3rd	Nottingham	2	Sheffield	3	
April 4th	Sheffield	4	Manchester	5	
April 4th	Coventry	3	Nottingham	1	
April 6th	Manchester	1	Nottingham	3	
April 7th	Sheffield	7	Coventry	2	
April 9th	Coventry	4	Manchester	5	OT
April 10th	Sheffield	8	Nottingham	4	
April 11th	Nottingham	1	Coventry	3	
April 11th	Manchester	4	Sheffield	6	
April 13th	Coventry	4	Sheffield	6	
April 14th	Nottingham	4	Manchester	3	OT
April 15th	Manchester	3	Coventry	4	
April 16th	Nottingham	4	Sheffield	3	
April 17th	Coventry	4	Nottingham	3	OT
April 18th	Sheffield	2	Manchester	3	
April 19th	Nottingham	4	Manchester	3	
April 20th	Sheffield	5	Coventry	3	
April 21st	Manchester	4	Nottingham	2	
April 22nd	Coventry	5	Sheffield	7	
April 24th	Coventry	6	Manchester	3	
April 24th	Sheffield	4	Nottingham	5	OT

April 25th	Nottingham	4	Coventry	3	OT
April 25th	Manchester	3	Sheffield	5	
April 27th	Coventry	0	Nottingham	2	SF1
April 27th	Manchester	4	Sheffield	5	SF1
April 28th	Nottingham	4	Coventry	1	SF2
April 29th	Sheffield	8	Manchester	3	SF2
May 1st May 2nd May 3rd (if needed)	Sheffield Nottingham Sheffield	3 5 void	Nottingham Sheffield Nottingham	5 2 void	Final 1,2,3.

ELITE 'Series' Trophy winners
The Nottingham Panthers by a 2 to 0 game win

****

AD

Pop into 'Mary's Kitchen' just across the road from the Parliament Street entrance. Sit in or take away drinks and eats before or after you venture anywhere in the area.
Opposite the Sneinton market area.

Player stats

Name	GP	GPi	Mins	Shots	GA	GAA	%sv	Pts	Pims	SO
Ben Bowns	15	8	437.36	233	26	3.57	88.84	0	2	0
Jackson Whistle	16	9	520.51	274	22	2.54	91.97	0	0	1
Will Kerlin	1	0								

Name…….	Games	Goals	Assists	Points	Penalties
Boivin	16	8	14	22	6
Domingue	16	10	10	20	10
Cangelosi	16	11	8	19	10
Mark Matheson	16	4	12	16	12
Brett Perlini	13	4	10	14	6
Talbot-Tassi	16	3	5	8	0
Lewis hook	16	3	4	7	8
Ellis	16	0	7	7	12
Ollie Betteridge	16	5	1	6	2
Dineen	16	3	3	6	11
Robert Lachowicz	15	0	6	6	4
Griffiths	15	0	4	4	0
May	16	1	1	2	12
Josh Tetlow	16	1	0	1	18
Kelsall	16	0	1	1	4
Clarke-Pizzo	5	0	0	0	0
Garrigan	13	0	0	0	0
Chamberlain	5	0	0	0	4
Garside	14	0	0	0	4
Stenton	16	0	0	0	4

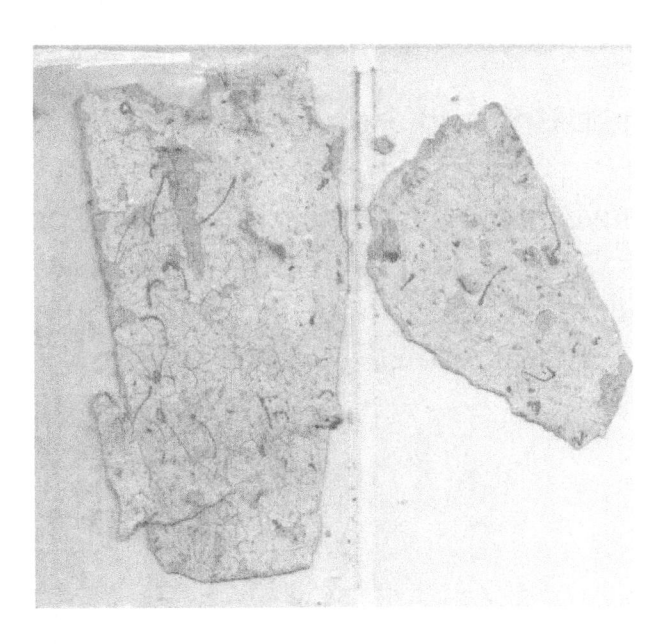

Actual paper/texture from the walls of the old stadium building

2021-22

e programme from the Official Website

Four UK challenge matches

Challenge Cup semi final
League placing 4th
Play offs quarter final

Elite All Star chosen:

Seasons Iron men: Brassard, Boivin, Kerlin (nm), Norrish, Tetlow

Player's player of the year – Kevin carr

Returnees: Betteridge, Boivin, Clarke-Pizzo, Domingue, Kelsall, Kerlin, Matheson, Tetlow, Wallace

Players IN	Players NOT returning
BAILLARGEON Robbie	BOWNS Ben n/m
CARR Kevin n/m	CHAMBERLAIN Bobby
BRASSARD Jean-Claude	CONGELOSI Austin
CARROZA Massimo	DINEEN Nick
DOHERTY Taylor	ELLIS Brendan
HEDBERG Edwin	GARRIGAN Craig
HOPKINS Jack	GARSIDE Mark
JOKINEN Tommi	GRIFFITHS Owen
LANE Matt	HOOK Lewis
LEE Stephen	LACHOWICZ Robert
MASSY Kevin	MAY Johno
MYERS Matthew	PERLINI Brett
NORRISH Brady	STENTON Liam
RICHARDS Sean	TALBOT-TASSI Dominic
SHELDON Luca n/m	WHISTLE Dave – co-coach
SOURANTA Simon	WHISTLE Jackson n/m
THOW Aaron	
TOUSIGNANT Mathieu	
WELSH Jeremy	

Net Minder Kevin Carr

2021-22

Challenge Cup

DATE		VERSUS	SCORE	HOME/AWAY
Oct	03	Manchester	7-3	A
	09	Manchester	3-1	H
	16	Sheffield	3-4ot	H
	23	Sheffield	3-2ot	A
Nov	07	Manchester	5-4ps	H
	13	Sheffield	1-3	H
	14	Manchester	3-7	A
	27	Sheffield	5-4ot	A

Q-Final

Semi-Final

UK League

DATE		VERSUS	SCORE	HOME/AWAY
Sept	26	Dundee	2-1	H
				H
Oct	02	Coventry	2-5	H
	17	Cardiff	5-2	H
	20	Guildford	4-3	H
	29	Belfast	0-5	H
	30	Cardiff	3-0	A
Nov	06	Dundee	4-3ot	H
	21	Glasgow	2-3	H
	28	Fife	2-4	H
Dec	03	Glasgow	4-1	H
	04	Dundee	1-4	A
	05	Fife	4-2	A
	11	Guildford	5-2	H
	12	Belfast	2-7	A
	26	Sheffield	3-5	A
	27	Sheffield	1-4	H
	31	Manchester	5-3	H
Jan	01	Manchester	0-4	A
	03	Belfast	2-7	H
	08	Guildford	4-3	A
	09	Fife	4-2	H
	14	Glasgow	5-2	A
	15	Fife	4-2	A
	16	Dundee	4-5ot	A
	22	Sheffield	2-4	A
	23	Glasgow	1-2	H
	29	Cardiff	1-5	A
	30	Dundee	5-2	H

Feb	05 Glasgow	1-2ot	H	
	06 Fife	1-2ot	H	
	11 Manchester	2-4	A	
	12 Cardiff	2-5	A	
	13 Cardiff	4-1	H	
	16 Manchester	4-2	H	
	19 Coventry	1-0	A	
	20 Belfast	2-3	H	
	26 Sheffield	3-7	H	
	27 Guildford	3-1	A	
Mar	02 Coventry	0-5	A	
	05 Manchester	4-7	A	
	06 Manchester	5-2	H	
	09 Fife	4-3ot	A	
	13 Guildford	4-5ot	A	
	19 Sheffield	3-0	H	
	20 Glasgow	4-3ot	A	
	25 Belfast	4-2	A	
	26 Belfast	1-4	A	
Apr	02 Sheffield	2-6	A	
	03 Coventry	4-10	H	
	06 Dundee	3-8	A	
	09 Coventry	6-4	A	
	10 Guildford	3-5	H	
	13 Coventry	9-1	H	
	17 Cardiff	3-7	H	
PlayOffs	Guildford	4-4	A	
	Guildford	2-3	H	

Challenge games

Sept 11 Cardiff	1-5	A	
12 Cardiff (Diamond Jubilee Cup)	2-4	H	
18 Sheffield	2-3	H	
19 Sheffield (Aladdin Cup)	5-3	A	

Domestic season
Challenge Cup
Quarter finals
Coventry 3 Belfast 2, Belfast 5 Coventry 1
Dundee 4 Cardiff 2, Cardiff 6 Dundee 1
Nottingham 4 Guildford 2, Guildford 3 Nottingham 2
Sheffield 5 Fife 1, Fife 2 Sheffield 4
Semi finals
Belfast 2 Nottingham 1
Sheffield 0 Cardiff 5
Final
Belfast 3 Cardiff 2

*****

League table
2021-22 Elite

Team	GP	RW	OTW	PSW	RL	OTL	PSL	GF	GA	-	GD	Pts
Belfast	54	37	3	3	9	1	1	224	108		+116	88
Sheffield	54	31	5	1	10	3	4	202	138		+64	81
Cardiff	54	30	2	3	15	3	1	188	131		+57	74
Nottingham	54	22	3	0	24	4	1	163	191		-28	55
Guildford	54	19	5	1	25	2	2	165	169		-04	54
Glasgow	54	21	2	0	24	6	1	150	182		-32	53
Dundee	54	19	5	1	26	1	2	160	185		-25	53
Coventry	54	19	1	3	26	2	3	154	173		-19	51
Manchester	54	14	1	3	32	3	1	150	210		-60	40
Fife	54	12	3	1	33	4	1	122	191		-69	37

Play offs

Quarter final
Belfast beat Coventry 4-3 on aggregate
Dundee beat Sheffield 5-3 on aggregate
Cardiff beat Glasgow 5-4 on aggregate
Guildford beat Nottingham 7-6 on aggregate

Semi final
Belfast 6 Dundee 0
Cardiff 3 Guildford 2

Final
Belfast 3 Cardiff 6

Player stats

Name	GP	GPi	Mins	Shots	GA	GAA	%sv	Pts	Pims	SO
Kevin Carr	59	57	3472.1	1879	167	2.89	91.11	1	20	3
Will Kerlin	67	10	539.42	266	51	5.67	80.83	1	2	0
Sheldon	4	0			4		80.49			
Dan Green	2	0								
Downie	2	2	120	41	8			0	0	0

Name…….	Games	Goals	Assists	Points	Penalties
Welsh	66	22	46	68	10
Boivin	67	29	39	68	36
Baillargeon	65	26	31	57	105
Lane	62	20	22	42	25
Matthew Myers	66	16	24	40	49
Brassard	67	7	32	39	24
Mark Matheson	65	4	24	28	36
Ollie Betteridge	56	16	11	27	10
Tousignant	64	13	13	26	80
Carozza	31	11	15	26	12
Thow	57	3	19	22	28
Norrish	67	3	17	20	62
Richards	47	9	10	19	47
Domingue	34	6	7	13	12
Kelsall	62	5	5	10	28
Souranta	19	4	6	10	8
Massy	29	2	8	10	19
Josh Tetlow	67	3	6	9	32
Doherty	24	2	7	9	18
Hedberg	29	2	2	4	4
Stephen Lee	6	1	2	3	6
Jokinen	8	0	3	3	0
Jack Hopkins	21	1	1	2	0
Clarke-Pizzo	16	1	0	1	6

2022-23 (this season)

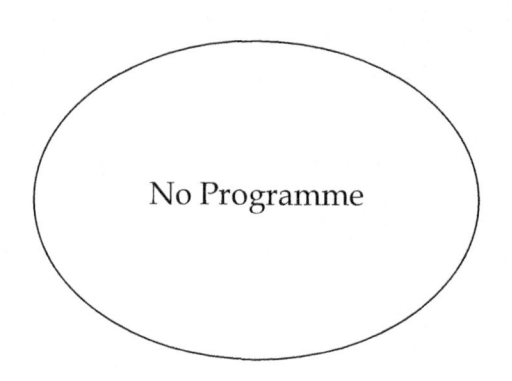

No Programme

Five UK challenge matches

Challenge Cup ?
League placing ?
Play offs ?

Elite All Star chosen: ?

Seasons Iron men: ?

Player's player of the year – ?

Returnees: Brassard, Hopkins, Kelsall, Myers, Sheldon, Welsh

Players IN	Players NOT returning
ANDERSON Stephen	BAILLARGEON Robert
BERRY Jack n/m	BETTERIDGE Oliver
BLOOR Mathew n/m	BOIVIN Christophe
BRADY Adam	CARR Kevin n/m
CARUSO Mike	CAROZZA Massimo
DUBEAU Alex n/m	DOHERTY Taylor
FERRARA Luke	DOMINGUE Kevin
GAGNON Mathieu	DOWNIE James n/m
GRAHAM GARY – Coach	DOUCET Guillaum – dir.of hoc.
HAMMOND Mike	GREEN Dan n/m
HAZLEDINE Archie	HEDBERG Edwin
JOHNSTON Andrew	JOKINEN Tommi
LAGRONE Duggie	KERLIN William n/m
LEVIN David	LEE Stephen
MOORE Craig	MASSY Kevin
PUFFER Craig	MATHESON Mark
SORENSON Tanner	NORRISH Brady
SUMMERS Kelly	RICHARDS Sean
WELYCHKA Brett	SAURANTA Simon
	TETLOW Joshua
	THOW Aaron
	TOUSIGNANT Mathieu
	WALLACE Tim – coach
	WHISTLE Dave – co-coach

Open training session to the public before the seasons start

Fixtures 2022-23

Detail	-	Versus	-	score	-	-	h/a
Challenge Cup							
Sept							
16		Manchester		1-5			A
25		Sheffield		3-2	ot		H
Oct							
01		Sheffield		1-2			A
15		Manchester		4-1			H
16		Manchester		2-3	ps		A
22		Sheffield		4-6			H
29		Sheffield		3-7			A
Nov							
06		Manchester		5-4			H
Quarter Final							
		Belfast					
		Belfast					
Semi-Final							
Final							

Detail	-	Versus	-	Score	-	-	h/a
League							
Sept							
10		Guildford		4-3	ot		H
11		Coventry		1-2			A
17		Coventry		1-6			H
30		Dundee		6-2			H
Oct							
7		Cardiff		1-5			A
8		Fife		1-3			H
14		Dundee		2-4			A
19		Glasgow		2-3	ps		A
25		Glasgow		6-2			H
30		Cardiff		5-2			H
Nov							
4		Cardiff		2-6			A
12		Belfast		5-4			H
13		Fife		1-6			A
18		Guildford		2-4			H
19		Guildford		2-4			A
26		Sheffield		2-3	ps		A
27		Manchester		1-3			H
Dec							
2		Fife					H
3		Dundee					A
10		Manchester					A
11		Cardiff					H
17		Fife					A
18		Fife					H
23		Glasgow					H
26		Sheffield					A
27		Sheffield					H

31		Coventry					H
Jan							
2		Coventry					A
7		Guilford					H
8		Guildford					A
13		Belfast					A
14		Belfast					A
20		Glasgow					A
21		Belfast					H
27		Dundee					A
28		Manchester					H
Feb							
4		Sheffield					H
5		Cardiff					A
14		Belfast					H
18		Coventry					H
19		Belfast					A
25		Cardiff					H
26		Dundee					H
Mar							
4		Sheffield					A
5		Guildford					A
11		Fife					A
12		Dundee					A
18		Sheffield					A
19		Manchester					H
22		Dundee					H
25		Glasgow					A
26		Coventry					A
31		Manchester					A
Apr							
1		Manchester					H
Play offs							

Detail	-	versus	-	Score	-	-	h/a
Challenge Games							
Aug							
27		Sheffield		4-5	ps		h
28		Sheffield		3-4			a
31		Coventry		4-1			a
Sept							
3		Cardiff		2-4			h
4		Cardiff		2-3			a

Domestic season (you can complete this one-ED)
Challenge Cup
Quarter finals

Semi finals

Final

*****

League Table
2022-23 Elite

Team	GP	RW	OTW	PSW	RL	OTL	PSL	GF	GA	-	GD	Pts

....

Play offs

Quarter final

Semi final

Final

Player stats – to be completed by the owner of this book

Name	GP	GPi	Mins	Shots	GA	%sv	GAA	Pts	Pims	SO
Dubeau										
Berry										
Sheldon										
Bloor										

Name…….	Games	Goals	Assists	Points	Penalties

New Chief Executive Officer
Omar Pacha

COMPETITION TITLES

1) CUP

English/International Tournament	1947-50
English /British Autumn Cup	1948-54 & 1955-60, 1981-01
Southern Cup + Playoff	1981-82
Icy-Smith Cup	1990
Express/Challenge Cup	1998-00, 2002-20, 2022-23
Elite 'series'	2021
Continental Cup	2000, 2005, 2007.2014.2018.2020
Champions Hockey League	2015, 2018
Charity Shield	2008, 2010
Midlands (Bass/Radio) Cup	1981-83 & 1990

2) LEAGUE

Inter-City/English League South	1981-82
English National League	1947-54, 1982
British/Super*/Elite**	1955-60, 1983-96, 1997-03* 2004-20**

2022-23**

3) PLAYOFFS

Inter-City/English League South	1981-82
British/Super*/Elite**	1960, 1983-96, 1997-03* 2004-20** 2022-23**

4) LOCAL (home cup)

Panther Trophy/Walker Cup   1949, 1981-85, 1990

In 48-49 v Brighton, London all-stars, Rest of England.
In 80-81 v Altrincham, Billingham, Crowtree (Sunderland), Solihull, Streatham, Southampton.
In 81-82 v Altrincham, Dundee, Whitley.
In 82-83 v Cleveland, Durham, Peterborough, Streatham, Southampton.
In 83-83 v Southampton.
In 84-85 v Lea Valley.
In 89-90 v Trafford.
In 2012-13 as Alladin Cup v Asiago (ITA)
In 2013-14 as Alladin Cup v Braehead and Amiens
In 2015-16 as Alladin Cup v Braehead
In 2016-17 as Alladin Cup v Braehead
In 2017-18 as Alladin Cup v Braehead and Cardiff
In 2021-22 as Alladin Cup v Sheffield (v Cardiff for the Diamond Jubilee Cup)

5) OTHER (away cups) – Nottingham being one of several teams invited to play.

Altrincham Cup	1981, 1983
Bristol Trophy	1982
London Cup	1954
Northumbria Cup (Whitley Bay)	1981, 1983
Sheffield Invitational Tournament	1992
Solihull Cup	1981, 1984
Streatham Cup	1981, 1983
Sussex Daily News Cup (Brighton)	1950, 1951
Top Rank Trophy (Southampton)	1981, 1982, 1983
Hull International tri tournament	2010

6) TRI-TOURNAMENTS

Brighton, Nottingham, Paisley	1956-57
Fife, Nottingham, Sheffield	1993
(x 2, 15 minute periods)	

7) INTERNATIONAL CHALLENGES
(as noted in season by season section)

8) CHALLENGE GAMES
(as noted in season by season section)

9) TESTIMONIALS

Neil Able at Ice Sheffield	2007
Paul Adey	1996
Mike Blaisdell at Sheffield	2004
Brent Bobyck at Sheffield	2005
Rick Brebant at Sheffield	2003
Steve Carpenter at Coventry	2005
Greg Hadden	2003
Simon Hunt	2000
Randall Weber	1999
Corey Neilson	2016
Steve Lee	2018
Robert Lachowicz	2019
Matthew Myers	2023

10) FOREIGN TOURS
- Canada — 1982
- Czechoslovakia — 1957-58
- France (Continental Cup* October1905, October 1906) 1984, 2005*, 2007 +2007* 2008, 2015, 2017
- Germany — 1957-58
- Holland — 2014
- Scotland — 1952
- Sweden (Ahearne Cup** December 1954) 1951-52, 1955**, 1959, 1981
- Switzerland — 1951, 1957
- Wales (Continental Cup* October 1999) 2000

Note that the Ahearne Trophy was played at home versus Germany 2002, 2006
Switzerland 2003

Above: left: admissions pass to the Heineken Championship finals 1989
Nottingham beat Ayr

Right: a commemorative medal for officiating.
Sheffield beat Nottingham

SEASON BY SEASON TOURNAMENTS

1) 1946/47 English National Tournament (**note. Panthers did not compete**
English National League **in English Autumn Cup.**)
International Challenge v U.S.A.

2) 1947/48 English National Tournament
English Autumn Cup
English National League

3) 1948/49 English International Tournament
English Autumn Cup
English National League
Panther (home) Trophy v Brighton (also League game)
London All Stars, Rest of England.
International Challenges v Sudbury Wolves (Canada),
Switzerland, U.S.A.

4) 1949/50 English National Tournament
English Autumn Cup
English National League
Sussex Daily News Cup (Brighton)

5) 1950/51 English Autumn Cup
English National League
Sussex Daily News Cup (Brighton)
International Challenges v Canada Representatives,
Switzerland Select.
Tours Abroad to Sweden and Switzerland.

6) 1951/52 English Autumn Cup
English National League
International Challenges v Edmonton Mercury's (Canada),
U.S.A.
Tours Abroad to Scotland and Sweden.

7) 1952/53 English Autumn Cup
English National league
Challenge Games v Dunfermline, Durham,
Murrayfield, Paisley, Wembley Lions,
Ice-Hockey World All Stars (IHW).

8) 1953/54 English Autumn Cup
English National League
London Cup with Brighton, Harringay, Streatham.
International Challenge v West Canada.
Challenge Games v Paisley x2, All Stars.

Left: League winners medal piping Streatham in 1954
Right: Runners up Medal 1955 behind Harringay Racers

9) 1954/55 British Autumn Cup
British League
Tour Abroad to Sweden (Ahearne Trophy).

10) 1955/56 British Autumn Cup
British League
International Challenges v Czechoslovakia, Sweden, U.S.A.
Tri-Challenge Competition with Brighton, Paisley.

11) 1956/57 British Autumn Cup
British League
International Challenges v Czechoslovakia, Sweden.
Tri-Challenge Competition with Brighton, Paisley.
Tours Abroad to Czechoslovakia, Germany,
Switzerland.

12) 1957/58 British Autumn Cup
British League
International Challenges in Czechoslovakia, Russia, U.S.A.
Challenge Game v Wembley Lions.
Tours Abroad to Czechoslovakia and Germany.

13) 1958/59 British Autumn Cup
British League
International Challenges v Canada, Russia.
Tour Abroad to Sweden.

14) 1959/60 British Autumn Cup
British League
British Play-Offs
International Challenge v RCAF Flyers (Canada)

15) 1980-81 Inter City League (ICL) Southern Cup
(Note: did not qualify for British play offs)
Inter City League and Play-Offs
Midlands Cup (Bass Worthington)
Walker (home) Cup v Altrincham, Billingham, Crowtree (Sunderland), Solihull, Streatham.
Altrincham Cup
Northumbria Cup (Whitley)
Solihull Cup
Streatham Cup
Top Rank Trophy (Southampton)
International Challenges v Baden Baden.
Challenge Games v Durham, Sheffield Sabres, Streatham.
Tour Abroad to Sweden.

16) 1981-82 Southern Cup and Play-Offs
(note. Panthers did not qualify for National Play-Offs)
English National League
English League South and Play-Offs
Midlands Cup (Bass Worthington)
Walker (home) Cup v Altrincham, Dundee, Whitley Bay.
Bristol Trophy
Top Rank Trophy (Southampton) - also league game.
International Challenge v Don Mills Comets (Canada).
Challenge Games v Altrincham, Dundee, Durham, Sheffield Sabres, Sheffield.
Tour Abroad to Canada.

17) 1982-83 British League **(note. Panthers did not qualify for**
Midlands Cup (Bass Worthington) **British League Play-offs)**
Walker (home) Cup v Cleveland, Durham, Peterborough, Southampton, Streatham.
Altrincham Cup
Northumbria Cup (Whitley Bay)
Streatham Cup
Top Rank Trophy (Southampton)
International Challenges v Air Canada, Don Mills Comets x2, (Canada).
Challenge Games v Peterborough, Streatham x3.

18) 1983-84 British Autumn Cup **(note. Panthers did not qualify for**
British League **British League Play-Offs.)**
Walker (home) Cup v Southampton.
Solihull Cup
International Challenges v Air Canada, Don Mills Comets, Rhode Island, All Stars.
Tour Abroad in France.

19) 1984-85 British Autumn Cup.(**note. Panthers did not qualify for British League Play-offs**)
British League
Walker (home) Cup v Lee Valley.
International Challenges v Air Canada and Mills Comets (Canada)
Challenge Games v Bournemouth and Solihull

20) 1985-86 British Autumn Cup
British League
British Play-Offs
International Challenge v East York Blackhawk's (Canada)
Challenge Games v Crowtree (Sunderland) and Dundee.

21) 1986-87 British Autumn Cup
British League
British Play-Offs
Challenge Games v Peterborough, Slough x2, Trafford.

22) 1987-88 British Autumn Cup
British League
British Play-Offs
International Challenge v Barden Rebels (Germany).
Challenge Games v Southampton x2, Trafford.

23) 1988-89 British Autumn Cup
British League
British Play-Offs
Challenge Games v Cardiff x2.

24) 1989-90 British Autumn Cup
British League
British Play-Offs
Midlands Radio Cup v Telford x4, Trafford x2, Solihull x2.
Icy-Smith Cup v Solihull x2, Whitley Bay x2.
Walker (home) Cup v Trafford.
Challenge Game v Humberside.

25) 1990-91 British Autumn Cup
British League
British Play-Offs
Challenge Game v Humberside.

26) 1991-92 British Autumn Cup
British League
British Play-Offs
International Challenges v Denmark, Romania.
Challenges Games v Humberside, Medway x2.

27) 1992-93 British Autumn Cup
British League
British Play-Offs
Challenge Competition with Fife/Sheffield x.2, 15 minute period games (Tri Tournament).
Challenge Games v Cardiff x2, Milton Keynes x2, Solihull x2.

28) 1993-94 British Autumn Cup
British League
British Play-Offs
International Challenge v Lada Togliatti (Russia).
Challenge Games v Humberside, Solihull x2, Trafford x2.

29) 1994-95 British Autumn Cup
British League
British Play-Offs
International Challenges v Manitoba Bison & Team Canada.
Challenge Games v Durham x2, Humberside x2.

30) 1995-96 British Autumn Cup
British League
British Play-Offs
Challenge Games v Durham, Milton Keynes x2.
Testimonial Paul Adey.

31) 1996-97 British Autumn Cup (B+H)
British Super League
British Play-Offs
International Challenges v University of Manitoba (Canada), and Team Japan.
Challenge Games v Kingston (Hull) x2, Newcastle x2.

32) 1997-98 British Autumn Cup (B+H)
Challenge Cup
British Super League
British Play-Offs
International Challenge v Interlarken (Switzerland).
Challenge Games v Guildford, Kingston (Hull).

33) 1998-99 British Autumn Cup (B+H)
Challenge Cup **note) Includes the mid section of league games**.
British Super League
British Play-Offs
International Challenge v Troja Ljungly (Sweden).
Challenge Games v London, Newcastle x2, Sheffield.
Testimonial Randall Weber.

34) 1999-00 British Autumn Cup (B+H)
Challenge Cup **note) Includes mid section of league games.**
British Super League
British Play-Offs
Continental Cup v Cardiff, Lada Togliatti.
International Challenge v Malmö Red hawks (Sweden).
Challenge Games v Guildford, Hull.
Testimonial Simon Hunt.

35) 2000-01 British Autumn Cup (B+H)
 (note. Panthers did not qualify for the Challenge Cup
British Super League
British Play-Offs
Challenge Games v Coventry, Sheffield.

36) 2001-02 Challenge Cup **note) Includes mid section of league games.**
British Super League
British Play-Offs
Ahearne Trophy v Germany.
International Challenges v AK Bars, Dynamo Moscow (Russia),
Huddinge (Sweden).
Challenge Game v Coventry.

37) 2002-03 Challenge Cup
British Super League
British Play-Offs
Ahearne Trophy v Switzerland.
International Challenge v Princeton University (U.S.A).
Challenge Games v Cardiff x2.
Testimonial Greg Hadden.

38) 2003-04 Challenge Cup **note)Includes mid section of league games.**
British Elite League
British Play-Offs
International Challenge v AIK Stockholm (Sweden).
Challenge Games v Newcastle x2.

39) 2004-05 Challenge Cup **note) Includes the first round of league games.**
British Elite League
British Play-Offs
Continental Cup v Amiens Gothiques (France),
Milano Vipers (Italy), Olimija Ljubliana (Slovenia).
Challenge Game v Peterborough.

40) 2005-06 Challenge Cup **(note. did not compete in Knock-Out Cup.)**
British Elite League
British Play-Offs
Ahearne Cup v Cologne (Germany).
Challenge Game v Peterborough.

41) 2006-07 Challenge Cup
   (note. Did not compete in K.O.Cup)
   British Elite League
   British Play-Offs
   Continental Cup v Dragons Rouen HE76 (France),
   Red Bull Saltsburg (Austria), Sønderjyske Vogen (Denmark).
   International Challenges v Morzine-Avoriaz (France).
   Geneve-Servette, Martigny, (Swiss).
   Challenge games v Bracknell, Romford.

42) 2007-08 Challenge Cup (did not play in knock out Cup)
   Elite league
   Play offs
   Charity Shield v Coventry
   Tour of France

43) 2008-09 Challenge Cup (did not play in knock Out Cup)
   Elite League
   Play offs
   Challenge v Manchester, Peterborough
   International challenge v Geneva

44) 2009-10 Challenge Cup
   Elite League
   Play offs
   Challenge v Sheffield x2
   International tri tour v Tilburg and Hull (Hull)
   20/20 fest - Sheffield

45) 2010-11 Challenge Cup
   Elite League
   Play offs
   International Challenge v Tilburg
   20/20 fest - Nottingham

46) 2011-12 Challenge Cup
   Elite League
   Play offs
   Challenge v Belfast x2

47) 2012-13 Challenge Cup
   Elite League
   Play offs
   Home tournament v Asiago (Italy) x2

48) 2013-14 Challenge Cup
             Elite League
             Play offs
             Continental Cup
             International challenge (tri) v Amiens and Braehead
             Tour of Holland
             Home Cup v Braehead and Asiago (Italy)

49) 2014-15 Challenge Cup
             Elite League
             Play offs
             CHL
             Tour of France v Amiens, Rouen, UQTR - Canada

50) 2015-16 Challenge Cup
             Elite League
             Play offs
             Challenge v Braehead, Coventry, Manchester
             Testimonial for Corey Neilson
             Home Cup v Braehead

51) 2016-17 Challenge Cup
             Elite League
             Play offs
             Continental Cup
             Challenge v Braehead, Coventry
             Tour of France v Amiens, Kassel Huskies, UQTR – Canada
             Home Cup v Braehead

52) 2017-18 Challenge Cup
             Elite League
             Play offs
             CHL
             Challenge v Braehead (Aladdin), Cardiff x2 (Aladdin x1)
             International challange v Krefield Penguin – Germany
             Home Cup v Braehead and Cardiff

53) 2019-19 Chalenge Cup
             Elite League
             Play offs
             Challenge v Cardiff x2
             International challenge v Dresden and Fistown (Germany),
              Stavenger – Norway and MAC – Budepest (Hungary)

154

54) 2019-20 Challenge Cup
             Elite League (incomplete – covid 19 pandemic)
             Play offs (not played – covid 19 pandemic)
             Continental Cup
             Challenge v Cardiff x2, Coventry x2

55) 2020-21 Elite 'series' Cup

56) 2021-22 Challenge Cup
             Elite League
             Play offs
             Challenge v Cardiff x2 (x1 Diamond Jubilee Cup), Sheffield x2 (x1 Alladin Cup)

57) 2022-23 Challenge Cup
             Elite League
             Play offs
             Challenge v Cardiff x2, Coventry and Sheffield x2

****

AD

The Nottingham legend public house which has supported the club throughout the years and been a place for fans to meet

NOTTINGHAM EUROPEAN ENTRIES

Season	Date	Competition	Place	Place
1999/00	Oct 1999	Continental Cup	Cardiff	2nd in group
2004-05	Oct 2004	Continental Cup	Amiens	2nd round
2006/07	Oct 2006	Continental Cup	Rouen	2nd round
2013/14	Oct 2013	Continental Cup	Nottingham/Asiago	3rd round
2014/15	Aug to Oct 2014	Champions Hockey League	Home and away	Bottom in group
2016/17	Oct 2016 to Jan 2017	Continental Cup	Jaca/Odense/Ritten	**Gold Medal**
2017/18	Aug to Nov 2018	Champions Hockey League	Home and away	Last 16
2019/20	Nov 2019	Continental Cup	Vojens/Vojens	**Silver Medal**

99/00 – Continental Cup – October 1999

Group L

(Cardiff, United Kingdom)

Team	Score	Team
Nottingham Panthers	8:6	Lada Togliatti
Cardiff Devils	9:2	Lyon HC
Lada Togliatti	12:1	Lyon HC
Cardiff Devils	5:3	Nottingham Panthers
Nottingham Panthers	5:3	Lyon HC
Cardiff Devils	2:8	Lada Togliatti

Group L standings

Rank	Team	Points	
1	Lada Togliatti (**Russia**)	4	(GF:14;GA:10)
2	**Nottingham Panthers**	4	(GF:11;GA:11)
3	**Cardiff Devils** (Wales)	4	(GF:7;GA:11)
4	**Lyon HC** (France)	0	(GF:6,GA:26)

Top Points scoring – Goals, Assists and Points -Greg Hadden with 4, 5 and 9
Penalties – with 20, Steve Carpenter

157

04-05 – Continental Cup
Second Round - Group D 2004/2005
France - Amiens - 15 October 2004 - 17 October 2004

	Team	Pts	GP	W	D	L	GF	GA	GD
1	**Milano Vipers (ITALY)**	5	3	2	1	0	15	4	+11
2	Nottingham Panthers	5	3	2	1	0	6	3	+3
3	HC Amiens (FRANCE)	2	3	1	0	2	4	7	-3
4	**HDD Olimpija Ljubljana (SLOVENIA)**	0	3	0	0	3	2	13	-11

15 October 2004

HC Amiens	3 - 0	HDD Olimpija Ljubljana
Milano Vipers	2 - 2	Nottingham Panthers

16 October 2004

Milano Vipers	4 - 0	HC Amiens
HDD Olimpija Ljubljana)	0 - 1	Nottingham Panthers

17 October 2004

Milano Vipers	9 - 2	HDD Olimpija Ljubljana
HC Amiens	1 - 3	Nottingham Panthers

Top Goals - John Craighead and Konstantin Kalmikov with 2
Top assists - and points Kim Alroos with 3 and 4
Penalties - with 45, John Craighead

06/07 – Continental Cup

Second Round - Group C (France - Rouen - 13/10/2006 - 15/10/2006)

	Team	Pts	MP	W	D	L	GF	GA	GD
1	Red Bulls Salzburg (AUSTRIA)	6	3	3	0	0	16	6	+10
2	SønderjyskE (DEN)MARK)	4	3	2	0	1	13	9	+4
3	Rouen HE (FRANCE)	2	3	1	0	2	8	13	-5
4	Nottingham Panthers	0	3	0	0	3	6	15	-9

13 October 2006

Nottingham Panthers	2 - 6	Rouen HE
Red Bulls Salzburg	5 - 2	Nottingham Panthers

14 October 2006

Rouen HE	2 - 5	SønderjyskE
SønderjyskE	4 - 5	Red Bulls Salzburg

15 October 2006

Rouen HE	0 - 6	Red Bulls Salzburg
Nottingham Panthers	2 - 4	SønderjyskE

Top assists and points – Corey Nielson and Sean McAslan with 2
Penalties - with 26, Matus Petricko

13/14 – Continental Cup
Second Round - Group B (Germany - Landshut - 18/10/2013 - 20/10/2013)

	Team	Pts	MP	W	D	L	GF	GA	GD
1	Nottingham Panthers	9	3	3	0	0	15	7	+8
2	Juniors Riga (LATVIA)	6	3	2	0	1	16	8	+8
3	HYS The Hague (NETHERLANDS)	3	3	1	0	2	11	18	-7
4	Bipolo Vitoria-Gasteiz (SPAIN)	0	3	0	0	3	8	17	-9

18 October 2013

	Bipolo Vitoria-Gasteiz	3 - 5	Nottingham Panthers
15h00	Juniors Riga	8 - 3	HYS The Hague

19 October 2013

14h00	Bipolo Vitoria-Gasteiz	2 - 7	Juniors Riga
18h00	Nottingham Panthers	7 - 3	HYS The Hague

20 October 2013

12h30	HYS The Hague	5 - 3	Bipolo Vitoria-Gasteiz
16h00	Nottingham Panthers	3 - 1	Juniors Riga

Third Round - Group D (Italy - Bolzano - 22/11/2013 - 24/11/2013)

	Team	Pts	MP	W	D	L	GF	GA	GD
1	Asiago Hockey (ITALY)	9	3	3	0	0	12	5	+7
2	Nottingham Panthers	3	3	1	0	2	7	8	-1
3	Ertis Pavlodar (KAZAKSTAN)	3	3	1	0	2	6	7	-1
4	Toros Neftekamsk (RUSSIA)	3	3	1	0	2	8	13	-5

FROM LAST PAGE:
Results
Toros Neftekamsk (Russia) 4 - 3 Nottingham Panthers
HC Asiago (Ita) 2 – 1 Ertis Paviodar (Kaz)
Nottingham Panthers 2 – 1 Ertis Paviodar
HC Asiago 6 – 2 Toros Neftekamsk
Ertis Paviodar 4 – 2 Toros Neftekamsk
HC Asiago 3 – 2 Nottingham Panthers

Top Goals - David Clarke 6, Assists Brandon Benedict and Matt Francis 5
Points Clarke/Francis 9   Penalties – with 26, Chris Murray

****

14/15 CHL – August to October 2014 Group K

Team	GP	W	OW	OL	L	GF	GA	GD	Pts
Lukko (FINLAND)	6	5	0	0	1	21	7	+14	15
Luleå HF (SWEDEN)	6	5	0	0	1	32	6	+26	15
Hamburg Freezers (GERMANY)	6	1	0	0	5	8	21	−13	3
Nottingham Panthers	6	1	0	0	5	9	36	−27	3

	HAM	LUK	LHF	NOT
Hamburg Freezers	—	0-3	1-4	6-0
Lukko	5-0	—	2-0	6-2
Luleå HF	6-0	3-1	—	9-1
Nottingham Panthers	3-1	2-4	1-10	—

Top Goals – Brandon Benedict, Stephen Lee and Cody Wild with 2
Top assists and points – Nathan Robinson with 4
Penalties with 26, Chris Lawrence

Continental Cup 2016-17

Second Round - Group B (Spain - Jaca - 21/10/2016 - 23/10/2016)

	Team	Pts	MP	W	D	L	GF	GA	GD
1	Nottingham Panthers	9	3	3	0	0	28	4	+24
2	Liepajas Metalurgs (LATVIA)	6	3	2	0	1	19	6	+13
3	Zeytinburnu Istanbul (TURKEY)	3	3	1	0	2	9	23	-14
4	CH Jaca (SPAIN)	0	3	0	0	3	7	30	-23

21 October 2016

15h30	Liepajas Metalurgs	8 - 1 (1-0, 4-1, 3-0)	Zeytinburnu Istanbul
19h00	Nottingham Panthers	13 - 2 (6-2, 5-0, 2-0)	CH Jaca

22 October 2016

15h30	Nottingham Panthers	12 - 1 (3-0, 5-0, 4-1)	Zeytinburnu Istanbul
19h00	Liepajas Metalurgs	10 - 2 (2-1, 4-0, 4-1)	CH Jaca

23 October 2016

15h30	Nottingham Panthers	3 - 1 (2-1, 1-0, 0-0)	Liepajas Metalurgs
19h00	Zeytinburnu Istanbul	7 - 3 (1-1, 3-2, 3-0)	CH Jaca

Third Round - Group D (Denmark - Odense - 18/11/2016 - 20/11/2016)

	Team	Pts	MP	W	D	L	GF	GA	GD
1	Odense Bulldogs (DENMARK)	6	3	2	0	1	9	8	+1
2	Nottingham Panthers	6	3	2	0	1	10	10	0
3	HC Donbass Donetsk (UKRAINE)	3	3	1	0	2	6	6	0
4	ASG Angers (FRANCE)	3	3	1	0	2	8	9	-1

18 November 2016

15h00	ASG Angers	3 - 2 (0-1, 2-1, 1-0)	HC Donbass Donetsk
19h00	Nottingham Panthers	5 - 4 (2-1, 2-1, 1-2)	Odense Bulldogs

19 November 2016

14h00	Nottingham Panthers	4 - 3 (1-2, 2-0, 1-1)	ASG Angers
18h00	Odense Bulldogs	2 - 1 (1-1, 0-0, 1-0)	HC Donbass Donetsk

20 November 2016

11h00	HC Donbass Donetsk	3 - 1 (0-0, 1-0, 2-1)	Nottingham Panthers
15h00	Odense Bulldogs	3 - 2 (1-0, 1-2, 1-0)	ASG Angers

Final Round - Group F (Italy - Ritten - 13/01/2017 - 15/01/2017)

	Team	Pts	MP	W	WO	L	LO	GF	GA	GD
1	Nottingham Panthers	8	3	2	1	0	0	9	3	+6
2	Odense Bulldogs (DENMARK)	4	3	1	0	1	1	6	6	0
3	HK Beibarys Atyrau (KAZAKSTAN)	4	3	0	1	0	2	7	8	-1
4	SV Ritten-Renon (ITALY)	2	3	0	1	2	0	5	10	-5

13 January 2017

15h00	Nottingham Panthers	2 - 0 (0-0, 1-0, 1-0)	Odense Bulldogs
19h00	SV Ritten-Renon	3 - 2 ot (2-1, 0-0, 0-1, 0-0, 2-0)	HK Beibarys Atyrau

14 January 2017

14h00	Nottingham Panthers	3 - 2 ot (1-1, 0-0, 1-1, 0-0, 2-1)	HK Beibarys Atyrau
18h00	Odense Bulldogs	4 - 1 (1-0, 1-0, 2-1)	SV Ritten-Renon

15 January 2017

14h00	HK Beibarys Atyrau	3 - 2 ot (0-1, 1-1, 1-0, 1-0)	Odense Bulldogs
18h00	Nottingham Panthers	4 - 1 (1-0, 2-1, 1-0)	SV Ritten-Renon

Top Goals and Points – Brad Moran with 8 and 15
Top assists – Jeff Brown and Alex Nikiforuk with 8
Penalties- with 10, Jeff Dimmen and Robert Farmer

Actual flowers thrown onto the ice at Wembley Arena 1989

>>>>>>>>>>>>>>>>>>>>>>>>

Whereas, the Champions hockey league is the top European competition for clubs, the British Championship play offs are our own.

It was Nottingham's first play off title in the second era in 1989.

Did you know there was a play offs in 1930?

That Nottingham was runner up in 1960.

British Championship play offs were played for again in 1966 and 1967.

The Northern League play offs were re-titled as the national play offs which continued to this season but for covid: 19 in season 2019/20.

Nottingham have triumphed six times, runners up eight.

17/18 CHL – August to November 2017

Champions Hockey League Group F

Pos	Team	Pld	W	OW	OL	L	GF	GA	GD	Pts	Qualification
1	Nottingham Panthers	6	3	1	0	2	18	17	+1	11	Advance to Playoffs
2	SC Bern (SWISS)	6	3	0	0	3	21	16	+5	9	
3	TPS (FINLAND)	6	3	0	0	3	12	15	−3	9	
4	Mountfield HK CECH)	6	2	0	1	3	18	21	−3	7	

	NOT	SCB	TPS	MHK
	—	4–2	2–0	4–3 (OT)
	5–2	—	4–0	5–2
	5–2	3–1	—	3–1
	2–4	5–4	5–1	—

Knock out stage – round of 16

ZSC LIONS 3 Nottingham 1
Nottingham 0 ZSC LIONS 3…lost 1-6 on aggregate

Top Goals and Points – Joshua Shalla with 5 and 8
Top Assists – Brett Perlini with 5
Penalties – with 29, Mathieu Gagnon

19/20 – Continental Cup

Third Round - Group E (Denmark - Vojens - 15/11/2019 - 17/11/2019)

Standing

	Team	Pts	MP	W	WO	L	LO	GF	GA	GD
1	Nottingham Panthers	6	3	2	0	1	0	10	7	+3
2	SønderjyskE (DENMARK)	6	3	2	0	1	0	8	6	+2
3	HC Amiens (FRANCE)	3	3	1	0	2	0	8	8	0
4	Ferencváros TC (HUNGARY)	3	3	1	0	2	0	5	10	-5

15 November 2019

15h00	Nottingham Panthers	4 - 2 (1-1, 2-0, 1-1)	HC Amiens
18h30	SønderjyskE	3 - 1 (1-0, 1-1, 1-0)	Ferencváros TC

16 November 2019

15h00	Ferencváros TC	3 - 2 (1-1, 2-0, 0-1)	Nottingham Panthers
18h30	SønderjyskE	3 - 1 (0-0, 0-1, 3-0)	HC Amiens

17 November 2019

14h00	HC Amiens	5 - 1 (0-0, 2-0, 3-1)	Ferencváros TC
17h30	Nottingham Panthers	4 - 2 (1-0, 3-1, 0-1)	SønderjyskE

Final Round - Group F (Denmark - Vojens - 10/01/2020 - 12/01/2020)

	Team	Pts	MP	W	WO	L	LO	GF	GA	GD
1	SønderjyskE (DENMARK)	7	3	1	2	0	0	9	5	+4
2	Nottingham Panthers	7	3	2	0	0	1	9	8	+1
3	Neman Grodno (BELARUS)	4	3	1	0	1	1	8	8	0
4	Cracovia Kraków (POLAND)	0	3	0	0	3	0	4	9	-5

10 January 2020

15h00	Neman Grodno	2 - 0 (0-0, 2-0, 0-0)	Cracovia Kraków
18h30	SønderjyskE	2 - 1 ot (0-0, 0-1, 1-0, 0-0, 2-0)	Nottingham Panthers

11 January 2020

15h00	Nottingham Panthers	4 - 3 (0-2, 1-1, 3-0)	Cracovia Kraków
18h30	SønderjyskE	4 - 3 ot (0-0, 1-1, 2-2, 1-0)	Neman Grodno

12 January 2020

14h30	SønderjyskE	3 - 1 (1-0, 1-0, 1-1)	Cracovia Kraków
18h00	Nottingham Panthers	4 - 3 (0-2, 3-1, 1-0)	Neman Grodno

Top Goals – Sam Herr with 5
Top Assists and points – xxx Hansen with 8 and 12
Penalties – with 18, Brian Connelly

Players in the GREAT BRITAIN team

Net minders for Great Britain

For each of these symbols (*), a tournament was played whereas no statistics were recorded or found. However in both cases of assists and Penalties, the totals will virtually be nought.

Name	GP	Gpi	A	Pim
Stephen Lyle	82	46	2	
Steven Murphy	66	39	1	2
Ben Bowns	63	49		
Bill Morrison	33	17		
William Clark	31	16**		*
John Puller	31	14*		
Stephen Foster	31	16		
Jimmy Foster	29/30	24	**	****
Jackson Whistle	29	9		
Derek Metcalf	26	2**		*
Joe Watkins	25	12		
John McCrone	23	17		
Ronnie Milne	16	9*	*	**
Martin McKay	15	8		
Stan Simon	13	13	**	**
Stan Christie	13	3*		
Harold Smith	13	3*		
Vic Gardner	10	10	**	**
David Graham	10	6		
Wayne Cowley	10	3		
Moray Hanson	9	6		
Mark Cavalin	9	5		
G English	9	4*	*	*
Scott O'Connor	9	5		
Glynn Thomas	9	4		*
B Anderson	9	0*	*	*
Reg Merrifield	8	0		*
Bethune Patton	7	7	*	*
Martin White	7	5		
Mike Ward	7	3		
William Speechley	7	0*	*	**
Ray Patridge	7	0		*
Roy Reid	7	0*		
Art Child	7	0	*	*
Jim Taylor	7	0		

Nathan Craze	6	1		
John Haney	6	1		
G Rogers	6	0*	*	*
Jody Lehman	5	5		
Lorne Carr-Harris	5	4	*	*
W Anderson	5	1	*	*
Barrie Holliehead	5	1		
Geoff Woolhouse	5	0	0	0
H C Caffyn	4	4	*	*
C Herbert Little	4	4	*	*
M F Agar	3	3	*	*
Thomas Sopwith	3	3	*	*
Jeff Smith	3	2		
Ricky Grubb	1	1		
Jim Hibbert	1	1		
John Rogers	1	0*		*
Thomas Murdy	1	0		
Jordan Hedley	1	0	0	0

It's stated that Jimmy Foster had 16 Shut outs in his 29 games.

Four gentlemen from Nottingham representing the club at national level
Here stood outside the Coventry Blaze rink

Myers, Meyers, Clarke and Ellis

Out skaters for GB

Player	GP	G	A	Pts	PIM
Jonathan Phillips	112	19	18	37	100
Ashley Tait	110	25	36	61	168
Matthew Myers	109	22	21	43	134
David Longstaff	101	32	45	77	88
Mark Richardson	100	7	21	28	14
David Phillips	96	7	22	29	84
Jonathan Weaver	96	21	48	69	66
Colin Shields	95	42	37	79	68
David Clarke	92	29	38	67	82
Ian Cooper	80	30	30	60	128
Robert Dowd	79	26	25	51	46
Ben O'Connor	76	18	32	50	62
Robert Lachowicz	73	4	18	22	22
Rick Strachan	66	7	10	17	20
Russell Cowley	66	10	18	28	28
Tony Hand	64	40	82	122	40
Stephen Cooper	61	11	27	38	54
Danny Meyers	59	6	12	18	32
Kevin Conway	58	33	33	66	54
Paul Dixon	58	5	16	21	26
Paul Adey	55	28	24	52	65
Shannon Hope	53	1	8	9	88
Robert Farmer	51	9	9	18	22
Alistair Brennan	50	5	3	8	**18
Doug McEwan	49	13	13	26	30
Steve Moria	49	22	13	35	30
Stephen Lee	49	0	9	9	20
Gerry Davey	45	43	*****9	52	********
Mark Garside	41	4	5	9	20
Mark Thomas	41	0	4	4	42
Benjamin Davies	40	4	3	7	20
Nicky Chinn	40	6	8	14	109
Craig Peacock	39	9	11	20	14
Gregory Owen	39	5	18	23	30
Mike Ellis	39	6	12	18	32
Tim Cranston	39	11	13	24	91
Andre Malo	37	2	7	9	40
Scott Neil	37	23	12	35	18
Darren Hurley	36	9	8	17	138
Gordon Dailley	36	15	***5	20	*****
Mike Bishop	36	5	8	13	109

Top to bottom – Peter Woods (coaching), Simon Hunt and Ashley Tait (icepix)

172

On the defence

Mike Bishop

- - -

Rick Strachan

*ALL Great Britain photos courtesy of Mike Smith (icepix)

Others with a Nottingham connection

Neil Morgan 35 games
Paul Swindlehurst 35
Rick Brebant 32
Chris Kelland 31
Brett Perlini 29
Terry Kurtenbach 29
Archie Stinchcombe 28
Graham Garden 27
Alex Archer 24
Evan Mosey 24
Darren Durdle 22
Mike Hammond 22
Oliver Betteridge 22
Jimmy Spence 20
Luke Ferrara 20
Warren Tait 20
Johnny Carlyle 19
Jamie Craiper 17
Paul Moran 15
Jeff Hoad 14
Joshua Tetlow 14
Jonathan Boxhill 13
Lawson Neil 12
Lewis Hook 11
Simon Hunt 11
Corey Neilson 10
Marc Levers 10
Mike O'Brian 9**
Adam Radmall 8
Brent Pope 8
Brent Bobyck 7
Neil McKay 7
Randall Weber 7
Robin Andrew 7
Doug Wilson 6
Tim Billingsley 6
Rupe Fresher 5**
Jack Prince 5
Clive Millard 4**
Grant Slater 4
Nigel Rhodes 4
Pat Mudd 4
Todd Bidner 4
Sam Oakford 3
Gerald Devereaux 3**

** Unsure of full total due to missing information

NOTTINGHAM PANTHERS ALL TIME STATS
A-Z Lists and registers plus non-iced players

Player Statistics (All-Time) Nottingham Panthers (Netminders) List

NAME	Mins	SOG	GLS	GAA	GA%	Sv%	Pts	Pims	SO
T.Askey	2050	950	77	2.25	8.11	91.91	0	4	4
A. Bastock	29	10	2	4.17	20.01	80.01	0	0	0
P.Blahyj	552	279	59	6.41	21.15	78.85	1	2	0
M. Boultby	40	33	9	13.43	27.27	72.73	0	0	0
B.Bowns	437.36	233	26	3.57	11.16	88.84	0	0	0
S. Butler	4147	1080	352	5.09	32.59	67.41	2	73	0
K Carr	6437 33	3410	293				3	34	7
N.Conway	1615 36	815	84	3.12	10.31	89.69	0	6	1
B.Cox	5636	3642	577	6.14	15.84	84.16	2	85	4
C.Cruikshank	6415	3013	215	2.01	7.14	92.86	4	18	14
D.Degeorgio	0	0	0	0	0	0	0	0	0
Downie	120	41	8				0	0	0
S.Ellis	0	0	0	0	0	0	0	0	0
H.Finch	3600	1919	316	5.27	16.47	83.53	0	8	0
J.Flynn	60	40	8	8	20.01	79.99	0	0	0
P.Galbraith	1932 30	1092	92	2.86	8.43	91.58	0	0	2
M.Garnett	5628 54	3961	279	2.97	7.04	92.96	1	8	4
S.Gospel	4015 6	201	27	4.04	13.43	86.57	0	0	0
D.Graham	12142	6886	1032	5.11	14.99	85.01	6	113	1
J.Graves	1037	627	112	6.48	17.86	82.14	0	0	0
D.Green	2236	1066	146	3.92	13.71	86.29	0	2	0
R.Griffiths	0	0	0	0	0	0	0	0	0
P.Hakkinen	329	168	18	3.29	10.71	89.29	0	0	0
D.Halverson	12540	6546	1054	5.04	16.1	83.9	0	3	3
M.Hartley	110	59	5	2.73	8.48	91.52	0	0	0
T.Heron	52 45	33	7	8.05	21.21	78.79	0	0	0
T.Hovall	0	0	0	0	0	0	0	0	0
T.Ingram	466 24	260	28	6.77	9.23	90.77	0	8	1
S.Inquanta	40	18	1	1.49	5.56	94.44	0	0	0
A.Jaszczyk	0	0	0	0	0	0	0	0	0
Ken.Johnson	6851	3194	514	4.51	16.09	83.91	0	22	1
Kyle Johnston	0	0	0	0	0	0	0	0	0

William Kerlin	5399	42	266	51			1	2	0
C.Keward	5545	21	4796	686	7.23	14.31 85.71	0	75	2
F.Killen	4733	30	3261	497	6.31	15.24 84.76	1	31	1
E.King	0		0	0	0	0 0	0	0	0
J.Kortesoja	365		186	33	5.43	17.74 82.26	0	0	0
C.Kowalski	15138	16	7199	603	2.39	8.38 91.62	10	64	29
L.Kurdna	452		280	17	2.26	6.07 93.93	0	0	0
A.Levers	0		0	0	0	0 0	0	0	0
E.Lindsey	1590		824	82	3.09	9.95 90.05	1	6	0
D.Lorenz	3031		1509	137	2.71	9.08 90.92	2	24	3
McInerney	1193		684	67	3.37	9.81 90.21	1	31	0
S Madolora	907		454	38	2.51	8.37 91.64	0	2	3
J.Mattson	60		33	5	5	15.15 84.85	0	0	0
M. Modig	1897		962	86	2.72	8.94 91.06	0	14	2
J.Moore	0		0	0	0	0 0	0	0	0
P.Munson	983	47	518	42	2.56	8.11 91.89	0	0	2
S.O'Conner	5419		3151	379	4.21	12.03 87.97	1	36	1
J.Pacl	1303	30	641	68	3.13	10.61 89.39	0	4	0
D.Parley	1251		599	66	3.17	11.02 88.98	0	4	1
M. Pietla	2588		1366	105	2.44	7.69 92.31	1	20	6
M.Raitums	37	44	29	6	9.68	20.69 79.31	0	0	0
D.Randall	1030		492	74	4.31	15.04 84.96	0	0	2
T.Robins	7638		4232	343	2.69	8.11 91.89	10	93	8
M.Robinson	2181		1107	86	2.37	7.77 92.23	1	18	4
G.Rockman	0		0	0	0	0 0	0	0	0
R.Rovnianek	3298		1583	138	2.51	8.72 91.28	0	56	5
John Russell	13		11	3	13.64	27.27 72.73	0	0	0
K.St.Pierre	4005		2071	195	2.92	9.42 90.58	3	12	2
N.Sandstrom	865		469	43	2.98	9.17 90.83	0	6	0
Sheldon	0		0	0	0	0	0	0	0
M.Snook	0		0	0	0	0 0	0	0	0
R.Spencer	20		15	2	6.06	13.33 86.67	0	0	0
B.Spours	469		310	62	7.93	20.01 80.01	0	0	0
S.Simon	120		51	7	3.51	13.73 86.27	0	0	0
J.Siemon	23040		12533	1615	4.21	12.89 87.11	1	7	3
M.Steeples	1337	50	931	188	8.43	20.19 79.81	1	16	0
N.Sundberg	3761		1783	154	2.46	8.64 91.36	3	8	4
R.Taylor	0		0	0	0	0 0	0	0	0
D.Thompson	1619		945	188	6.97	19.89 80.11	0	8	0
D.Todd	1140		620	95	5.01	15.32 84.68	0	0	0
J.Warwick	600		334	72	7.21	21.56 78.44	0	0	0
A.Watson	540		254	46	5.11	18.11 81.89	0	0	0

J.Whistle	1418.4141	691	60	2.54	8.68	91.32	0	0	2
M.Wiikman	570522	2786	247	2.61	8.87	91.13	2	6	7
J.Willis	5914	3155	340	3.45	10.78	89.22	2	51	5
I.Woodward	182217	1214	201	6.62	16.56	83.44	0	33	1
G.Woolhouse	2080	988	104	3.01	10.53	89.47	3	24	3
K.Wotherspoon?	0	0	0	0	0	0	0	0	0 nets?
I.Young	1732	945	141	4.88	14.92	85.08	0	2	1
M.Zanier	1518	814	80	3.16	9.83	90.17	5	2	2

g=games

?=unknown

* = seasons unknown

Player Statistics (All-Time) Nottingham Panthers (Netminders)　　　Reg.

xxx　　　　　　　　　　　　x

NAME	Mins	SOG	GLS	GAA	GA%	Sv%	Pts	Pims	so	App/GPI.	
Askey Tom	2050	950	77				0	4	4	36(34)	2007-08
	Total= 2050	950	77	2.25	8.11	91.91	0	4	4	36(34)	1
Bastock Andrew	29	10	2				0	0	0	'-	1995-96
	29	10	2	4.17	20.01	80.01	0	0	0	0	1
Blahyj Paul	552	279	59				1	2	0	55(-)	1994-95
	552	279	59	6.41	21.15	78.85	1	2	0	55(-)	1
Boultby Matt	0	0	0				0	0	0	4 (0)	1985/86
	40	33	9				0	0	0	5(-)	1986-87
	40	33	9	13.43	27.27	72.73	0	0	0	9(-)	2
Bowns Ben	437.36	233	26				0	0	0	15(8)	2020-21
	437.36	233	26	3.57	11.16	88.84	0	0	0	15(8)	1'
Butler Steve	1343	826	128				0	18	0	28(-)	1993-94
	2804	254	224				2	55	0	59(-)	1994-95
	4147	1080	352	5.09	32.59	67.41	2	73	0	87(-)	2
Carr Kevin	2965.23	1531	127				2	14	4	62(49)	2019-20
	3472.1	1879	166+1ps				1	20	3	59(57)	2021-22
	6437.33	3410	293				3	34	7	121(106)	2
Conway Neil	1615.36	815	84				0	6	1	28(28)	2013-14
	1615.36	815	84	3.12	10.31	89.69	0	6	1	28(28)	1

Player										
Cox Brian	1730	1095	155			1	30	2	45(-)	1985-86
	1435	917	148			0	21	0	42(-)	1986-87
	1674	1194	211			1	4	1	40(-)	1987-88
	484	254	37			0	26	1	15(-)	1994-95
	284	171	24			0	4	0	8(-)	1995-96
	30	11	2			0	0	0	'-	1996-97
	5636	3642	577	6.14	15.84 84.16	2	85	4	150	6
Cruikshank Curtis	3171	1437	106			1	2	6	54(-)	2004-05
	3244	1576	109			3	16	8	57(55)	2005-06
	6415	3013	215	2.01	7.14 92.86	4	18	14	111 (-)	2
Degeargio Dominic	0	0	0			0	0	0	1(1)	2001-02
	0	0	0	0	0 0	0	0	0	1(1)	1
Downie	120	41	8			0	0	0	2(2)	
	120	41	8			0	0	0	2(2)	1'
Ellis Stephen	0	0	0			0	0	0	1(-)	2004-05
	0	0	0	0	0 0	0	0	0	1(-)	1
Finch Hap	3600	1919	316			0	8	0	60(60)	1952-53
	3600	1919	316	5.27	16.47 83.53	0	8	0	60(60)	1
Flynn Johnny	49	40	8			0	0	0	1(1)	1951-52
	49	40	8	8	20.01 79.99	0	0	0	1(1)	1
Galbraith Patrick	1932.3	1092	92			0	0	2	48(35)	2017-18
	1932.3	1092	92	2.86	8.43 91.58	0	0	2	48(35)	1

Player										
Garnett Mike		2481.26	1289	129			0	6 1	61(44)	2017-18
		3147.28	1672	150			1	2 3	61(53)	2018-19
		5628.54	2961	279	2.97	7.04 92.96	1	8 4	122(97)	2
Gospel Sam		0	0	0			0	0 0	1(0)	2011-12
		4	5	0			0	0 0	5(1)	2012-13
		0	0	0			0	0 0	1(0)	2014-15
		235.43	123	15			0	0 0	39(6)	2017-18
		162.13	73	12			0	0 0	50(4)	2018-19
		401.56	201	27	4.04	13.43 86.57	0	0 0	96(11)	5
Graham David		756	628	100			1	4 0	20	1987-88
		2475	1468	211			0	49 1	43	1988-89
		2299	1292	184			1	28 0	37(-)	1989-90
		2156	1252	188			1	22 0	39(-)	1990-91
		2638	1321	207			1	10 0	48(-)	1991-92
		2058	1056	156			2	0 0	38(-)	1993-94
		12142	6886	1032	5.11	14.99 85.01	6	113 1	225	6
Graves Jim		1037	627	112			0	0 0	'-	1992-93
		1037	627	112	6.48	17.86 82.14	0	0 0	0	1
Green Dan		376	205	30			0	2 0	67(13)	2010-11
		356	190	31			0	0 0	67(19)	2011-12
		342	157	17			0	0 0	67(17)	2012-13
		296	147	22			0	0 0	71(18)	2013-14
		342	137	17			0	0 0	61(11)	2014-15
		437	196	20			0	0 0	60(12)	2015-16
		87	34	9			0	0 0	30(3)	2016-17
		0	0	0			0	0 0	0	2021-22
		2236	1066	146	3.92	13.71 86.29	0	2 0	423(93)	8

Name											
Griffiths Richard	0	0	0				0	0	0	1(0)	2006-07
	0	0	0	0	0	0	0	0	0	1(0)	1
Hakkinen Pasi	329	168	18				0	0	0	'-	2000-02
	329	168	18	3.29	10.71	89.29	0	0	0	0	1
Halverston Dick	1920	1073	178				0	0	0	32(32)	1946-47
	3420	1782	295				0	0	1	57(57)	1947-48
	3360	1670	236				0	0	2	56(56)	1948-49
	3840	2021	345				0	0	0	64(64)	1949-50
	12540	6546	1054	5.04	16.1	83.9	0	0	3	209(209)	4
Hartley Mark	0	0	0				0	0	0	2(0)	2005-06
	0	0	0				0	0	0	3(0)	2007-08
	110	59	5				0	0	0	67(6)	2009-10
	110	59	5	2.73	8.48	91.52	0	0	0	72(6)	3
Heron Tim	10.45	6	0				0	0	0	1(1)	1981-82
	0	0	0				0	0	0	4(-)	1982-83
	41.34	27	7				0	0	0	18(-)	1983-84
	52.45	33	7	8.05	21.21	78.79	0	0	0	5(-)	3
Hovel Tom	0	0	0				0	0	0	1(0)	2012-13
	0	0	0				0	0	0	3(0)	2015-16
	0	0	0				0	0	0	1(0)	2019-20
	0	0	0	0	0	0	0	0	0	5(0)	3

Name											
Ingram Tim	406.24	260	24				0	8	1	18(7)	1980-81
	406.24	260	24	6.77	9.23	90.77	0	8	1	18(7)	1
Inguanta Salvatouri	40	18	1				0	0	0	3(1)	1981-82
	40	18	1	1.49	5.56	94.44	0	0	0	3(1)	1
Jaszczyk Andrew	0	0	0				0	0	0	1(-)	2004-05
	0	0	0				0	0	0	4(0)	2007-08
	0	0	0	0	0	0	0	0	0	5(-)	2
Johnson Ken	3600	1633	239				0	12	0	60(60)	1950-51
	3251	1561	275				0	10	1	55(55)	1951-52
	6851	3194	514	4.51	16.09	83.91	0	22	1	115(115)	2
Johnston Kyle	0	0	0				0	0	0	1(0)	2015-16
	0	0	0	0	0	0	0	0	0	1(0)	1
Kerlin William	0	0	0	0	0	0	0	0	0	1(0)	2020-21
	539.42	266	51				1	2	0	67(10)	2021-22
	539.42	266	51	0	0	0	1	2	0	68(10)	2
Keward Chris	393.36	208*	36				0	0	0	20(13)	1980-81
	844.45	539	63				0	2	0	40(14)	1981-82
	590	447	48				0	0	1	25(-)	1982-83
	364	289	50				0	2	0	24(-)	1983-84
	2088	1340	193				0	18	1	40(-)	1984-85
	1265	1973	296				0	53	0	44(-)	1985-86
	5545.21	4796	686	7.23	14.3	85.71	0	75	2	193(-)	6
Killen Frank	1294.3	865*	108				0	11	0	29(22)	1981-82
	1139	779	95				0	4	1	30(-)	1982-83
	1994	1445	263				1	16	0	40(-)	1983-84
	306	172	31				0	0	0	11(-)	1984-85
	4733.3	3261	497	6.31	15.24	84.76	1	31	1	110(-)	4

Name											
King Ewan	0	0	0				0	0	0	3(-)	2004-05
	0	0	0	0	0	0	0	0	0	3(-)	1
Kortesoya Jarrko	365	186	33				0	0	0	15(-)	1999-00
	365	186	33	5.43	17.74	82.26	0	0	0	15(-)	1
Kowalski Graig	3397	1806	150				1	18	5	61(59)	2010-11
	3686	1579	120				3	4	10	66(64)	2011-12
	3721	1583	128				1	18	8	64(64)	2012-13
	2374	1248	110				5	12	2	43(41)	2013-14
	1960.16	983	95				0	12	4	37(35)	2014-15
	15138.16	7199	603	2.39	8.38	91.62	10	64	29	271(263)	5
Kudrna Ladislav	452	280	17				0	0	0	8(-)	2004-05
	452	280	17	2.26	6.07	93.93	0	0	0	8(-)	1
Levers Alan	0	0	0				0	0	0	1(0)	2000-01
	0	0	0				0	0	0	'-	2001-02
	0	0	0				0	0	0	1(-)	2004-05
	0	0	0				0	0	0	1(0)	2005-06
	0	0	0				0	0	0	6(0)	2006-07
	0	0	0				0	0	0	3(0)	2007-08
	0	0	0				0	0	0	1(0)	20010-11
	0	0	0	0	0	0	0	0	0	13(-)	7

Player										
Lindsey Evan	1590	824	82			1	6	0	27 (26)	2006-07
	1590	824	82	3.09	9.95 90.05	1	6	0	27 (26)	1
Lorenz Danny	3031	1509	137			2	24	3	52(-)	2001-02
	3031	1509	137	2.71	9.08 90.92	2	24	3	52(-)	1
McInerney	1193	684	67			1	31	0	23(-)	2000-01
	1193	684	67	3.37	9.81 90.21	1	31	0	23(-)	1
Madolora Shane	907	454	38			0	2	3	20(15)	2015-16
	907	454	38	2.51	8.37 91.64	0	2	3	20(15)	1
Mattson Jim	60	33	5			0	0	0	1(1)	1958-59
	60	33	5	5	15.15 84.85	0	0	0	1(1)	1
Modig Mattias	1897	962	86			0	14	2	38(34)	2014-15
	1897	962	86	2.72	8.94 91.06	0	14	2	38(34)	1
Moore James	0	0	0			0	0	0	5(-)	2004-05
	0	0	0	0	0 0	0	0	0	5(-)	1
Munson Patrick	983.47	518	42			0	0	2	31(17)	2018-19
	983.47	518	42	2.56	8.11 91.89	0	0	2	31(17)	1
O'Connor Scott	3107	1836	214			1	10	1	56(-)	1995-96
	915	560	70			0	26	0	26(-)	1996-97
	1397	755	95			0	0	0	'-	1997-98
	5419	3151	379	4.21	12.03 87.97	1	36	1	82(-)	3
Pacl Jindrich	1303.3	641	68			0	4	0	56(27)	2016-17
	1303.3	641	68	3.13	10.61 89.39	0	4	0	56(27)	1
Parley Davis	1251	599	66			0	4	1	23(21)	2008-09
	1251	599	66	3.17	11.02 88.98	0	4	1	23(21)	1

Name									
Pietila Mika	2588	1366	105			1	20 6	47(-)	2002-03
	2588	1366	105	2.44	7.69 92.31	1	20 6	47(-)	1
Raitums Martin	37.44	29	6			0	0 0	2(1)	2014-15
	37.44	29	6	9.68	20.69 79.31	0	0 0	2(1)	1
Randall Dave	730	384	63			0	0 1	23(16)	1980-81
	300	108	11			0	0 1	11(5)	1981-82
	1030	492	74	4.31	15.04 84.96	0	0 2	34(21)	2
Robins Trevor	2755	1715	129			5	28 2	45(-)	1996-97
	2390	1262	111			2	59 2	35(-)	1997-98
	2493.45	1255	103			3	6 4	39(-)	1998-99
	7638.45	4232	343	2.69	8.11 91.89	10	93 8	119(-)	3
Robinson Michel	2181	1107	86			1	18 4	38(36)	2008-09
	2181	1107	86	2.37	7.77 92.23	1	18 4	38(36)	1
Rockman Greg	0	0	0			0	0 0	'-	2000-02
	0	0	0	0	0 0	0	0 0	'-	1
Rovnianek Rastislav	1853	944	70			0	30 2	31(31)	2006-07
	1445	639	68			0	26 3	26(24)	2007-08
	3298	1583	138	2.51	8.72 91.28	0	56 5	56(54)	2
Russell John	13	11	3			0	0 0	1(1)	1997-98
	0	0	0			0	0 0	0	2019-20
	13	11	3	13.64	27.27 72.73	0	0 0	1(1)	1

Name										
St.Pierre Kevin	3712	1923	174			3	10	2	62(62)	2009-10
	293	148	21			0	2	0	5(5)	2010-11
	4005	2071	195	2.92	9.42 90.58	3	12	2	66(66)	2
Sandstrom Petter	865	469	43			0	6	0	18(-)	2002-03
	865	469	43	2.98	9.17 90.83	0	6	0	18(-)	1
Selby David	0	0	0			0	0	0	1(0)	1989-90
	0	0	0	0	0 0	0	0	0	1(0)	1
Sheldon	0	0	0	0	0 0	0	0	0	4(0)	2021-22
	0	0	0	0	0 0	0	0	0	4(0)	1
Siemon Jack	3600	1621	221			1	0	0	60(60)	1953-54
	3720	1864	244			0	7	1	62(62)	1954-55
	3360	1882	259			0	0	0	56(56)	1955-56
	3360	2050	297			0	0	1	56(56)	1956-57
	3360	2048	158			0	0	0	56(56)	1957-58
	2040	1110	169			0	0	0	34(34)	1958-59
	3600	1958	267			0	0	1	60(60)	1959-60
	23040	12533	1615	4.21	12.89 87.11	1	7	3	384(384)	7
Simon Stan	120	51	7			0	0	0	2(2)	1949-50
	120	51	7	3.51	13.73 86.27	0	0	0	2(2)	1
Snook Michael	0	0	0			0	0	0	5(-)	2004-05
	0	0	0	0	0 0	0	0	0	5(-)	1
Spencer Richard	0	0	0			0	0	0	1(0)	1987-88
	20	15	2			0	0	0	4(0)	1989-90
	20	15	2	6.06	13.33 86.67	0	0	0	5(0)	2

Name										
Spours Barry	469	310	62			0	0	0	'-	1989-90
	469	310	62	7.93	20.01 80.01	0	0	0	0	1
Steeples Mark	0	0	0			0	0	0	1(0)	1983-84
	119.47	95	22			0	0	0	28(-)	1984-85
	60	28	2			0	0	0	6(-)	1986-87
	275.5	249	69			0	2	0	25(23)	1987-88
	525	336	58			0	12	0	12(-)	1988-89
	352	224	39			1	2	0	9(-)	1989-90
	1337.5	931	188	8.43	20.19 79.81	1	16	0	81(-)	6
Sundberg Niklas	3761	1783	154			3	8	4	64(-)	2003-04
	3761	1783	154	2.46	8.64 91.36	3	8	4	64(-)	1
Taylor R.	0	0	0	0	0 0					
Thompson Danny	280	176	32			0	0	0	'-	1989-90
	662	392	71			0	2	0	16	1991-92
	677	377	85			0	6	0	16(-)	1992-93
	1619	945	188	6.97	19.89 80.11	0	8	0	35(-)	3
Todd Dick	1140	620	95			0	0	0	19(19)	1958-59
	844	480	87			0	2	0	19(-)	1990-91
	1140	620	95	5	15.32 84.68	0	2	0	38	2
Warwick Jack	600	334	72			0	0	0	10(10)	1946-47
	600	334	72	7.21	21.56 78.44	0	0	0	10(10)	1
Watson Alan	240	106	22			0	0	0	4(4)	1949-50
	300	148	24			0	0	0	5(5)	1951-52
	540	254	46	5.11	18.11 81.89	0	0	0	9(9)	2

Name										
Whistle Jackson	897.49	417	38			0	0	1	64(15)	2019-20
	520.51	274	22	2.54	8.03 91.97	0	0	1	16(9)	2020-21
	1418.41	691	60	2.54	8.68 91.32	0	0	2	80(24)	2
Wilkman Mikka	2698	1248	110			0	4	4	59(47)	2015-16
	3007.22	1538	137			2	2	3	60(55)	2016-17
	5705.22	2786	247	2.61	8.87 91.13	2	6	7	119-102	2
Willis Jordon	3214	1676	200			2	8	3	59(-)	1999-00
	2700	1479	140			0	43	2	47(-)	2000-01
	5914	3155	340	3.45	10.78 89.22	2	51	5	106(-)	2
Woodward Ian	128.57	119	30			0	2	0	9(-)	1984-85
	0	0	0			0	0	0	2(0)	1985-86
	1525	984	158			0	27	1	49(-)	1986-87
	175.2	111	13			0	0	0	10(-)	1987-88
	1822.17	1214	201	6.62	16.56 83.44	0	33	1	32(-)	4
Woolhouse Geoff	240	111	16			0	0	0	9(-)	2003-04
	325	155	17			1	0	1	38(-)	2004-05
	133	54	8			1	22	1	53(7)	2005-06
	398	197	17			0	0	0	61(8)	2006-07
	430	194	15			0	0	1	58(9)	2007-08
	260	133	13			0	2	0	56(5)	2008-09
	294	144	18			1	0	0	7(5)	2009-10
	2080	988	104	3.01	10.53 89.47	3	24	3	282(-)	7
Wotherspoon Ken	0	0	0			0	0	0	'-	2001-02
	0	0	0	0	0 0	0	0	0	'-	1

Young Ian	1473	813	122			0	2	1	26(-)	1992-93
	259	132	19			0	0	0	'-	1993-94
	1732	945	141	4.88	14.92 85.08	0	2	1	26(-)	2
Zanier Mike	1518	814	80			5	2	2	26(-)	1998-99
	1518	814	80	3.16	9.83 90.17	5	2	2	26(-)	1

and out = played as a skater also
* one game 1982 (mids Cup final) SOG guess
*** One match in 80-81 with Ingram (unsure who played.
*** one match in 80-81 with Randall unsure who played

mids cup — so mins etc not added

mids cup

END OF NET MINDING STATS　　　　START OF SKATER STATS (next page)

189

Player Statistics (All Time) Skaters A-Z list   notes

NAME		GP	G	A	Pts	Pims	
Abel	Neil	14	8	5	13	24	
Adams	Phil	44	14	21	35	46	
Adey	Paul	593	796	751	1547	669	
Adolfsson	Marcus	10	1	2	3	12	
Allen	Bill	414	81	109	190	466	
Allison	Scott	51	9	20	29	150	
Alroos	Kim	101	45	62	107	46	
Anderson	Nic	15	2	4	6	20	
Andison	Jeff	45	27	34	61	187	
Andrew	Robin	104	25	75	100	46	
Archer	Alex	1	0	0	0	0	
Baillargeon	Robert	65	26	31	57	105	
Balchin	Nicky	129	7	8	15	49	
Barnes	Steve	26	7	7	14	16	
Barr	Ron	3	2	2	4	2	
Batham	Bob	27	3	5	8	45	
Baxter	Chris	23	6	4	10	47	
Beach	George	19	10	13	23	2	
Beardsley	Brian	8	0	0	0	0	
Beaudoin	Yves	24	20	28	48	38	
Beaulieu	Corey	44	2	6	8	109	
Beauregard	David	141	79	77	156	142	
Beckett	Jason	66	5	12	17	192	
Belanger	Mario	39	46	55	101	54	
Bell	Jonathan	1					Ch only
Bellamy	Rob	56	23	32	55	84	
Benedict	Brandon	244	67	135	202	168	
Bergin	Kevin	168	69	84	153	281	
Berube	Mike	67	2	14	16	36	
Betteridge	Ollie	439	60	57	117	135	
Bidner	Todd	26	24	32	56	77	
Biggs	Tyler	27	4	7	11	61	
Billingsley	Tim	141	14	41	55	115	
Binkley	Jason	6	0	1	1	6	
Bishop	Mike	167	26	38	64	256	
Bissonnette	Dan	6	12	8	20	6	
Black	Wally	168	102	70	172	159	
Blaisdell	Mike	84	52	67	119	202	
Bobyck	Brent	216	41	80	121	116	
Bohmbach	Andy	66	23	27	50	49	
Boivin	Christoph.	83	37	53	90	42	
Bolduc	Alexandre	48	9	17	26	70	
Booth	Rod	51	11	11	22	57	

190

Boston	Martyn	2	0	0	0	0
Bouchard	John	51	38	29	67	38
Bougie	George	29	11	14	25	16
Bowen	Curtis	104	23	50	73	219
Bowley	Callam	5	0	0	0	0
Boxhill	Jonathan	135	15	34	49	111
Boynton	Nick	20	4	5	9	26
Brassard	J.C.	67	7	32	39	24
Bradbury	Matt	18	0	0	0	0
Brebant	Rick	59	85	156	241	106
Bremner	John	495	60	132	192	696
Brinster	Chris	4	1	7	8	4
Brisebois	Mathieu	37	3	9	12	43
Broadhead	Mick	25	2	10	12	2
Broadhurst	Pete	56	1	5	6	81
Brown	Jeffrey	149	36	55	91	216
Brown	Hal	171	39	81	120	56
Buckman	Jason	17	0	1	1	0
Buckman	Lewis	22	0	2	2	16
Budd	Grant	37	1	1	2	4
Bullas	Sam	54	1	1	2	2
Bulmer	Brett	46	13	17	30	20
Burke	George	40	17	9	26	39
Burke	Greg	64	2	14	16	118
Bury	Ed	58	26	34	60	80
Bussieres	Raphael	70	7	22	29	57
Butler	Phillip	80	9	4	13	205
Caddotte	Marc	176	67	124	191	101
Cain	Aarron	59	9	12	21	86
Calvert	Ashley	1	0	0	0	0
Cangelosi	Austin	16	11	8	19	10
Capraro	Chris	28	10	16	26	18
Carderelli	Joe	94	39	56	95	64
Carlsson	Calle	290	40	91	131	218
Carlyle	Johnny	27	1	6	7	14
Carozza	Massimo	31	11	15	26	12
Carpenter	Steve	153	17	65	82	353
Carr	Adam					Ch only?
Carter	Matt	67	22	17	39	20
Casey	Gerry	47	19	30	49	13
Casey	Pat	175	105	124	229	286
Ceman	Dan	25	7	15	22	32
Cernich	Kord	33	6	12	18	58
Chamberlain	Bobby	5	0	0	0	4
Champagne	Scott	29	9	28	37	22
Charron	Eric	54	3	10	13	118
Chin	George	60	35	40	75	24
Chinn	Nicky	11	0	0	0	6
Churchill	John	18	0	0	0	0
Ciarelli	Peter	4	4	9	13	2

Clarke	David	786	381	371	752	900
Clarke	Jason	55	19	20	39	213
Clarke-Piz	Morgan	21	1	0	1	6
Clarson	Gary	61	2	9	11	24
Clay	Stu (John?)	1	0	0	0	0
Cockburn	Steve	122	7	13	20	58
Cohen	Colby	18	2	6	8	37
Coleman	Joe/john	19	4	5	9	12
Connelly	Brian	64	7	29	36	42
Cook	Brendan	61	34	41	75	39
Cooke	James	99	8	8	16	29
Cooney	Pat	62	51	28	79	67
Cooper	Stephen	62	2	12	14	46
Cote	Brandin	40	15	21	36	66
Cotton	Darren	2	0	1	1	0
Cownie	Jordan	4	1	0	1	2
Coyston	Art	42	15	10	25	29
Craighead	John	86	55	42	97	362
Crapier	Jamie	57	106	106	212	97 Crapper
Da Costa	Jeff	54	4	18	22	28
Dalgliesh	Ross	53	4	4	8	50
Dallman	Marty	110	58	74	132	60
D'Amour	Dominic	65	13	24	37	219
Darling	Dion	37	5	16	21	48
De Angelis	Mike	24	2	5	7	16
Derlago	Mark	73	27	42	69	49
DeSantis	Jason	47	4	12	16	27
Desilets	Mike	52	21	18	39	110
Deutsch	Adam	47	9	13	22	49
Devreaux	Red	2	0	1	1	0
Dickson	Brian	39	22	22	44	92
Dilks	Chris	23	0	1	1	0
Dimmen	Jeff	85	11	31	42	78
Dineen	Nick	16	3	3	6	11
Doherty	Taylor	24	2	7	9	18
Domingue	Kevin	50	16	17	33	22
Dorian	Dan	77	144	104	248	121
Doty	Jacob	23	2	1	3	43
Doucet	Guillaume	27	19	10	29	34
Dougherty	Ernie	106	69	51	120	20
Doyle	Perry	59	3	5	8	161
Drolet	Jimmy	56	7	16	23	86
Drouin	PC	141	57	91	148	222
Dryburgh	Jim	7	1	3	4	0
Dubois	Eric	57	1	20	21	34
Ducharme	Dave	24	44	43	87	43
Dunnigan	Dick	59	30	36	66	6
Durdle	Darren	99	109	170	279	204
Easson	Darryl	235	51	44	95	154
Elders	Jason	53	22	20	42	36

Elliott	James	145	14	17	31	148	Hunt
Ellis	Brendan	16	0	7	7	12	
Ellis	Mike	35	4	6	10	20	
Emersic	Blaz	79	13	29	42	44	
Eratt	Layton	171	39	34	73	298	
Evans	Frank	36	3	6	9	53	
Farley	Shaun	6	9	6	15	0	
Farmer	Robert	348	80	138	218	604	
Farnsworth	Darren	14	0	0	0	0	
Ferrara	James	198	11	15	26	50	
Ferrara	Luke	2				Ch only	
Ferrara	Robert	1	0	0	0	0	
Fick	Danny	62	0	11	11	99	
Flavill	John	173	13	14	27	23	
Flichel	Martyn	50	20	26	46	100	
Flint	Matt	18	0	0	0	0	
Flint	Nick	14	0	0	0	0	
Flint	Tim	2	0	0	0	2	
Flynn	Ron	39	29	17	46	20	
Foord	Matt	1	0	0	0	0	
Fornica	Joe	24	17	7	24	9	
Fothergill	Paul	2	0	0	0	0	
Fox	Jordon	130	45	107	152	129	
Francis	Matt	201	85	123	208	209	
Fraser	Gavin	409	216	219	435	609	
Fresher	Rupe	165	51	44	95	71	
Gagnon	Mathieu	75	2	11	13	142	
Galbraith	Jade	187	76	193	269	258	
Galivan	Pat	62	24	35	59	31	
Gallant	trevor	10	3	15	18	36	
Garden	Graham	178	19	46	66	414	
Garrigan	Craig	13	0	0	0	0	
Garside	Mark	14	0	0	0	4	
Gascon	Marty	66	16	49	65	26	
Gascoyne	Russ	5	0	0	0	0	
Gauthier	Jim	19	36	19	55	18	
Gavrilenko	Sergei	2	0	1	1	2	
Gawthrop	Les	3	0	1	1	4	
Gebhardt	Jim	77	14	22	36	83	
Gillis	Ryan	46	2	13	15	122	
Gilmartin	John	1	0	0	0	0	
Glossop	Connor	3				Ch only	
Goldby	Mark	171	6	6	12	23	
Golicic	Juri	6	2	1	3	8	
Golovkovs	Georgs	51	9	23	32	20	
Goodman	Roger 'George'	177	23	30	53	180	
Gordon	Rhett	23	4	17	21	12	
Grace	Peter	4	0	0	0	0	
Graham	Bruce	121	58	62	120	129	

Graham	Joe	66	0	2	2	29
Greaves	Simon	137	2	1	3	0
Grieg	Tommy	60	14	8	22	86
Griffiths	Owen	15	0	4	4	0
Griffiths	Tony	17	5	4	9	20
Grimaldi	Joe	7	2	6	8	110
Gudziunas	Terry	34	47	45	92	28
Guptill	Alex	67	39	26	65	72
Hadden	Greg	395	177	180	357	379
Hall	Fred	55	18	24	42	66
Hamilton	Bruce	8	7	6	13	0
Hamilton	Doug	38	2	2	4	72
Hansen	Jake	51	22	38	60	45
Hardy	Kyle	10	0	4	4	10
Harper	Tristan	1	0	0	0	2
Hazeldine	Joseph	73	0	1	1	2
Hedberg	Edwin	29	2	2	4	4
Heerema	Jeff	66	35	43	78	87
Henderson	Jim	21	5	9	14	60
Henderson	Kevin	50	5	17	22	18
Henley	Brent	42	0	4	4	294
Herr	Sam	64	41	44	85	56
Herriot	Jim	213	26	42	68	319
Higgins	Chris	38	11	22	33	30
Hill	Ed	20	0	7	7	16
Hoad	Jeff	57	21	17	38	95
Hobson	John	193	11	28	39	67
Hodgins	Art	51	4	7	11	14
Hoffman	Kevin	15	6	5	11	0
Hoffman	Walt	3	0	0	0	0
Hook	Lewis	19	3	4	7	10
Hopkins	Jack	21	1	1	2	0
Horb	George	60	34	28	62	40
Horvat	Ryan	34	5	13	18	41
Howard	Reg	99	15	20	35	157
Howarth	Andrew	2	0	0	0	0 Ch? only
Hudson	Gerry	112	64	94	158	83
Hughes	Tommy	65	6	18	24	62
Hunt	Simon	517	246	153	399	1259
Hurtubise	Mark	71	16	39	55	54
Hussey	Marc	56	10	13	23	48
Hutchinson	Dave	182	3	14	17	148
Hutchinson	James	2	0	0	0	0
Hutchinson	Phil					Ch?
Ingram	John	8	4	3	7	27
Ingram	Tim	10	1	0	1	22
Innes	Bill	60	19	15	34	24
Ivan	Merek	56	26	22	48	143
Jacina	Greg	94	19	39	58	194
Jakobs	Jens	11	1	0	1	13

James	Budd	114	14	29	43	203
Janssen	Cam	66	5	6	11	122
Jeffrey	Mike	23	48	36	84	62
Jennings	Jason	33	9	18	27	18
Jenson	Joe	19	4	13	17	50
Jinman	Lee	140	59	125	184	160
Jokinen	Tommi	8	0	3	3	0
Jones	Scott	1	2	0	2	0
Kalmikov	Konstantine	63	28	19	47	22
Kalus	Petre	60	21	27	48	76
Kasun	Mark	46	17	17	34	83
Kelham	A J	70	17	27	44	22
Kelland	Chris	92	25	114	139	256
Kelsall	Jordan	154	8	7	15	38
Keys	Jimmy	92	165	155	320	379
Keyward	Chris	41	0	1	1	2
Keyward	Dwayne	278	209	204	413	435
King	Duncan	191	6	12	18	156
Knox	Blake	54	20	29	49	107
Koivanoirau	Miko	57	13	46	59	117
Kolesar	Mark	63	25	40	65	58
Kolnik	Juraj	65	33	40	73	44
Kovacs	Justin	60	15	32	47	14
Krajicek	Jan	59	11	32	43	194
Krullis	Jan	43	7	10	17	70
Kudroc	Kristian	12	1	5	6	12
Kurtenbach	Terry	355	290	432	722	454
Kwong	Larry	55	55	24	79	10
Lachowicz	Robert	780	121	236	357	142
LaForge	Maurice	135	53	45	98	62
Lambert	Ross	123	122	203	325	365
Landry	Charles	66	6	11	17	60
Lane	Matthew	62	20	22	42	25
Lang Pa.	Maxime	51	11	12	23	81 Langlier-Parent Maxime
Larocque	Mario	21	2	5	7	80
Larter	Ron	23	4	2	6	8
Larter	Tyler	5	7	6	13	12
Lattimer	Keith	17	3	2	5	4
Lavinge	Eric	58	1	10	11	210
Lavoie	Daryl	61	2	7	9	90
Lawrence	Chris	163	53	81	134	265
Laxdal	Derek	112	55	53	108	247
Leach	Jamie	234	100	117	217	126
Leak	Sean	9	0	0	0	2
LeClair	Corey	6	1	1	2	4
Lee	Mark	1	0	0	0	0
Lee	Rod	60	31	28	59	17
Lee	Stephen	618	33	154	187	665

Lepine	Guillaume	315	18	65	83	814
L'Esperance	Gilles	9	10	7	17	14
Levers	Marc	454	64	111	175	378
Lindhagen	Erik	150	15	42	57	84
Ling	David	101	52	102	154	243
Linton	Andy	85	24	38	62	61
Liscak	Robert	4	0	1	1	6
Loewen	Darcy	40	3	8	11	68
Loiseau	Alex	5	1	1	2	2
Longley	Andrew	1	0	0	0	0
Lund	Martin	21	2	4	6	32
Lundmark	Herb	27	3	6	9	29
Lyons	Bob	41	2	8	26	30
Lyons	Lynn	52	15	18	33	16
Machin	Keith	1	0	0	0	0
Magdosko	Jan	38	2	4	6	107
Makela	Tuuka	7	0	1	1	38
Malo	Andre	56	26	50	76	40
Malo	Tony	21	8	6	14	8
Malmquist	Dylan	63	9	25	34	8
Malone	Russ	60	53	30	83	88
Maloney	Darren	47	2	3	5	16
Mann	Cameron	61	36	33	69	107
Mansoff	Jason	21	2	4	6	6
Martel	Paul	55	19	28	47	37
Martin	Jason	141	0	10	10	133
Maslanko	Bill	34	16	23	39	8
Massy	Kevin	29	20	8	10	19
Masters	Cason	51	3	9	12	24
Matheson	Mark	145	19	81	100	78
Mathieson	Jim	57	2	11	13	76
Matthews	Rod	116	57	45	102	56
May	Johno	16	1	1	2	12
Maynard	Marcus	49	0	2	2	4
McAslan	Shaun	194	130	131	261	293
McDonald	Bill	112	25	30	55	243
McDonald	Franklin	18	1	3	4	6
McDonald	Greg	46	57	48	105	202
McDonald	Ian	34	12	17	29	16
McDonald	Kenny	50	59	33	92	84
McDonald	Tony	10	0	0	0	0
McGrattan	Brian	66	19	8	27	149
McHugh	Ron	42	11	13	24	23
McKay	Larry	46	14	14	28	20
McKay	Neil	69	113	105	219	217
McKenna	Steve	51	8	13	21	28
McKie	Kenny	46	20	23	43	130
McLachlan	Mac	98	52	49	101	82
McLinchey	Randy	17	23	29	52	55

Randy						
McMillan	Logan	126	15	32	47	44
McNiven		1	0	0	0	0
McWilliams	Rhys	10	0	0	0	0
Melancon	Craig	28	49	74	123	66
Messier	Doug	53	5	35	40	107
Meyers	Danny	358	25	100	125	253
Millard	Clive/nip	62	19	6	25	45
Miller	Cam	19	2	1	3	18
Mitchell	Roy	66	6	11	17	58
Mokshantsev	Alexander	77	28	27	55	57
Molin	Johan	131	62	71	133	54
Mollard	Hutch	38	6	10	16	6
Monk	Arnie	61	9	6	15	50
Moran	Brad	132	41	73	114	58
Moran	Ian	21	2	7	9	10
Moran	Paul	262	17	41	58	262
Morgan	Ian	11	1	0	1	2
Morgan	James	44	3	2	5	57
Morgan	Neil	156	63	113	176	153
Moria	Steve	62	24	24	48	22
Mosey	Evan	198	55	73	128	124
Moulden	Pete	59	6	9	15	97
Moxon	Daryle	18	2	3	5	33
Mudd	Pat	3	0	4	4	0
Murray	Chris	45	9	35	44	152
Myers	Matt	620	139	261	400	784
Ndur	Ruman	36	2	4	6	198
Neil	James	171	3	2	5	0
Neil	Lawson	146	10	31	41	50
Neilsson	Corey	399	86	293	379	821
Nelson	Eric	19	1	8	9	20
Nemirovski	Michail	11	3	2	5	8
Nieckar	Barry	151	21	33	54	797
Nienhuis	Kraig	60	25	33	58	53
Nikiforuk	Alex	70	22	32	54	77
Nikolov	Angel	53	2	27	29	40
Nordmark	Robert	35	5	7	12	20
Norris	Clayton	49	5	7	12	188
Norrish	Brady	67	3	17	20	62
Norton	Tom	229	5	13	18	59
Oakford	Sam	135	3	8	11	37
O'Brian	Mike	10	3	3	6	2
Odelein	Selmar	30	22	28	50	60
O'Higgins	Paul	136	71	69	140	88
Olsen	Darryl	58	14	37	51	32
Olsen	Dylan	56	9	15	24	49
Oreskovic	Phil	26	0	3	3	31
Pachal	Vern	30	29	29	58	8
Paek	Jimmy	132	8	51	59	78

Parker	Stuart	82	14	19	33	34
Parkes	Andrew	2	0	0	0	0
Patricko	Matus	60	17	22	39	131
Patterson	Brad	42	6	14	20	40
Paterson	Duncan	28	1	3	4	18
Paterson	Gordon	61	8	14	22	165
Peacock	Tim	53	82	47	129	175
Pelletier	Steve	65	8	24	32	83
Penner	Alex	30	4	5	9	289
Perkins	Simon	284	101	103	204	378
Perlini	Brett	214	68	97	165	81
Perlini	Fred	42	99	95	194	149
Peters	Keith	29	8	6	14	12
Phillips	Dave	35	2	1	3	11
Phillips	Zack	77	18	39	57	20
Pither	Luke	98	34	54	88	78
Plata	Eddie	55	24	33	57	63
Podlesak	Martin	2	0	0	0	0
Poirier	Joel	53	6	13	19	84
Pope	Brent	118	4	23	27	179
Precenicks	Stanislaus	3				Ch only
Premak	Garth	274	87	138	225	268
Prince	Jack	2				Ch only
Purves	John	51	19	17	36	96
Putszai	Johnny	13	0	0	0	0 Bennett
Pyryhora	Johnny	92	25	29	54	75
Quick	Kevin	18	2	6	8	8
Quist	William	30	6	2	8	10
Radmall	Adam	2	0	0	0	0
Rapley	Dave	7	5	4	9	0
Raynor	Kieran	3				Ch only
Rees	Mike	54	4	12	16	195
Rendell	John	55	30	31	61	59
Reynolds	Kurt	2	0	0	0	0
Rheault	Jon	86	12	21	33	42
Rhodes	Nigel	382	248	281	529	350
Ricci	Scott	65	3	18	21	12
Richard	Dylan	43	10	13	23	4
Richardson	Bruce	124	32	93	125	265
Richardson	Mark	92	12	20	32	26
Richardson	Sean	47	9	10	19	47
Richie	Dave	131	2	3	5	2
Ringer	Bill	355	164	194	358	119
Rippingale	Gary	95	1	1	2	38
Rissling	Jaynen	62	4	20	24	124
Roberts	Mark	71	2	3	5	2
Roberts	Steve	51	21	16	37	22
Robinson	Adam	1	0	0	0	0 ?Ch only
Robinson	Nathan	24	6	15	21	40
Rose	Danny	6	0	0	0	0

Rusnell	Dave	56	47	55	102	36
Ryan	Billy	67	31	48	79	64
Ryan	Cliff	28	18	13	31	14
Ryan	Matt	68	19	45	64	83
Ryhanen	Sami	33	9	28	37	22
Saari	Joonas	54	0	4	4	13
St.John	Del	31	17	16	33	10
Salonen	Joel	61	16	30	46	32
Salmi	Jarmie	11	1	2	3	4
Salt	John	1	0	0	0	0
Salter	Steve	27	45	20	65	68
Salters	Lee	65	28	34	62	148
Sarkanis	Deivids	13	2	4	6	2
Sauve	Yann	74	17	33	50	110
Savoie	Claude	52	14	13	27	35
Schmidt	Bryan	137	7	23	30	120
Schwarz	Darren	7	15	5	20	18
Schultz	Stephan	94	34	53	87	66
Scott	Daniel	142	0	3	3	38
Sebastian	Jeff	118	17	51	68	127
Selby	David	1	0	0	0	
Semeniuk	Ted	61	39	38	77	32
Sertich	Andy	72	5	28	33	22
Sevcik	Jaroslav	7	9	9	18	0
Shalla	Josh	40	10	12	22	17
Shepherd	Jim	7	0	3	3	35
Shmyr	Ryan	125	15	31	46	515
Simoes	Steve	43	7	9	16	107
Simon	Stan	10	1	1	2	2 also n/m
Sjogren	Christian	26	2	11	13	79
Sjogren	Stefan	21	2	4	6	28
Slater	Grant	4	1	1	2	2
Smith	Ged	84	20	26	46	120
Smith	Julian	5	0	0	0	0
Smith	Lorne	423	85	149	234	534
Smith	Tony	2	0	0	0	0
Soar	Tom	5	0	1	1	0
Spang	Dan	140	19	48	69	85
Spence	Jimmy	57	44	27	71	18
Sproat	Dustin	17	6	12	18	33
Stancok	Robert	99	7	21	28	207
Steen	Don	5	0	0	0	6
Stenton	Liam	16	0	0	0	4
Stevens	George	33	21	16	37	4
Stevens	Rod	61	22	36	58	60
Stevenson	Richard	29	2	1	3	2
Stewart	Anthony	19	6	5	11	14
Stewart	Chris	27	7	9	16	27
Stewart	Keith	33	17	24	41	50
Stinchcombe	Archibald	51	3	22	25	6

Strachan	Rick	23	11	25	36	16
Strachan	Sam	44	2	1	3	4
Strongman	Les	507	400	330	730	330
Strongman	Mark	3	0	0	0	0
Struch	David	191	49	88	137	128
Souranta	Simon	19	4	6	10	8
Sutter	Shaun	43	16	18	34	50
Swindlehurst	Paul	48	3	13	16	36
Taggart	Kenny	19	0	0	0	4
Tait	Ashley	482	167	265	431	724
Tait	Warren	1	0	1	1	4
Talbot	Jullian	45	18	19	37	38
Talbot-Ta	Dominic	16	3	5	8	0
Taubert	Kristian	114	8	17	25	154
Taylor	Chuck	109	37	74	111	328
Taylor	Richard	1	0	0	0	0 ?Ch only
Tessier	Dan	76	36	70	116	170
Tetlow	Josh	255	5	20	25	114
Theriault	Paul	54	28	19	47	12
Thompson Brian	Briane	110	22	46	68	299
Thompson	Bruce	8	6	11	17	35
Thompson	Shaun	3	1	1	2	0
Thow	Aaron	57	3	19	22	28
Timmins	Russ	189	9	22	31	34
Tkaczuk	Daniel	12	2	11	13	18
Toneys	Nick	94	4	14	18	112
Tousignant	Mathieu	75	16	14	30	97
Townsend	George	54	37	27	64	20
Trickett	Matt	358	49	50	99	491
Tuma	Martin	12	0	1	1	43
Tvrdon	Marek	16	4	6	10	8
Tvrdon	Roman	10	2	5	7	6
Twaite	Marc	324	35	29	64	243
Unkuri	Passi	23	1	7	8	37
Urquhart	Mike	115	71	137	208	228
Van Hoof	Jeremy	18	1	3	4	10
Van Kleef	Tyler	19	1	1	2	4
Vaskivuo	Mike	20	9	9	18	10
Virta	Pekka	51	13	10	23	26
Waghorn	Graham	436	59	183	242	935
Walker	Rob	65	2	12	14	52
Wallenberg	Patrik	120	58	74	132	151
Ward	Josh	129	3	9	12	12
Watson	Gerry	401	140	215	355	388
Waugh	Geoff	97	10	22	32	83
Weaver	Jason	34	12	18	30	87
Weaver	Jonathan	126	19	74	93	83
Weber	Randall	856	326	517	843	518
Webster	Dave	22	1	0	1	0

Welch	Dan	13	1	7	8	20	
Welch	Dave	54	4	7	11	40	
Weldon	Will	5	1	0	1	0	
Welsh	Jeremy	66	22	46	68	10	
Werner	Eric	105	11	40	51	46	
Westman	Ken	480	169	240	409	286	
Wetzel	Todd	17	4	4	8	8	
Whyatt	Nicky	1	0	0	0	0	Ch only
Wiedergut	Andreas	2	0	0	0	0	
Wightman	Oscar						Ch only
Wild	Cody	52	13	30	43	18	
Williams	Jason	17	6	13	19	0	
Willock	Elden	52	23	24	47	36	
Wilson	Brock	67	7	29	36	127	
Wilson	Dick	23	9	10	19	26	
Wilson	Doug	174	2	17	19	170	
Wilson	Kelsey	34	10	9	19	112	
Withenshaw	Doug	44	55	63	118	70	
Wojciak	Richard	109	6	8	14	28	
Wood	Dodi	51	4	15	19	222	
Wood	Shaun	23	3	4	7	33	
Woods	Gyle	60	19	23	42	54	
Worthington	Robert	80	3	4	7	8	
Wren	Bob	20	7	15	22	39	
Wright	Jason	36	7	13	20	12	
Wright	Mark	25	1	1	2	6	
Yardley	Shaun	5	0	1	1	0	
Young	Ed	132	96	73	169	36	
Zamick	Chick	624	778	645	1423	192	
Zamick	Joe	18	1	2	3	26	
Zann	Tony	28	4	3	7	49	
Zion	Jonathan	39	9	24	33	22	
Zukiwsky	Jarret	58	12	25	37	169	

Non Iced players	Only challenge games	GP	
Oscar Wightman		?	1989-90
Scott Jones, Adam		?	1980-81
Robinson		1	2002-03
Richard Taylor		1	2003-04
Nicky Whyatt		1	2003-04
Adam Carr		?	2004-05
Johnathan Bell		1	2006-07
Jack Prince		2	2006-07
Luke Ferrara		2	2012-13
Connor Glossop		3	2015-16
Kieran Raynor		?	2015-16
Stanislaus Precenicks		3	2015-16
Phil Hutchinson		?	?
Andy Howarth			
?n/m		2	?

If anyone feels that there are missing players from this list please get in touch. The same goes for anything throughout the book in as regards detail that omits factual content.

Actual stats, game splayed or other I would be pleased to update my files on players accounts.

Skater Registry

	Seasons	GP	Goals	Assists	Points	Pens.	GP	G	A	PTS	PEN.
Able Neil	1981-82	14	8	5	13	24	14	8	5	13	24
Adams Phil	1984-85	44	14	21	35	46	44	14	21	35	46
Adey Paul	1988-89	40	88	83	171	105					
	1989-90	55	94	88	182	86					
	1990-91	50	90	61	151	12					
	1991-92	55	81	79	160	44					
	1992-93	51	83	84	167	82					
	1993-94	45	70	63	133	58					
	1994-95	64	120	103	223	66					
	1995-96	56	85	69	154	81					
	1996-97	53	38	40	78	73					
	1997-98	62	22	36	58	24					
	1998-99	61	25	45	70	38					
	2003-04	1	0	0	0	0	593	796	751	1547	669
Adolfsson Marcus	1999-00	10	1	2	3	12	10	1	2	3	12
Allen Bill.......	1948-49	56	15	8	23	18					
	1949-50	70	20	31	51	46					
	1950-51	60	15	16	31	96					
	1951-52	60	10	14	24	82					
	1952-53	59	10	17	27	116					
	1953-54	47	4	7	11	40					
	1954-55	62	7	16	23	68	414	81	109	190	466
Allison Scott	2002-03	51	9	20	29	150	51	9	20	29	150
Alroos Kim	2003-04	66	34	42	76	36					
	2004-05	35	11	20	31	10	101	44	62	106	46
Anderson Nic	2013-14	15	2	4	6	20	15	2	4	6	20
Andison Jeff	1981-82	23	18	24	42	116					

	1984-85	22	9	10	19	71	45	27	34	61	187
Andrew Robin	1984-85	36	7	13	20	12					
	1985-86	50	14	48	62	22					
	1986-87	18	4	14	18	12	104	25	75	100	46
Archer Alex	1946-47	1	0	0	0	0	1	0	0	0	0
Baillargeon Robert	2021-22	65	26	31	57	105	65	26	31	57	105
Balchin Nicky	1989-90	47	0	2	2	0					
	1990-91	32	3	3	6	10					
	1991-92	44	4	3	7	35					
	1992-93	5	0	0	0	4					
	1993-94	1	0	0	0	0	129	7	8	15	49
Barnes Steve	1996-97	26	7	7	14	16	26	7	7	14	16
Barr Ron	1958-59	3	2	2	4	2	3	2	2	4	2
Batham Bob	1980-81	25	3	5	8	45					
	1981-82	2	0	0	0	0	27	3	5	8	45
Baxter Chris	2000-01	23	6	4	10	47	23	6	4	10	47
Beach George	1956-57	19	10	13	23	2	19	10	13	23	2
Beardsley Brian	1953-54	8	0	0	0	0	8	0	0	0	0
Beaudoin Yves	1989-90	24	20	28	48	38	24	20	28	48	38
Beaulieu Corey	1998-99	44	2	6	8	109	44	2	6	8	109
Beauregard David	2010-11	66	34	35	69	68					
	2011-12	67	44	36	80	72					
	2012-13	8	1	6	7	2	141	79	77	156	142

Beckett Jason	2012-13	66	5	12	17	192	66	5	12	17	192
Belanger Mario	1994-95	39	46	55	101	54	39	46	55	101	54
Bell Jonathan	2006-07	1									
Bellamy Rob	2010-11	56	23	32	55	84	56	23	32	55	84
Benedict Brendan	2011-12	66	23	40	63	50					
	2012-13	65	19	37	56	42					
	2013-14	52	13	33	46	36					
	2014-15	61	12	25	37	40	244	67	135	202	168
Bennett Johnny	1980-81	13	0	0	0	0	13	0	0	0	0
Bergin Kevin	2007-08	52	24	20	44	49					
	2008-09	61	29	37	66	126					
	2009-10	55	16	27	43	106	168	69	84	153	281
Berube Mike	2014-15	67	2	14	16	36	67	2	14	16	36
Betteridge Ollie	2011-12	5	0	0	0	0					
	2012-13	2	0	0	0	0					
	2013-14	3	0	0	0	0					
	2014-15	11	0	0	0	2					
	2015-16	61	3	2	5	13					
	2016-17	73	7	13	20	32					
	2017-18	77	6	9	15	26					
	2018-19	71	10	12	22	22					
	2019-20	64	13	9	22	28					
	2020-21	16	5	1	6	2					
	2021-22	56	16	11	27	10	439	60	57	117	135
Bidner Todd	1990-91	26	24	32	56	77	26	24	32	56	77
Biggs Tyler	2018-19	27	4	7	11	61	27	4	7	11	61

Player	Season	GP	G	A	Pts	PIM	Tot GP	Tot G	Tot A	Tot Pts	Tot PIM
Billinsley Tim	2017-18	77	10	24	34	66					
	2018-19	64	4	17	21	49	141	14	41	55	115
Binkley Jason	2019-20	6	0	1	1	6	6	0	1	1	6
Bishop Mike	1996-97	60	12	20	32	130					
	1997-98	42	3	3	6	60					
	1998-99	65	11	15	26	66	167	26	38	64	256
Bissonette Dan	1987-88	6	12	8	20	6	6	12	8	20	6
Black Wally	1947-48	55	23	9	32	46					
………………..	1948-49	43	24	15	39	46					
………………..	1949-50	70	55	46	101	67	168	102	70	172	159
Blaisdell Mike	1994-95	14	11	14	25	66					
	1995-96	52	35	46	81	124					
	1996-97	15	6	6	12	12					
	1998-99	3	0	1	1	0	84	52	67	119	202
Bobyck Brent	1996-97	53	10	11	21	28					
	1997-98	55	10	21	31	20					
	1998-99	54	9	16	25	28					
	1999-00	54	12	32	44	40	216	41	80	121	116
Bohmbach Andy	2015-16	66	23	27	50	49	66	23	27	50	49
Boivin Christophe	2020-21	16	8	14	22	6					
	2021-22	67	29	39	68	36	83	37	53	90	42
Bolduc Alexandre	2018-19	48	9	17	26	70	48	9	17	26	70
Booth Rod	1951-52	51	11	11	22	57	51	11	11	22	57
Boston Martin	1993-94	2	0	0	0	0	2	0	0	0	0
Bouchard John	1959-60	51	38	29	67	38	51	38	29	67	38

206

Name	Season	GP	G	A	Pts	PIM	Career GP	Career G	Career A	Career Pts	Career PIM
Bougie George	1958-59	29	11	14	25	16	29	11	14	25	16
Bowen Curtis	1999-00	50	8	20	28	141					
	2005-06	54	15	30	45	78	104	23	50	73	219
Bowley Callum	2009-10	2	0	0	0	0					
	2010-11	1	0	0	0	0					
	2011-12	2	0	0	0	0	5	0	0	0	0
	2012-13	1									
Boxhill Jonathan	2007-08	3									
	2013-14	65	8	8	16	37					
	2014-15	70	7	26	33	74	135	15	34	49	111
Boynton Nick	2004-05	20	4	5	9	26	20	4	5	9	26
Bradbury Matt	1990-91	18	0	0	0	0	18	0	0	0	0
Brassard J.C.	2021-22	67	7	32	39	24	67	7	32	39	24
Brebant Rick	1994-95	59	85	156	241	106	59	85	156	241	106
Bremner John	1981-82	41	10	15	25	90					
	1982-83	25	3	10	13	68					
	1983-84	37	6	7	13	63					
	1984-85	44	2	11	13	63					
	1985-86	43	0	10	10	101					
	1986-87	48	6	17	23	67					
	1987-88	48	8	20	28	64					
	1988-89	50	6	14	22	40					
	1989-90	56	10	15	25	48					
	1990-91	49	4	6	10	76					
	1991-92	54	5	5	10	16	495	60	132	192	696
Brinster Chris	1985-86	4	1	7	8	4	4	1	7	8	4
Brisbois Mathieu	2017-18	37	3	9	12	43	37	3	9	12	43
Broadhead Mick	1981-82	22	2	10	12	2					

	1983-84	3	0	0	0	0	25	2	10	12 2
Broadhurst Pete	1984-85	40	0	3	3	48				
	1985-86	16	1	2	3	33	56	1	5	6 81
Brown Hal	1947-48	50	12	21	33	12				
....	1948-49	56	10	23	33	16				
....	1949-50	65	17	37	54	28	171	39	81	120 56
Brown Jeff	2016-17	72	17	26	44	128				
	12017-18	77	19	29	48	88	149	36	55	91 216
Buckman Jason	2003-04	2	0	0	0	0				
	2004-05	14	0	1	1	0				
	2005-06	1	0	0	0	0	17	0	1	1 0
Buckman Lewis	2003-04	10	0	1	1	14				
	2004-05	11	0	1	1	0				
	2005-06	1	0	0	0	2	22	0	2	2 16
Budd Grant	1987-88	1	0	0	0	0				
	1988-89	25	0	0	0	4				
	1989-90	11	1	1	2	0	37	1	1	2 4
Bullas Sam	2007-08	26	1	1	2	0				
	2008-09	22	0	0	0	2				
	2009-10	6	0	0	0	0	54	1	1	2 2
Bulmer Brett	2019-20	46	13	17	30	20	46	13	17	30 20
Burke George	1946-47	40	17	9	26	39	40	17	9	26 39
Burke Greg	2000-01	64	2	14	16	118	64	2	14	16 118
Bury Ed	1952-53	58	26	34	60	80	58	26	34	60 80
Bussieres Raphael	2017-18	70	7	22	29	57	70	7	22	29 57
Butler Phillip	1993-94	19	1	1	2	75				

	1994-95	61 8 3 8 3 3	11 130 80 9 4 13 205

Player	Season	Stats	
Cadotte Mark	2002-03	54 21 32 53 33	
	2003-04	65 35 55 90 46	
	2004-05	57 11 37 48 22	176 67 124 191 101
Cain Aaron	1999-00	59 9 12 21 86	59 9 12 21 86
Calvert Ashley	2007-08	1 0 0 0 0	1 0 0 0 0
Cangelosi Austin	2020-21	16 11 8 19 10	16 11 8 19 10
Capraro Chris	2013-14	28 10 16 26 18	28 10 16 26 18
Carderelli Joe	2005-06	56 29 29 58 50	
	2006-07	38 10 27 37 14	94 39 56 95 64
Carlsson Calle	1999-00	57 18 18 36 30	
	2001-02	56 7 11 18 56	
	2003-04	65 7 31 38 56	
	2004-05	65 5 21 26 40	
	2005-06	47 3 10 13 36	290 40 91 131 218
Carlyle Johnny	1958-59	27 1 6 7 14	27 1 6 7 14
Carozza Massimo	2021-22	31 11 15 26 12	31 11 15 26 12
Carpenter Steve	1997-98	57 8 15 23 77	
	1998-99	50 4 27 31 80	
	1999-00	46 5 23 28 196	153 17 65 82 353
Carr Adam	2004-05		
Carter Matt	2016-17	67 22 17 39 20	67 22 17 39 20
Casey Gerry	1958-59	47 19 30 49 13	47 19 30 49 13

Name	Season	Stats	Totals
Casey Pat	1950-51	58 41 56 97 91	
....	1951-52	58 48 46 94 104	
....	1952-53	59 16 22 38 91	175 105 124 229 286
Ceman Dan	2005-06	25 7 15 22 32	25 7 15 22 32
Cernich Kord	1993-94	33 6 12 18 58	33 6 12 18 58
Chamberlain Bobb	2020-21	5 0 0 0 4	5 0 0 0 4
Champagne Scott	2011-12	29 9 28 37 22	29 9 28 37 22
Charron Eric	2002-03	54 3 10 13 118	54 3 10 13 118
Chiarelli Peter	1987-88	4 4 9 13 2	4 4 9 13 2
Chinn George	1954-55	60 35 40 75 24	60 35 40 75 24
Chinn Nicky	2003-04	11 0 0 0 6	11 0 0 0 6
Churchill John	1990-91	18 0 0 0 0	18 0 0 0 0
Clarke David	2003-04	52 17 21 38 55	
	2004-05	65 32 30 62 34	
	2005-06	44 13 13 26 77	
	2006-07	59 37 25 62 120	
	2008-09	41 28 21 49 48	
	2009-10	67 37 39 76 106	
	2010-11	67 46 39 85 61	
	2011-12	63 43 32 75 60	
	2012-13	61 27 38 65 65	
	2013-14	69 39 34 73 126	
	2014-15	25 11 14 25 16	
	2015-16	63 21 29 50 75	
	2016-17	39 18 14 32 21	
	2017-18	71 12 22 34 36	786 381 371 752 900
Clarke Jason	2002-03	55 19 20 39 213	55 19 20 39 213

Name	Season	Stats								
Clarke-Pizzo Morga	2020-21	5	0	0	0					
	2021-22	16	1	0	1	6	21	1	0	1	6
Clarson Gary	1980-81	24	0	1	1	2					
	1981-82	13	0	0	0	0					
	1982-83	23	2	8	10	22					
	1983-84	2	0	0	0	0	62	2	9	11	24
Clay John (stu?)	1956-57	1	0	0	0	0	1	0	0	0	0
Cockburn Steve	1985-86	5	0	0	0	0					
	1986-87	2	0	0	0	0					
	1987-88	24	0	1	1	14					
	1988-89	2	1	0	1	0					
	1989-90	2	0	0	0	0					
	1990-91	41	2	6	8	14					
	1991-92	30	2	6	8	24					
	1993-94	16	2	0	2	6	122	7	13	20	58
Cohen Colby	2014-15	18	2	6	8	37	18	2	6	8	37
Coleman John	2007-08	19	4	5	9	12	19	4	5	9	12
Connelly Brian	2019-20	64	7	29	36	42	64	7	29	36	42
Cook Brendan	2008-09	61	34	41	75	39	61	34	41	75	39
Cooke James	2004-05	10	0	0	0	0					
	2005-06	30	4	2	6	10					
	2006-07	59	4	6	10	19	99	8	8	16	29
Cooney Pat	1954-55	62	51	28	79	67	62	51	28	79	67
Cooper Stephen	1999-00	62	2	12	14	46	62	2	12	14	46
Cote Brandin	2005-06	40	15	21	36	66	40	15	21	36	66
Cotton Darren	2001-02	2	0	1	1	0	2	0	1	1	0

211

Cownie Jordan	2014-15	4	1	0	1	2	4	1	0	1	2
Coyston Art	1946-47	42	15	10	25	29	42	15	10	25	29
Craighead John	2003-04	63	45	32	77	228					
	2004-05	23	10	10	20	134	86	55	42	97	362
Crapier Jamie	1985-86	49	97	89	186	87					
	1986-87	8	9	17	26	10	57	106	106	212	97
Dalgleish Ross	2009-10	53	4	4	8	50	53	4	4	8	50
Dallman Marty	1996-97	59	33	44	77	38					
	1997-98	51	25	30	55	22	110	58	74	132	60
D'Amour Dominic	2009-10	65	13	24	37	219	65	13	24	37	219
Darling Dion	2005-06	37	5	16	21	48	37	5	16	21	48
De Angelis Mike	1997-98	24	2	5	7	16	24	2	5	7	16
De Costa Jeff	1998-99	54	4	18	22	28	54	4	18	22	28
Derlago Mark	2017-18	73	27	42	69	49	73	27	42	69	49
DeSantis Jason	2019-20	47	4	12	16	27	47	4	12	16	27
Desilets Mike	1957-58	52	21	18	39	110	52	21	18	39	110
Deutsch Adam	2019-20	47	9	13	22	49	47	9	13	22	49
Devereaux Red	1958-59	2	0	1	1	0	2	0	1	1	0
Dilks Chris	1989-90	21	0	1	1	0					
	1993-94	2	0	0	0	0	23	0	1	1	0
Dimmen Jeff	2015-16	36	2	12	14	40					
	2016-17	49	9	19	28	38	85	11	31	42	78

Player	Season Stats
Dineen Nick	2020-21 16 3 3 6 11 16 3 3 6 11
Dixon Brian	1983-84 39 22 22 44 92 39 22 22 44 92
Doherty Taylor	2021-22 24 2 7 9 18 24 2 7 9 18
Domingue Kevin	2020-21 16 10 10 20 10
	2021-22 34 6 7 13 12 50 16 17 33 22
Dorian Dan	1991-92 54 94 85 179 91
	1992-93 23 50 19 69 30 77 144 104 248 121
Doty Jacob	………..2018-19 23 2 1 3 43 23 2 1 3 43
Doucet Guillaume	2014-15 27 19 10 29 34 27 19 10 29 34
Dougherty Ernie	1953-54 60 29 20 49 12
	1955-56 46 40 31 71 8 106 69 51 120 20
Doyle Perry	1993-94 59 3 5 8 161 59 3 5 8 161
Drolet Jimmy	2001-02 56 7 16 23 86 56 7 16 23 86
Drouin P C	2000-01 64 29 39 68 104
	2001-02 56 20 38 58 82
	2007-08 21 8 14 22 36 141 57 91 148 222
Dryburgh Jim	1956-57 5 1 3 4 0
……………………..	1959-60 2 0 0 0 0 7 1 3 4 0
Dubois Eric	1998-99 57 1 20 21 34 57 1 20 21 34
Ducharme Dave	1987-88 24 44 43 87 43 24 44 43 87 43
Dunnigan Dick	1959-60 59 30 36 66 6 59 30 36 66 6
Durdle Darren	1988-89 50 78 105 183 146
	1995-96 49 31 65 96 58 99 109 170 279 204

213

Easson Darryl	1980-81	25	22 15 37 79
	1981-82	33	8 5 13 14
	1986-87	40	3 6 9 13
	1987-88	44	11 9 20 22
	1988-89	43	5 4 9 12
	1989-90	50	2 5 7 14 235 51 44 95 154
Elders Jason	2002-03	53	22 20 42 36 53 22 20 42 36
Elliott (Hunt) James	1984-85	9	0 1 1 16
	1985-86	30	1 3 4 11
	1986-87	42	5 2 7 38
	1987-88	41	7 5 12 42
	1988-89	23	1 6 7 41 145 14 17 31 148
Ellis Brendan	2020-21	16	0 7 7 12 16 0 7 7 12
Ellis Mike	2006-07	15	3 3 6 4
	2007-08	20	1 3 4 16 35 4 6 10 20
Emersic Blaz	2005-06	56	12 27 39 22
	2006-07	23	1 2 3 22 79 13 29 42 44
Eratt Layton	1980-81	26	5 3 8 14
	1981-82	11	5 3 8 21
	1984-85	44	10 7 17 75
	1985-86	45	10 9 19 103
	1986-87	45	9 12 21 85 171 39 34 73 298
Evans Frank	2001-02	36	3 6 9 53 36 3 6 9 53
Farley Sean	1991-92	6	9 6 15 0 6 9 6 15 0
Farmer Robert	2013-14	35	11 15 26 70
	2014-15	59	16 29 45 178

214

	2015-16 55 9 14 23 100		
	2016-17 67 19 28 47 90		
	2017-18 68 12 24 36 97		
	2018-19 64 13 28 41 69	348 80 138 218 604	
Farnsworth Darren	1983-84 14 0 0 0 0	14 0 0 0 0	
Ferrara James	2005-06 4 0 0 0 0		
	2006-07 53 2 3 5 16		
	2007-08 63 2 9 11 14		
	2008-09 57 7 3 10 16		
	2009-10 21 0 0 0 4	198 11 15 26 50	
Ferrara Luke	2012-13 2		
Ferrara Robert	2007-08 1 0 0 0 0	1 0 0 0 0	
Fick Danny	2019-20 62 0 11 11 99	62 0 11 11 99	
Flavill John	1987-88 1 0 0 0 0		
	1988-89 13 0 0 0 4		
	1989-90 55 4 9 13 12		
	1990-91 49 4 1 5 7		
	1991-92 54 5 4 9 0		
	1992-93 1 0 0 0 0	173 13 14 27 23	
Flint Matt	1987-88 18 0 0 0 0	18 0 0 0 0	
Flint Nick	1983-84 9 0 0 0 0		
	1987-88 5 0 0 0 0	14 0 0 0 0	
Flint Tim	1987-88 2 0 0 0 2	2 0 0 0 2	
Flitchel Martin	1999-00 50 20 26 46 100	50 20 26 46 100	
Flynn Ron	1956-57 39 29 17 46 20	39 29 17 46 20	
Foord Matt	2006-07 1 0 0 0 0	1 0 0 0 0	

Name	Season	GP	G	A	Pts	PIM					
Fornica Joe	1958-59	24	17	7	24	9	24	17	7	24	9
Fothergill Paul	1981-82	2	0	0	0	0	2	0	0	0	0
Fox Jordan	2011-12	67	29	56	85	82					
	2012-13	63	16	51	67	47	130	45	107	152	129
Francis Matt	2011-12	67	28	40	68	33					
	2012-13	67	26	41	67	61					
	2013-14	67	31	42	73	115	201	85	123	208	209
Fraser Gavin	1982-83	29	19	10	29	50					
	1983-84	29	17	25	42	10					
	1984-85	40	12	20	32	84					
	1985-86	47	13	10	23	78					
	1986-87	51	47	39	86	80					
	1987-88	37	27	30	57	121					
	1988-89	48	38	34	72	55					
	1989-90	58	19	24	43	56					
	1990-91	24	9	7	16	32					
	1991-92	43	15	20	35	43					
	1992-93	4	0	0	0	0	409	216	219	435	609
Fresher Rupe	1957-58	54	12	16	28	6					
....	1958-59	52	27	17	44	30					
....	1959-60	59	12	11	23	35	165	51	44	95	71
Gagnon Mathieu	2017-18	75	2	11	13	142	75	2	11	13	142
Galbraith Jade	2008-09	59	23	52	75	53					
	2009-10	68	25	72	97	106					
	2010-11	60	28	69	97	99	187	76	193	269	258
Galivan Pat	2012-13	62	24	35	59	31	62	24	35	59	31
Gallant Trevor	2006-07	10	3	15	18	36	10	3	15	18	36
Garden Graham	1998-99	65	9	16	25	98					
	1999-00	53	7	18	25	175					

	2000-01 60 3 13 16 141 178 19 47 66 414
Garrigan Craig	2020-21 13 0 0 0 0 13 0 0 0 0
Garside Mark	2020-21 14 0 0 0 4 14 0 0 0 4
Gascon Marty	2009-10 66 16 49 65 26 66 16 49 65 26
Gascoyne Russ	1983-84 5 0 0 0 0 5 0 0 0 0
Gautier Jim	1984-85 19 36 19 55 18 19 36 19 55 18
Gavrilenko Sergei	1992-93 2 0 1 1 2 2 0 1 1 2
Gawthrop Les	1949-50 3 0 1 1 4 3 0 1 1 4
Gebhardt Jim	1955-56 21 5 3 8 24 1956-57 56 9 19 28 59 77 14 22 36 83
Gillis Ryan	2000-01 46 2 13 15 122 46 2 13 15 122
Gilmartin John	1983-84 1 0 0 0 0 1 0 0 0 0
Glossop Connor	2015-16 3
Goldby Mark	1984-85 36 0 0 0 6 1985-86 37 1 1 2 4 1986-87 33 0 2 2 7 1987-88 29 2 2 4 2 1988-89 14 0 0 0 2 1990-91 22 3 1 4 2 171 6 6 12 23
Golicic Juri	2008-09 6 2 1 3 8 6 2 1 3 8
Golovkovs Georgs	2019-20 51 9 23 32 20 51 9 23 32 20
Goodman Roger	1947-48 54 11 7 18 38 1948-49 56 8 15 23 76 1949-50 67 4 8 12 76 177 23 30 53 190

Gordon Rhett	2011-12	23	4	17	21	12	23	4	17	21	12
Grace Peter	1981-82	4	0	0	0	0	4	0	0	0	0
Graham Bruce	2012-13	66	42	37	79	59					
	2014-15	55	16	25	41	70	121	58	62	120	129
Graham Joe	2007-08	29	0	0	0	4					
	2008-09	36	0	2	2	25					
	2009-10	1	0	0	0	0	66	0	2	2	29
Greaves Simon	1995-96	42	2	1	3	0					
	1996-97	28	0	0	0	0					
	1997-98	67	0	0	0	0	137	2	1	3	0
Greig Tommy	1952-53	60	14	8	22	86	60	14	8	22	86
Griffiths Owen	2020-21	15	0	4	4	0	15	0	4	4	0
Griffiths Tony	1980-81	17	5	4	9	20	17	5	4	9	20
Grimaldi Joe	2013-14	7	2	6	8	110	7	2	6	8	110
Gudzuinas Terry	1981-82	7	17	10	27	4					
	1982-83	27	30	35	65	24	34	47	45	92	28
Guptill Alex	2018-19	67	39	26	65	72	67	39	26	65	72
Hadden Greg	1996-97	59	21	14	35	65					
	1997-98	58	24	32	56	38					
	1998-99	57	37	37	74	94					
	1999-00	55	32	30	62	34					
	2000-01	58	22	20	42	81					
	2001-02	54	21	22	43	15					
	2002-03	54	20	25	45	52	395	177	180	357	379
Hall Fred	1955-56	55	18	24	42	66	55	18	24	42	66

Name	Season	GP	G	A	Pts	PIM					
Hamilton Bruce	1958-59	8	7	6	13	0	8	7	6	13	0
Hamilton Doug	1953-54	38	2	2	4	72	38	2	2	4	72
Hansen Jake	2019-20	51	22	38	60	45	51	22	38	60	45
Hardy Kyle	2015-16	10	0	4	4	10	10	0	4	4	10
Harper Tristan	2009-10	1	0	0	0	2	1	0	0	0	2
Hazledine Joseph	2017-18	8	0	0	0	0					
	2018-19	24	0	0	0	0					
	2019-20	41	0	1	1	2	73	0	1	1	2
Hedberg Edwin	2021-22	29	2	2	4	4	29	2	2	4	4
Heerema Jeff	2010-11	35	22	20	42	38					
	2011-12	31	13	23	36	49	66	35	43	78	87
Henderson Jim	2009-10	21	5	9	14	60	21	5	9	14	60
Henderson Kevin	2018-19	50	5	17	22	18	50	5	17	22	18
Henley Brent	2013-14	42	0	4	4	294	42	0	4	4	294
Herr Sam	2019-20	64	41	44	85	56	64	41	44	85	56
Herriott Jim	1946-47	42	1	6	7	34					
	1947-48	55	10	14	24	120					
	1948-49	55	4	11	15	83					
	1949-50	61	11	11	22	82	213	26	42	68	319
Higgins Chris	2014-15	38	11	22	33	30	38	11	22	33	30
Hill Ed	2008-09	20	0	7	7	16	20	0	7	7	16
Hoad jeff	1996-97	57	21	17	38	95	57	21	17	38	95
Hobson John	1983-84	2	0	0	0	0					

	1984-85 3 0 1 1 0	
	1985-86 38 2 5 7 4	
	1986-87 36 2 4 6 8	
	1987-88 47 4 12 16 12	
	1988-89 16 1 1 2 16	
	1989-90 51 2 5 7 27	193 11 28 39 67
Hodgins Art	1959-60 51 4 7 11 14	51 4 7 11 14
Hoffman Kevin	2000-01 15 6 5 11 0	15 6 5 11 0
Hoffman Walt	1959-60 3 0 0 0 0	3 0 0 0 0
Hook Lewis	2012-13 2	
	2014-15 3 0 0 0 2	
	2020-21 16 3 4 7 8	19 3 4 7 10
Hopkins Jack	2021-22 21 1 1 2 0	21 1 1 2 0
Horb George	1953-54 60 34 28 62 40	60 34 28 62 40
Horvat Ryan	2019-20 34 5 13 18 41	34 5 13 18 41
Howard Reg	1946-47 42 9 9 18 77	
	1947-48 57 6 11 17 80	99 15 20 35 157
Howarth Andy	2003-04 2 0 0 0 0	2 0 0 0 0
Hudson Gerry	1955-56 56 35 45 80 46	
	1956-57 56 29 49 78 37	112 64 94 158 83
Hughes Tommy	2018-19 65 6 18 24 62	65 6 18 24 62
Hunt Simon	1988-89 14 3 3 6 8	
	1989-90 48 14 10 24 98	
	1990-91 35 21 23 44 141	
	1991-92 51 42 23 65 231	
	1992-93 44 34 15 49 149	
	1993-94 46 35 11 46 169	

	1994-95 52 51 38 89 121	
	1995-96 43 34 18 52 154	
	1996-97 50 1 3 4 86	
	1997-98 44 2 6 8 28	
	1998-99 62 7 2 9 28	
	1999-00 28 2 1 3 46	517 246 153 399 1259
Hurtubise Mark	2018-19 71 16 39 55 54	71 16 39 55 54
Hussey Marc	2002-03 56 10 13 23 48	56 10 13 23 48
Hutchinson Dave	1983-84 3 0 0 0 0	
	1984-85 9 0 0 0 17	
	1985-86 48 1 2 3 64	
	1986-87 50 1 5 6 14	
	1987-88 47 0 4 4 39	
	1988-89 25 1 3 4 14	182 3 14 17 148
Hutchinson James	2007-08 2 0 0 0 0	2 0 0 0 0
Hutchinson Phil		
Ingram John	1980-81	8 4 3 7 27 8 4 3 7 27
Ingram Tim	1980-81	10 1 0 1 22 10 1 0 1 22
Innes Bill	1951-52	60 19 15 34 24 60 19 15 34 24
Ivan Marek	2004-05	56 26 22 48 143 56 26 22 48 143

AD

Player	Season	Stats									
Jacina Greg	2013-14	30	5	15	20	61					
	2014-15	64	14	24	38	133	94	19	39	58	194
Jakobs Jens	2019-20	11	1	0	1	13	11	1	0	1	13
James Bud	1950-51	60	9	19	28	98					
…………………..	1951-52	54	5	10	15	105	114	14	29	43	203
Janssen Cam	2015-16	66	5	6	11	122	66	5	6	11	122
Jeffrey Mike	1987-88	23	48	36	84	62	23	48	36	84	62
Jennings Jason	1996-97	33	9	18	27	18	33	9	18	27	18
Jenson Joe	2013-14	19	4	13	17	50	19	4	13	17	50
Jinman lee	2001-02	49	12	36	48	84					
	2002-03	55	22	48	70	30					
	2002-03	36	25	41	66	46	140	59	125	184	160
Jokinen Tommi	2021-22	8	0	3	3	0	8	0	3	3	0
Jones Scott	1980-81	1	2	0	2	0	1	2	0	2	0
Kalmikov Konstantin	2004-05	63	28	19	47	22	63	28	19	47	22
Kalus Petre	2013-14	47	18	22	40	63					
	2016-17	13	3	5	8	13	60	21	27	48	76
Kason Mark	1980-81	11	6	4	11	22					
	1981-82	35	11	13	24	61	46	17	17	35	83
Kelham A J	1995-96	52	15	26	41	22					
	2001-02	18	2	1	3	0	70	17	27	44	22
Kelland Chris	1991-92	55	14	67	81	174					
	1992-93	37	11	47	58	82	92	25	114	139	256

Player	Season	GP	G	A	Pts	PIM	Totals
Kelsall Jordon	2017-18	12	2	0	2	0	
	2019-20	64	1	1	2	6	
	2020-21	16	0	1	1	4	
	2021-22	62	5	5	10	28	154 8 7 15 38
Keward Chris	1986-87	39	0	1	1	2	
	1994-95	2	0	0	0	0	41 0 1 1 2
Keward Dwayne	1980-81	26	39	19	58	55	
	1981-82	41	44	31	75	96	
	1982-83	22	32	27	59	39	
	1983-84	36	30	18	48	48	
	1984-85	32	14	21	35	42	
	1985-86	35	7	14	21	60	
	1986-87	48	25	43	68	57	
	1988-89	23	7	21	28	28	
	1989-90	15	11	10	21	10	278 209 204 413 435
Keyes Jimmy	1985-86	42	71	69	140	212	
	1986-87	50	94	86	180	167	92 165 155 320 379
King Duncan	1989-90	4	0	0	0	4	
	1990-91	43	1	1	2	26	
	1991-92	39	0	2	2	18	
	1992-93	51	4	8	12	88	
	1993-94	18	1	1	2	20	191 6 12 18 156
Knox Blake	1997-98	54	20	29	49	107	54 20 29 49 107
Koivonarou Mikko..	2003-04	57	13	46	59	117	57 13 46 59 117
Kolesar Mark	1998-99	63	25	40	65	58	63 25 40 65 58
Kolnik Juraj	2015-16	65	33	40	73	44	65 33 40 73 44
Kovacs Justin	2018-19	60	15	32	47	14	60 15 32 47 14
Krajicek Jan	2006-07	59	11	32	43	194	59 11 32 43 194

Krulis Jan 2004-05		43	7	10	17	70	43	7	10	17	70
Kudroc Kristian 2016-17		12	1	5	6	12	12	1	5	6	12
Kurtenbach Terry	1986-87	51	44	83	127	76					
	1987-88	45	45	66	111	66					
	1988-89	50	44	78	122	62					
	1989-90	52	58	50	108	60					
	1990-91	50	32	46	78	60					
	1991-92	54	32	56	88	62					
	1992-93	53	35	53	88	68	355	290	432	722	454
Kwong Larry	1957-58	55	55	24	79	10	55	55	24	79	10

Lachowicz Robert	2006-07	1								
	2007-08	31	1	0	1	0				
	2008-09	36	1	3	4	2				
	2009-10	12	1	3	4	2				
	2010-11	67	12	18	30	6				
	2011-12	67	23	33	56	14				
	2012-13	67	20	31	51	8				
	2013-14	69	21	42	63	38				
	2014-15	70	15	31	46	18				
	2015-16	64	5	14	19	8				
	2016-17	73	5	20	28	14				
	2017-18	77	10	15	25	10				
	2018-19	68	3	9	12	8				
	2019-20	64	4	11	15	10				
	2020-21	15	0	6	6	4	780	121	236	357	142

LaForge Maurice	1947-48	55	25	19	44	30					
………………………	1948-49	54	20	19	39	24					
……………………	1952-53	26	8	7	15	8	135	53	45	98	62
Lambert Ross	1993-94	60	69	100	169	184					
	1994-95	63	53	103	156	181	123	122	203	325	365
Landrey Charles	2014-15	66	6	11	17	60	66	6	11	17	60
Lane Matthew	2021-22	62	20	22	42	25	62	20	22	42	25
Lang Parent. Maxime	2014-15	51	11	12	23	81	51	11	12	23	81
Larocque Mario	2009-10	21	2	5	7	80	21	2	5	7	80
Larter Ron	1953-54	23	4	2	6	8	23	4	2	6	8
Larter Tyler	1993-94	5	7	6	13	12	5	7	6	13	12
Lattimer Keith	1959-60	17	3	2	5	4	17	3	2	5	4
Lavinge Eric	2000-01	58	1	10	11	210	58	1	10	11	210
Lavoie Daryl	2000-01	61	2	7	9	90	61	2	7	9	90
Lawrence Chris	2014-15	67	25	39	64	151					
	2015-16	40	6	18	24	42					
	2016-17	56	22	24	46	72	163	53	81	134	265
Laxdell Derek	1996-97	50	23	18	41	118					
	1997-98	62	32	35	67	129	112	55	53	108	247

Player	Season	GP	G	A	Pts	PIM					
Leach Jamie	1997-98	55	27	33	60	40					
	1998-99	55	30	28	58	24					
	1999-00	62	24	40	64	38					
	2000-01	62	19	16	35	24	234	100	117	217	126
Leak Sean	1993-94	9	0	0	0	2	9	0	0	0	2
LeClair Corey	2008-09	6	1	1	2	4	6	1	1	2	4
Lee Mark	2014-15	1	0	0	0	0	1	0	0	0	0
Lee Rod	1959-60	60	31	28	59	17	60	31	28	59	17
Lee Stephen	2009-10	64	3	6	9	112					
	2010-11	61	3	19	22	100					
	2011-12	63	5	16	21	102					
	2012-13	58	2	11	13	45					
	2013-14	51	4	15	19	71					
	2014-15	47	5	15	20	33					
	2015-16	62	5	23	28	42					
	2016-17	64	3	21	24	45					
	2017-18	75	1	15	16	73					
	2018-19	67	1	11	12	36					
	2021-22	6	1	2	3	6	618	33	154	187	665
Lepine Guillaume	2010-11	62	4	8	12	245					
	2011-12	66	7	18	25	191					
	2012-13	60	4	17	21	165					
	2018-19	65	2	8	10	131					
	2019-20	62	1	14	15	82	315	18	65	83	814

L'Esperance Gilles	1980-81	9	10	7	17	14	9	10	7	17	14
Levers Marc	2000-01	25	0	0	0	0					
	2003-04	54	6	4	10	44					
	2007-08	63	10	16	26	52					
	2008-09	57	11	19	30	54					
	2009-10	68	16	19	35	131					
	2010-11	54	10	26	36	24					
	2011-12	66	11	20	31	57					
	2012-13	67	0	7	7	16	454	64	111	175	378
	2016-17	1									
Lindhagan Eric	2016-17	73	8	25	33	44					
	2017-18	77	7	17	24	40	150	15	42	57	84
Ling David	2012-13	67	38	70	108	160					
	2015-16	34	14	32	46	83	101	52	102	154	243
Linton Andy	1981-82	14	12	14	26	19					
	1982-83	26	10	12	22	12					
	1983-84	32	2	11	13	24					
	1984-85	13	0	1	1	6	85	24	38	62	61
Liscak Robert	2010-11	4	0	1	1	6	4	0	1	1	6
Loiseau Alex	2019-20	5	1	1	2	2	5	1	1	2	2
Longley Andrew	1993-94	1	0	0	0	0	1	0	0	0	0
Lowen Darcy	1998-99	40	3	8	11	68	40	3	8	11	68

Lyons Bob	1946-47	41	2	8	10	30	41	2	8	10	30
Lyons Lynn	2013-14	52	15	18	33	16	52	15	18	33	16
Lund Martin	1980-81	21	2	4	6	32	21	2	4	6	32
Lundmark Herb	1958-59	27	3	6	9	29	27	3	6	9	29
McAslan Sean	2006-07	57	45	30	75	113					
	2007-08	65	41	56	97	114					
	2009-10	68	43	44	87	64					
	2011-12	4	1	1	2	2	194	130	131	261	293
McDonald Bill	1950-51	57	16	13	29	163					
………………………..	1951-52	55	9	17	26	80	112	25	30	55	243
McDonald Franklin	2015-16	18	1	3	4	6	18	1	3	4	6
McDonald Greg	1983-84	36	41	40	81	182					
	1984-85	10	16	8	24	20	46	57	48	105	202
McDonald Ian	2010-11	34	12	17	29	16	34	12	17	29	16
McDonald Kenny	1981-82	25	33	18	51	34					
	1982-83	25	26	15	41	50	50	59	33	92	84
McDonald Tony	1980-81	10	0	0	0	0	10	0	0	0	0
McGratton Brian	2016-17	66	19	8	27	149	66	19	8	27	149
McHugh Ron	1959-60	42	11	13	24	23	42	11	13	24	23

McKay Larry	1948-49	46	14	14	28	20	46	14	14	28	20
McKay Neil	1982-83	29	60	48	108	105					
	1983-84	40	53	57	110	112	69	113	105	219	217
McKenna Steve	2004-05	51	8	13	21	28	51	8	13	21	28
McKie Kenny	1982-83	15	9	11	20	16					
	1983-84	31	11	12	23	114	46	20	23	43	130
McLinchey Randy	1981-82	17	23	29	52	55	17	23	29	52	55
McMillan Logan	2015-16	60	12	15	27	36					
	2016-17	66	3	17	20	8	126	15	32	47	44
McNiven ..	1956-57	1	0	0	0	0	1	0	0	0	0
McWilliams Rhys	2003-04	2	0	0	0	0					
	2004-05	7	0	0	0	0					
	2005-06	1	0	0	0	0	10	0	0	0	0
Machin Keith	1956-57	1	0	0	0	0	1	0	0	0	0
McLachlan Mac	1946-47	42	23	25	48	34					
....	1947-48	56	29	24	53	48	98	52	49	101	82
Magdosko Jan	2004-05	38	2	4	6	125	38	2	4	6	125
Makela Tuukka	2013-14	7	0	1	1	38	7	0	1	1	38
Malmquist Dylan	2019-20	63	9	25	34	8	63	9	25	34	8
Malo Andre	1993-94	56	26	50	76	40	56	26	50	76	40

Malo Tony	1951-52 21 8 6 14 8 21 8 6 14 8
Malone Russ	1959-60 60 53 30 83 88 60 53 30 83 88
Maloney Darren	2001-02 47 2 3 5 16 47 2 3 5 16
Mann Cameron	2009-10 61 36 33 69 107 61 36 33 69 107
Mansoff Jason	1999-00 21 2 4 6 6 21 2 4 6 6
Martel Paul	1957-58 55 19 28 47 37 55 19 28 47 37
Martin Jason	1985-86 12 0 0 0 2
	1986-87 26 0 0 0 2
	1987-88 29 0 2 2 49
	1988-89 45 0 7 7 54
	1989-90 28 0 1 1 26
	1994-95 1 0 0 0 0 141 0 10 10 133
Maslanko Bill	1953-54 34 16 23 39 8 34 16 23 39 8
Massy Kevin	2021-22 29 2 8 10 19 29 2 8 10 19
Masters Casson	2000-01 51 3 9 12 24 51 3 9 12 24
Matheson Mark	2019-20 64 11 45 56 30
	2020-21 16 4 12 16 12
	2021-22 65 4 24 28 36 155 19 81 100 78
Mathieson Jim	1997-98 57 2 11 13 76 57 2 11 13 76
Matthews Rod	1951-52 60 26 21 47 32
....	1952-53 56 31 24 55 24 116 57 45 102 56
May Johno	2020-21 16 1 1 2 12 16 1 1 2 12
Maynard Marcus	2011-12 49 0 2 2 4 49 0 2 2 4
Meloncon Craig	1987-88 28 49 74 123 66 28 49 74 123 66

Messier Doug	1957-58 53 5 35 40 107 53 5 35 40 107
Meyers Danny	2006-07 62 2 17 19 36
	2007-08 63 1 21 22 51
	2008-09 55 6 16 22 55
	2009-10 62 2 9 11 44
	2010-11 60 7 18 25 40
	2011-12 56 7 19 26 27 358 25 100 125 253
Millard Clive (nip)	1956-57 2 1 0 1 0
	1959-60 60 18 6 24 45 62 19 6 25 45
Miller Cam	1953-54 19 2 1 3 18 19 2 1 3 18
Mitchell Roy	1998-99 66 6 11 17 58 66 6 11 17 58
Mollard Hutch	1946-47 38 6 10 16 6 38 6 10 16 6
Moira Steve	1992-93 7 9 12 21 6
	2001-02 55 15 12 27 16 62 24 24 48 22
Monk Arnie	1949-50 61 9 6 15 50 61 9 6 15 50
Mokshantsev Alex.	2017-18 77 28 27 55 57 77 28 27 55 57
Molin Johan	2007-08 62 30 32 62 28
	2008-09 53 28 32 60 20
	2009-10 16 4 7 11 6 131 62 71 133 54
Moran Brad	2015-16 60 19 35 54 18
	2016-17 72 22 38 60 40 132 41 73 114 58
Moran Ian	2004-05 21 2 7 9 10 21 2 7 9 10
Moran Paul	2000-01 30 0 0 0 2
	2001-02 6 0 0 0 0
	2002-03 18 1 1 2 2

	2003-04	66	7	14	21	80				
	2004-05	53	6	8	14	46				
	2005-06	51	2	11	13	62				
	2006-07	38	1	7	8	70	262	17	41	58	262
Morgan Ian	1995-96	11	1	0	1	2	11	1	0	1	2
Morgan James	2002-03	21	1	0	1	15				
	2003-04	23	2	2	4	42	44	3	2	5	57
Morgan Neil	1995-96	56	33	68	101	95				
	1996-97	60	20	32	52	30				
	1997-98	40	10	13	23	28	156	63	113	176	153
Mosey Evan	2014-15	68	13	17	30	38				
	2015-16	67	19	33	52	34				
	2017-18	63	23	23	46	52	198	55	73	128	124
Moulden Pete	1950-51	59	6	9	15	97	59	6	9	15	97
Moxam Darryl	2000-01	18	2	3	5	33	18	2	3	5	33
Mudd Pat	1952-53	3	0	4	4	0	3	0	4	4	0
Murray Chris	2013-14	45	9	35	44	152	45	9	35	44	152
Myers Matt	2004-05	64	5	23	28	89				
	2005-06	54	10	5	15	60				
	2006-07	58	6	20	26	129				
	2007-08	65	10	21	31	76				
	2008-09	51	13	33	46	87				
	2010-11	64	25	46	71	115				
	2011-12	64	20	40	60	50				
	2012-13	67	19	29	48	74				
	2015-16	67	15	20	35	55				
	2021-22	66	16	24	40	49	620	139	261	400	784

Ndur Ruman	2008-09	36 2 4 6 198 36 2 4 6 198
Neil James	2004-05	4 0 1 1 0
	2005-06	30 0 0 0 0
	2006-07	42 0 0 0 0
	2007-08	6 1 1 1 2 0
	2008-09	28 2 0 2 0
	2009-10	6 0 0 0 0 171 3 2 5 0
Neil Lawson	1956-57	38 3 1 11 14 12
....	1957-58	56 4 8 12 16
....	1958-59	24 1 10 11 12
....	1959-60	28 2 2 4 10 146 10 31 41 50
Neilson Corey	2006-07	63 13 35 48 125
	2007-08	65 17 50 67 156
	2008-09	61 16 52 68 145
	2009-10	68 16 50 66 143
	2010-11	67 11 52 63 120
	2011-12	66 13 48 61 119
	2012-13	9 0 6 6 18 399 86 293 379 826
Nelson Eric	2007-08	19 1 8 9 20 19 1 8 9 20
Nemirosky Michail	2004-05	11 3 2 5 8 11 3 2 5 8
Nieckar Barry	2000-01	56 5 14 19 351
	2001-02	53 5 6 11 224
	2002-03	42 11 13 24 222 151 21 33 54 797
Nienhous Kraig	1997-98	60 25 33 58 53 60 25 33 58 53
Nikiforuk Alex	2016-17	70 22 32 54 77 70 22 32 54 77
Nikolov Angel	2010-11	53 2 27 29 40 53 2 27 29 40
Nordmark Robert	2000-01	35 5 7 12 20 35 5 7 12 20

Name	Season	GP	G	A	P	PIM	GP	G	A	P	PIM
Norris Clayton	2001-02	49	5	7	12	188	49	5	7	12	188
Norrish Brady	2021-22	67	3	17	20	62	67	3	17	20	62
Norton Tom	2007-08	4	0	0	0	0					
	2008-09	16	0	0	0	2					
	2009-10	58	0	2	2	4					
	2010-11	65	2	1	3	18					
	2011-12	12	0	2	2	4					
	2012-13	3	0	0	0	0					
	2013-14	71	3	8	11	31	229	5	13	18	59
	2016-17	1									
Oakford Sam	2014-15	60	2	5	7	14					
	2015-16	67	1	3	4	16					
	2016-17	8	0	0	0	7	135	3	8	11	37
O'Brian Mike	1956-57	10	3	3	6	2	10	3	3	6	2
Odelein Selmar	1992-93	30	22	28	50	60	30	22	28	50	60
O'Higgins Paul	1980-81	26	13	12	25	20					
	1981-82	42	36	31	67	20					
	1982-83	28	10	19	29	18					
	1983-84	40	12	7	19	30	136	71	69	140	88
Olsen Darryl	1996-97	58	14	37	51	32	58	14	37	51	32
Olsen Dylan	2018-19	56	9	15	24	49	56	9	15	24	49
Oreskovic Phil	20013-14	26	0	3	3	31	26	0	3	3	31
Pachal Vern	1958-59	30	29	29	58	8	30	29	29	58	8
Paek Jimmy	2000-01	63	5	27	32	36					
	2001-02	12	1	3	4	8					
	2002-03	57	2	21	23	34	132	8	51	59	78

Player	Season	Stats	Totals
Parker Stuart	1987-88	20 1 3 4 2	
	1988-89	35 7 9 16 30	
	1991-92	27 6 7 13 2	82 14 19 33 34
Parkes Andrew	1989-90	2 0 0 0 0	2 0 0 0 0
Patterson Brad	2005-06	42 6 14 20 40	42 6 14 20 40
Patterson Duncan	2000-01	28 1 3 4 18	28 1 3 4 18
Patterson Gordon	1982-83	24 5 3 8 33	
	1983-84	37 3 11 14 132	61 8 14 22 165
Peacock Tim	1980-81	10 10 6 16 31	
	1981-82	37 64 37 101 135	
	1982-83	6 8 4 12 9	53 82 47 129 175
Pelletier Steve	2007-08	65 8 24 32 83	65 8 24 32 83
Penner Alex	2010-11	30 4 5 9 289	30 4 5 9 289
Perkins Simon	1987-88	13 1 1 2 0	
	1988-89	41 14 15 29 66	
	1989-90	55 15 20 35 50	
	1990-91	48 21 14 35 69	
	1991-92	53 19 26 45 112	
	1992-93	43 21 23 44 54	
	1993-94	31 10 4 14 27	284 101 103 204 378
Perlini Brett	2017-18	76 23 46 69 22	
	2018-19	70 18 22 40 39	
	2019-20	55 23 19 42 14	
	2020-21	13 4 10 14 6	214 68 97 165 83
Perlini Fred	1986-87	42 99 95 194 149	42 99 95 194 149

Peters Keith	1952-53	29	8	6	14	12	29	8	6	14	12
Petriko Matus	2006-07	60	17	22	39	131	60	17	22	39	131
Phillips David	1986-87	14	0	0	0	5					
	1987-88	21	2	1	3	6	35	2	1	3	11
Phillips Zack	2017-18	77	18	39	57	20	77	18	39	57	20
Pither Luke	2017-18	27	12	23	35	18					
	2018-19	71	22	31	53	60	98	34	54	88	78
Plata Eddie	1957-58	55	24	33	57	63	55	24	33	57	63
Podlesak Martin	20014-15	2	0	0	0	0	2	0	0	0	0
Poirier Joel	2001-02	53	6	13	19	84	53	6	13	19	84
Pope Brent	1999-00	62	3	11	14	108					
	2001-02	56	1	12	13	71	118	4	23	27	179
Precenicks Stanis.	2015-16	3									
Premack Garth	1993-94	32	26	30	56	36					
	1994-95	64	25	58	83	71					
	1995-96	56	19	20	39	77					
	1996-97	60	11	21	32	50					
	1997-98	62	6	9	15	34	274	87	138	225	268
Prince Jack	2006-07	2									
Purves John	2002-03	51	19	17	36	96	51	19	17	36	96
Pyryhora Johnny	1949-50	33	9	10	19	26					
....	1950-51	59	16	19	35	49	92	25	29	54	75
Quick Kevin	2015-16	18	2	6	8	8	18	2	6	8	8

Quist William	2019-20	30	6	2	8	10	30	6	2	8	10
Radmall Adam	2005-06	2	0	0	0	0	2	0	0	0	0
Rapley Dave	1982-83	7	5	4	9	0	7	5	4	9	0
Raynor Kieran	12015-16	3									
Rees Mike	2006-07	54	4	12	16	195	54	4	12	16	195
Rendell John	1957-58	55	30	31	61	59	55	30	31	61	59
Reynolds Kurt	2007-08	2	0	0	0	0	2	0	0	0	0
Rheault Jon	2018-19	36 6		12	18	28					
	2019-20	50	6	9	15	14	86	12	21	33	42
Rhodes Nigel	1983-84	3	0	0	0	0					
	1984-85	38	2	2	4	4					
	1985-86	37	27	23	50	35					
	1986-87	47	19	33	52	44					
	1987-88	48	39	38	77	45					
	1988-89	44	44	42	86	40					
	1989-90	52	46	55	111	42					
	1992-93	52	33	39	72	71					
	1993-94	61	38	49	87	69	382	248	281	529	350
Ricci Scott	2004-05	65	3	18	21	12	65	3	18	21	12
Richard Dylan	2018-19 43 10			13	23	4	43	10	13	23	4
Richards Sean	2021-22	47	9	10	19	47	47	9	10	19	47
Richardson Bruce	2008-09	61	14	47	61	133					
	2009-10	63 18		46	64	132	124	32	93	125	265
Richardson Mark	2007-08	47	8	14	22	16					
	2008-09	45	4	6	10	10	92	12	20	32	26

Ringer Bill	1950-51	60	22	24	46	14					
	1951-52	60	35	23	58	22					
	1952-53	60	32	36	68	28					
	1953-54	60	21	39	61	25					
	1954-55	61	34	52	86	22					
	1958-59	54	20	20	40	8	355	164	194	358	119
Rippingale Gary	1989-90	10	1	0	1	0					
	1990-91	38	0	0	0	8					
	1991-92	37	0	1	1	6					
	1992-93	10	0	0	0	24	95	1	1	2	38
Rissling Jaynen	2018-19	62	4	20	24	124	62	4	20	24	124
Ritchie Dave	1953-54	7	0	0	0	0					
……………………	1954-55	58	0	0	0	0					
…………………	1955-56	56	2	2	4	2					
………………..	1956-57	10	0	1	1	0	131	2	3	5	2
Roberts Mark	1990-91	1	0	0	0	0					
	1992-93	35	2	2	4	0					
	1993-94	35	0	1	1	2	71	2	3	5	2
Roberts Steve	1998-99	13	11	5	16	4					
	1999-00	38	10	11	21	18	51	21	16	37	22
Robinson A.	2002-03										
Robinson Nathan	2014-15	24	6	15	21	40	24	6	15	21	40
Rose Danny	2011-12	6	0	0	0	0	6	0	0	0	0
Rusnell Dave	1955-56	56	47	55	102	36	56	47	55	102	36
Ryan Billy	2010-11	67	31	48	79	64	67	31	48	79	64
Ryan Cliff	1955-56	6	6	4	10	4					
……………………	1956-57	22	12	9	21	10	28	18	13	31	14

Name	Season	Stats									
Ryan Matt	2013-14	68	19	45	64	83	68	19	45	64	83
Ryhanen Sami	2011-12	33	9	28	37	22	33	9	28	37	22
Saari Joonas	2013-14	54	0	4	4	13	54	0	4	4	13
St.John Del	1956-57	31	17	16	33	10	31	17	16	33	10
Salmi Jarmie	1956-57	11	1	2	3	4	11	1	2	3	4
Salonen Joel	2003-04	61	16	30	46	32	61	16	30	46	32
Salt John	1956-57	1	0	0	0	0	1	0	0	0	0
Salter Steve	1984-85	27	45	20	65	68	27	45	20	65	68
Salters Leigh	2013-14	65	28	34	62	148	65	28	34	62	148
Sarkanis Deivids	2016-17	13	2	4	6	2	13	2	4	6	2
Sauve Yann	2017-18	74	17	33	50	110	74	17	33	50	110
Savoie Claude	2001-02	52	14	13	27	35	52	14	13	27	35
Schmidt Bryan	2014-15	70	2	8	10	65					
	2015-16	67	5	15	20	55	137	7	23	30	120
Schwarz Darren	1994-95	7	15	5	20	18	7	15	5	20	18
Schultz Stephen	2015-16	47	19	21	40	34					
	2016-17	46	15	35	50	32	93	34	56	90	66
Scott Daniel	2002-03										
	2003-04	29	0	0	0	2					
	2004-05	59	0	3	3	14					
	2005-06	54	0	0	0	22	142	0	3	3	38
Sebastian Jeff	1997-98	62	12	30	42	109					
	2005-06	56	5	21	26	18	118	17	51	68	127

Player	Season	Stats
Selby David	1989-90	1 0 0 0 0 1 0 0 0 0
Semeniuk Ted	1949-50	61 39 38 77 32 61 39 38 77 32
Sertich Andy	2016-17	72 5 28 33 22 72 5 28 33 22
Sevcik Jaroslav	1992-93	7 9 9 18 0 7 9 9 18 0
Shalla Josh	2017-18	40 10 12 22 17 40 10 12 22 17
Shepheard Jim	2007-08	7 0 3 3 35 7 0 3 3 35
Shmyr Ryan	2006-07	60 9 18 27 236
	2007-08	65 6 13 19 279 125 15 31 46 515
Simoes Steve	2006-07	43 7 9 16 107 43 7 9 16 107
Simon Stan	1949-50	10 1 1 2 2 10 1 1 2 2
Sjorgren Christian	2001-02	26 2 11 13 79 26 2 11 13 79
Sjorgren Stefan	2005-06	21 2 4 6 28 21 2 4 6 28
Slater Grant	1991-92	4 1 1 2 2 4 1 1 2 2
Smith Ged	1984-85	41 12 18 30 40
	1985-86	43 8 8 16 80 84 20 26 46 120
Smith Julian	2007-08	5 0 0 0 0 5 0 0 0 0
Smith Lorne	1952-53	58 15 13 28 102
……………………..	1953-54	22 6 13 19 48
…………………	1954-55	61 6 26 32 110
…………………	1955-56	56 10 20 30 64
…………………	1956-57	56 14 14 28 66
…………………..	1957-58	56 12 27 39 58
………………..	1958-59	54 11 17 28 42
…………………..	1959-60	60 11 19 30 44 423 85 149 234 534

Name	Season	Stats	Totals
Smith Tony	1954-55	2 0 0 0 0	2 0 0 0 0
Soar Tom	2009-10	3 0 1 1 0	
	2010-11	1 0 0 0 0	
	2011-12	1 0 0 0 0	5 0 1 1 0
Souranta Simon	2021-22	19 4 6 10 8	19 4 6 10 8
Spang Dan	2016-17	72 9 26 35 26	
	2017-18	68 10 22 32 61	140 19 48 67 87
Spence Jimmy	1955-56	56 44 27 71 18	
....	1956-57	1 0 0 0 0	57 44 27 71 18
Sproat Dustin	2010-11	17 6 12 18 33	17 6 12 18 33
Stancok Robert	2003-04	60 3 16 19 92	
	2007-08	39 4 5 9 115	99 7 21 28 207
Steen Don	1959-60	5 0 0 0 6	5 0 0 0 6
Stenton Liam	2020-21	16 0 0 0 4	16 0 0 0 4
Stevens George	1946-47	33 21 16 37 4	33 21 16 37 4
Stevens Rod	2006-07	61 22 36 58 60	61 22 36 58 60
Stevenson Richard	1983-84	2 0 0 0 0	
	1985-86	11 1 1 2 0	
	1987-88	12 0 0 0 2	
	1988-89	4 1 0 1 0	29 2 1 3 2
Stewart Anthony	2012-13	19 6 5 11 14	19 6 5 11 14
Stewart Chris	2018-19	27 7 9 16 27	27 7 9 16 27
Stewart Keith	1989-90	33 17 24 41 50	33 17 24 41 50
Stinchcombe Archie	1948-49	17 1 5 6 2	
	1949-40	31 2 16 18 2	

	1951-52	3	0	1	1	2	51	3	22	25	6
Strachen Rick	1990-91	23	11	25	36	16	23	11	25	36	16
Strachan Sam	1953-54	43	2	1	3	4					
....	1954-55	1	0	0	0	0	44	2	1	3	4
Strongman Les	1946-47	42	22	16	38	16					
	1947-48	54	37	31	68	39					
	1949-50	49	29	27	56	22					
	1950-51	60	61	41	102	32					
	1951-52	60	52	42	94	69					
	1952-53	52	40	36	76	76					
	1953-54	59	63	42	105	36					
	1954-55	62	53	56	109	28					
	1955-56	1	1	0	1	0					
	1958-59	48	34	23	57	10					
	1959-60	20	8	16	24	2	507	400	330	730	330
Strongman Mark	1982-83	3	0	0	0	0	3	0	0	0	0
Struch David	1999-00	62	14	24	38	34					
	2000-01	63	22	31	53	70					
	2003-04	66	13	33	46	24	191	49	88	137	128
Sutter Shaun	2005-06	43	16	18	34	50	43	16	18	34	50
Swindlehurst Paul	2015-16	48	3	13	16	36	48	3	13	16	36
Taggert Ken	1980-81	19	0	1	1	4	19	0	1	1	4
Tait Ashley	1990-91	38	6	5	11	14					
	1991-92	16	5	2	7	6					
	1992-93	48	21	26	47	71					
	1993-94	50	18	46	64	132					
	1994-95	60	43	61	104	167					
	1995-96	45	29	43	72	147					
	1996-97	60	7	21	28	62					
	1999-00	61	15	25	39	54					

Player	Season	Stats									
	2000-01	53	15	21	36	40					
	2001-02	51	8	15	23	31	482	167	265	431	724
Tait Warren	1995-96	1	0	0	0	0	1	0	0	0	0
Talbert Jullian	2019-20	45	18	19	37	38	45	18	19	37	38
Talbot-Tassi Domin	2020-21	16	3	5	8	0	16	3	5	8	0
Taubert Kristian	2002-03	55	3	6	9	91					
	2003-04	59	5	11	16	63	114	8	17	25	154
Taylor Chuck	1994-95	64	29	55	84	251					
	1995-96	45	8	19	27	77	109	37	74	111	328
Taylor Richard	2003-04	1	0	0	0	0	1	0	0	0	0
Tessier Dan	2005-06	23	15	17	32	71					
	2008-09	53	21	53	74	99	76	36	70	106	170
Tetlow Josua	2017-18	41	1	2	3	6					
	2018-19	71	0	6	6	43					
	2019-20	60	0	6	6	15					
	2020-21	16	1	0	1	18					
	2021-22	67	3	6	9	32	255	5	20	25	114
Theriault Paul	1948-49	54	28	19	47	12	54	28	19	47	12
Thompson Brian	2002-03	48	7	14	21	151					
	2003-04	62	15	32	47	148	110	22	46	68	299
Thompson Bruce	1988-89	8	6	11	17	35	8	6	11	17	35
Thompson Shaun	2007-08	3	1	1	2	0	3	1	1	2	0
Thow Aaron	2021-22	57	3	19	22	28	57	3	19	22	28
Timmins Russell	1980-81	26	2	8	10	12					

	1981-82	14	0	0	0	0				
	1982-83	22	1	6	7	0				
	1983-84	37	1	5	6	12				
	1984-85	38	2	1	3	0				
	1985-86	37	3	2	5	8				
	1986-87	15	0	0	0	2	189	9	22	31	34
Tkaczuk Daniel	2010-11	12	2	11	13	18	12	2	11	13	18
Toneys Nick	2008-09	61	3	8	11	84					
	2009-10	33	1	6	7	28	94	4	14	18	112
Tousignant Mathieu	2019-20	10	3	1	4	17					
	2021-22	65	13	13	26	80	75	16	14	30	97
Townsend George	1956-57	54	37	27	64	20	54	37	27	64	20
Trickett Matt	1989-90	10	0	0	0	2					
	1990-91	42	6	7	13	37					
	1991-92	52	12	5	17	63					
	1992-93	53	7	3	10	42					
	1993-94	60	17	15	32	137					
	1994-95	61	6	10	16	124					
	1995-96	55	1	9	10	66					
	1996-97	25	0	1	1	20	358	49	50	99	491
Tuma Martin	2012-13	12	0	1	1	43	12	0	1	1	43
Tvrdon Marek	2018-19	16	4	6	10	8	16	4	6	10	8
Tvrdon Roman	2004-05	10	2	5	7	6	10	2	5	7	6
Twaite Marc	1990-91	1	0	0	0	0					
	1991-92	9	0	0	0	0					
	1992-93	36	1	2	3	4					
	1993-94	60	8	6	14	47					
	1994-95	62	9	9	18	43					
	1995-96	53	14	8	22	84					
	1996-97	48	2	1	3	24					

		1997-98	55 1 3 4 41 324 35 29 64 243
Unkuri Pasi		1995-96	23 1 7 8 37 23 1 7 8 37
Urquhart Mike		1982-83	26 19 27 46 82
		1983-84	34 32 42 74 50
		1984-85	9 2 10 12 10
		1985-86	46 18 58 76 86 115 71 137 208 228
Van Hoof Jeremy		2010-11	18 1 3 4 10 18 1 3 4 10
Vankleef Tyler		2018-19	19 1 1 2 4 19 1 1 2 4
Vaskivuo Mike		2017-18	20 9 9 18 10 20 9 9 18 10
Virta Pekka		1998-99	51 13 10 23 26 51 13 10 23 26
Waghorn Graham		1990-91	49 6 25 31 136
		1991-92	53 11 28 39 116
		1992-93	53 10 38 48 58
		1993-94	61 12 36 48 143
		1994-95	63 10 33 43 135
		1995-96	44 6 8 14 145
		1996-97	59 4 8 12 109
		1997-98	54 0 7 7 93 436 59 183 242 935
Walker Rob		1980-81	26 1 5 6 32
		1981-82	36 1 7 8 18
		1982-83	3 0 0 0 2 65 2 12 14 52
Wallenberg Patrik		2001-02	56 24 28 52 77
		2007-08	64 34 46 80 74 120 58 74 132 151
Ward Josh		2009-10	22 1 0 1 2
		2010-11	39 0 4 4 6
		2011-12	7 0 2 2 2
		2012-13	61 2 3 5 2 129 3 9 12 12

Watson Gerry	1950-51	60 21 21 42 22	
	1951-52	58 8 24 32 80	
	1952-53	58 21 31 52 114	
	1953-54	60 32 35 67 75	
	1954-55	62 8 49 57 61	
	1955-56	48 34 31 65 10	
	1956-57	55 16 24 40 26	401 140 215 355 388
Waugh Geoff	2015-16	54 7 16 23 59	
	2016-17	43 3 6 9 24	97 10 22 32 83
Weaver Jason	1998-99	34 12 18 30 87	34 12 18 30 87
Weaver Jonathan	2012-13	55 10 35 45 27	
	2013-14	71 9 39 48 56	126 19 74 93 83
Webber Randall	1985-86	43 5 11 16 21	
	1986-87	49 15 35 50 26	
	1987-88	31 16 34 50 20	
	1988-89	48 48 54 102 45	
	1989-90	56 41 54 95 50	
	1990-91	44 28 42 70 44	
	1991-92	50 32 53 85 40	
	1992-93	53 23 38 61 38	
	1993-94	44 23 40 63 58	
	1994-95	57 41 69 110 28	
	1995-96	57 21 30 51 60	
	1996-97	53 8 14 22 40	
	1997-98	60 7 16 23 16	
	1998-99	58 5 10 15 10	
	1999-00	51 4 5 9 4	
	2000-01	55 7 8 15 12	
	2001-02	47 2 4 6 6	856 326 517 843 518
Webster Dave	1980-81	22 1 0 1 0	22 1 0 1 0
Welch Dan	2005-06	13 1 7 8 20	13 1 7 8 20
Welch Dave	1982-83	24 3 6 9 18	

	1983-84	31 2 1 3 24	55 5 7 12 42
Weldon Will	2009-10	3 0 0 0 0	
	2010-11	2 1 0 1 0	5 1 0 1 0
Welsh Jeremy	2021-22	66 22 46 68 10	66 22 46 68 10
Werner Eric	2012-13	67 7 33 40 28	
	2013-14	38 4 7 11 18	105 11 40 51 46
Westman Kenny	1946-47	42 11 12 23 23	
	1947-48	56 21 32 53 49	
	1948-49	45 25 26 51 24	
	1949-50	69 34 35 69 44	
	1954-55	54 47 52 99 32	
	1955-56	45 5 20 25 38	
	1956-57	56 12 16 28 38	
	1957-58	56 7 31 38 24	
	1958-59	36 3 12 15 14	
	1959-60	21 4 4 8 0	480 169 240 409 286
Wetzel Todd	2002-03	17 4 4 8 8	17 4 4 8 8
Whyatt Nicky	2003-04	1 0 0 0 0	1 0 0 0 0
Wiedergut Andreas	2015-16	2 0 0 0 0	2 0 0 0 0
Wightman Oscar	1989-90		
Wild Cody	2014-15	52 13 30 43 18	52 13 30 43 18
Willaims Jason	2016-17	17 6 13 19 0	17 6 13 19 0
Willock Elden	1958-59	52 23 24 47 36	52 23 24 47 36
Wilson Brock	2011-12	67 7 29 36 127	67 7 29 36 127
Wilson Dick	1958-59	23 9 10 19 26	23 9 10 19 26

Wilson Doug	1953-54	60	2	5	7	72					
....	1954-55	62	0	6	6	64					
....	1955-56	52	0	6	6	34	174	2	17	19	170
Wilson Kelsey	2012-13	34	10	9	19	112	34	10	9	19	112
Withenshaw Doug	1980-81	5	4	3	7	6					
	1981-82	39	51	60	111	64	44	55	63	118	70
Wojciak Richard	2004-05	55	6	4	10	10					
	2005-06	54	0	4	4	18	109	6	8	14	28
Wood Dodi	2002-03	51	4	15	19	222	51	4	15	19	222
Wood Shaun	1980-81	23	3	4	7	33	23	3	4	7	33
Woods Gyle	1950-51	60	19	23	42	54	60	19	23	42	54
Worthington Rob	1993-94	4	0	0	0	0					
	1994-95	39	0	1	1	8					
	1995-96	32	1	3	4	0					
	1996-97	5	2	0	2	0	80	3	4	7	8
Wren Bob	2013-14	20	7	15	22	39	20	7	15	22	39
Wright Jason	1984-85	36	7	13	20	12	36	7	13	20	12
Wright Mark	1992-93	25	1	1	2	6	25	1	1	2	6
Yardley Shaun	2003-04	1	0	1	1	0					
	2004-05	4	0	0	0	0	5	0	1	1	0
Young Ed.......	1946-47	40	27	19	46	14					
....	1947-48	40	28	14	42	8					
....	1948-49	52	41	40	81	14	132	96	73	169	36

Zamick Chick	1947-48	56 65 59 124 8
…………………..	1948-49	56 80 54 134 22
…………………	1949-50	70 87 61 148 26
…………………….	1950-51	58 78 61 139 34
…………………	1951-52	41 47 51 98 22
……………………	1952-53	60 74 57 131 20
…………………	1953-54	57 69 55 124 12
…………………	1954-55	62 94 75 169 16
…………………	1955-56	56 62 73 135 12
…………………	1956-57	53 50 53 103 9
…………………	1957-58	55 72 46 118 11 624 778 645 1423 192
Zamick Joe	1949-50	18 1 2 3 26 18 1 2 3 26
Zann Tony	1959-60	28 4 3 7 49 28 4 3 7 49
Zion Jonathan	2010-11	39 9 24 33 22 39 9 24 33 22
Zukiwsky Jarrett	1998-99	58 12 25 38 169 58 12 25 38 169

Graham Waghorn who appears in my book 'Ice Cold Murder' see page 294
Copies available £4 plus postage email **spikc2004@yahoo.co.uk** (Pic by icepix)

249

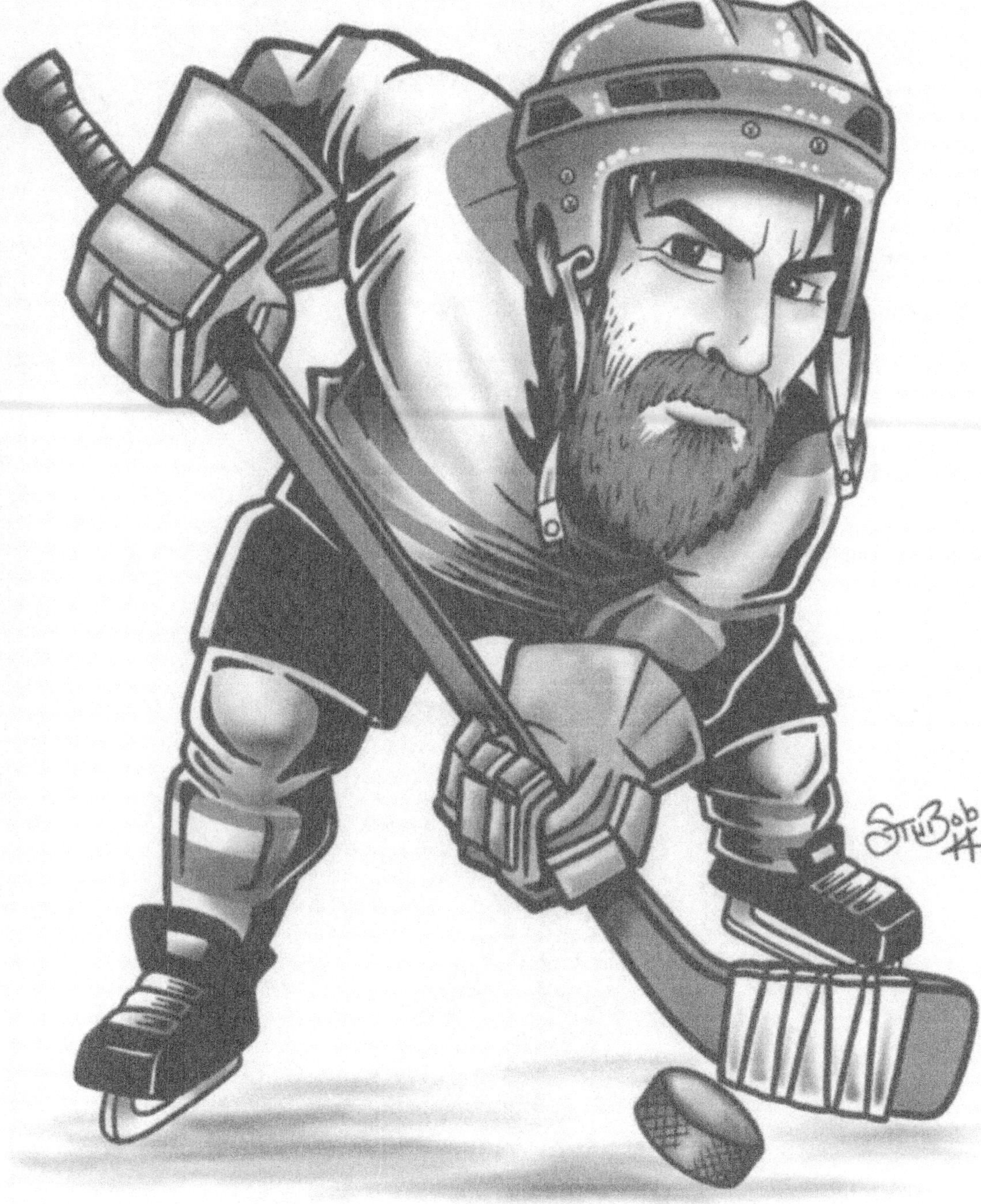
StuBob

All time top lists by end of season 21-22

Top net men

Name	Seasons	Time on ice
Jack Siemon	SEVEN	23040
Craig Kowalski	FIVE	15138
Dick Halverson	FOUR	12540
David Graham	SIX	12142
Trevor Robins	THREE	7638
Ken Johnson	TWO	6851
Kevin Carr	TWO	6437.33
Curtis Cruikshank	TWO	6415
Jordan Willis	TWO	5914
MiKka Wiikman	TWO	5705

Top appearances
* still playing

NAME		GP
Weber	Randall	856
Clarke	David	786
Lachowicz	Robert	780
Zamick	Chick	624
Myers*	Matt	620
Lee	Stephen	618
Adey	Paul	593
Hunt	Simon	517
Strongman	Les	507
Bremner	John	495

Top goals

NAME		G
Adey	Paul	796
Zamick	Chick	778
Strongman	Les	400
Clarke	David	381
Weber	Randall	326
Kurtenbach	Terry	290
Rhodes	Nigel	248
Hunt	Simon	246
Fraser	Gavin	216
Keyward	Dwayne	209

Top Assists

NAME		GP	G	A
Adey	Paul	593	796	751
Zamick	Chick	624	778	645
Weber	Randall	856	326	517
Kurtenbach	Terry	355	290	432
Clarke	David	786	381	371
Strongman	Les	507	400	330
Neilsson	Corey	399	86	293
Rhodes	Nigel	382	248	281
Tait	Ashley	482	167	265
Myers	Matt	620	139	260

Top Points

NAME		GP	G	A	Pts
Adey	Paul	593	796	751	1547
Zamick	Chick	624	778	645	1423
Weber	Randall	856	326	517	843
Clarke	David	786	381	371	752
Strongman	Les	507	400	330	730
Kurtenbach	Terry	355	290	432	722
Rhodes	Nigel	382	248	281	529
Fraser	Gavin	409	216	219	435
Tait	Ashley	482	167	265	431
Keyward	Dwayne	278	209	204	413

Top Pims

NAME		GP	G	A	Pts	Pims
Hunt	Simon	517	246	153	399	1259
Waghorn	Graham	436	59	183	242	935
Clarke	David	786	381	371	752	900
Neilsson	Corey	399	86	293	379	821
Lepine	Guillaume	315	18	65	83	814
Nieckar	Barry	151	21	33	54	797
Myers	Matt	620	139	260	399	782
Tait	Ashley	482	167	265	431	724
Bremner	John	495	60	132	192	696
Adey	Paul	593	796	751	1547	669

UNIVERSITY/OLYMPIAD

University Hockey – by the author

Senior, Junior, Sledge, Recreational, there have been various types of hockey. I have seen them all but in all the 43 years I have been puck watching, have never been to a Oxford versus Cambridge University game as yet.

It has a great history with Oxford versus Cambridge being instrumental since 1885. Yet a 6-0 score line for the dark blues has not been confirmed as a true Ice Hockey game.

The first recorded game being on 16th March 1900. Another Oxford win although only by the odd goal in 13. Using a lacrosse ball and bandy sticks or hockey ones cut down at Oxfords insistence. The very next evening a combined 'Oxbridge' team played the Princes Club, a ball being used for the first half of the game.

In 1901 they played with a rubber puck with bevelled edges and regulation sticks. The combined team verses Princes became a regular occurrence thereafter.

The University teams started playing abroad. But in 1902 Cambridge invited Oxford for another Varsity Bash. Oxford agreed on condition of playing the game of Bandy also, which was done, yet Oxford pulled out of the Ice Hockey game. Tut.

1903, Cambridge had joined the first Ice Hockey League finishing 5th and last.

Varsity matches were then not played or we have no record. An Oxford Canadians team existed playing consistently more in European competitions. Not until 1909 did Oxford University win 5-3 in a game versus Cambridge in Switzerland using bandy/hockey sticks again and a wooden block. Because of a thaw two other games had to be cancelled.

By 1911 onwards Varsity got back on track more regularly but for the war, with Cambridge coming out on top mostly to be reversed by 1913 as Oxford emerged with the upper hand.
Experimentation of three ten minute periods were used in 1920 followed by five minutes each way of extra time but the final score line was still 0-0.

On the 23/10/21 Oxford University Ice Hockey Club formed officially and entered Continental Tours. By 9/11/21 Cambridge affiliated to the British Hockey Association.
Points of interest: - 1921 Oxford beat Switzerland's National Team 9-0, Germanys National Team and the Army, a great era for them.
Players were assisting the British National team in representation too.
Both Universities were touring and winning effectively. By the end of 1923 both were playing against the British Olympic Team and in 1925 arrangements and terms no agreed upon meant games between the sides were not being played.
1930 saw a combined team playing the visiting 'Canadas' but were defeated 0-13.

1932. Whilst back in England competing in National Leagues until 1935 Cambridge were keen in travelling to practices in Purly but Oxford had its own rink, the light blues playing out of Peterborough as a home venue. As you can guess Oxford were more self sufficient and financially self supporting. But both teams would play out of other rinks over the years.

Cambridge won over the varsity title by a 2-0 score line in 1936 by the time Great Britain were World Champions. Oxford though had 13 wins to 8 with a drawn game.

Moving on…..Apart from a 2-9 loss in 1952 Oxford had a mini run of wins from 1947 after the war until 1957. After this decade Cambridge came to the fore winning 5 of 6 games. But then it all went pear shaped, they won only one game from 1964 to 1979.

Thereafter things evened out a little more. During which Oxford had eight double figure score lines, Cambridge only achieving this in an 11-1 1962 'Hurrah'. Oxford even topped their 1921 27-0 route by 2 extra goals in 1955.

Moving on again …..Both teams toyed once more in league play in the 1976-77 season till the mid 80's with affiliation to The Southern Ice Hockey Association. Playing in the 80-81 Inter-city League and 81-82 English National League with our very own Nottingham Panthers.
By 1986 Oxford's own home town gained a regular League team, 'The City Stars' playing at the Oxford Rink and the University sides Varsity score lines continued though on a yearly basis. The light blues endured a poor period of losses including huge score lines against the 'darks', winning only one in ten until 1997. The latest round of games however had them evened out again.

Remarkably a lost 1913 'varsity 'silver trophy was found and given to the curators of the Hall of Fame. No student gains an athletic scholarship at Campus but players are taking degrees. The centenary (anniversary) game in the year 2000 quoted in its programme notes that a 1902 'mistaken' bandy match was struck from the varsity records and so it was the 80th game that day.

Universities all around the country have big set ups of there own now.
The British University Ice Hockey Association (BUIHA) with various leagues for different levels of players and local universities have built up their own rivalries – for example Nottingham's University and the local Trent University.

Great Britain's student populous even enters The World Olympiad Games now. Matt Bradbury and Mike Urquhart have been a big organisational part.
*From 1933 until 1947 there had been' University games' held, however in that period our universities did not enter.

Nottingham Club players by Simon Hopkins

From memory, the following all played for Great Britain University (GBU) (most of them also played for the Nottingham Universities Mavericks Ice Hockey Club, apart from Geoff Woolhouse and Josh Crane):

Rich Griffiths - Lions and Panthers played for GBU in World University Games (WUGs) 2007 (Torino) & Reserve 2009 (Harbin)

Stewart Bliss - Lions played for GBU in WUGs 2007 (Torino) & 2009 (Harbin)

Marcus Maynard - Lions and Panthers played for GBU in WUGs 2007 (Torino) & 2009 (Harbin)

Colm Cannon - Luxembourg and Lions played for GBU in WUGs 2007 (Torino) & 2009 (Harbin)

Adam Robinson - Lions played for GBU in WUGs 2007 (Torino) & 2009 (Harbin)

Geoff Woolhouse - Lions and Panthers played for GBU in WUGs 2009 (Harbin)

Tom Norton - Lions and Panthers played for GBU in WUGs 2009 (Harbin)

Robert Lachowicz - Lions and Panthers played for GBU in WUGs 2009 (Harbin)

Cam Good - Lions played for GBU in WUGs 2013 (Trentino)

Christy Johnson-Brown - Lions played for GBU in WUGs 2013 (Trentino)

Jack Baveystock - Lions played for GBU in WUGs 2013 (Trentino)

James Francis-Barrie - Lions played for GBU in WUGs 2013 (Trentino)

Stephen Breisner - Lions played for GBU in WUGs 2013 (Trentino)

Luke Branin - Lions played for GBU in WUGs 2017 (Almaty)
Tom Parkinson - Lions played for GBU in WUGs 2017 (Almaty)

Tom Hovell - Lions and Panthers played for GBU in WUGs 2017 (Almaty) & 2019 (Krasnoyarsk)

Joe Gretton - Lions played for GBU in WUGs 2019 (Krasnoyarsk)

Cam Pywell - Lions played for GBU in WUGs 2019 (Krasnoyarsk)

Ruskin Springer-Hughes - Lions played for GBU in WUGs 2019 (Krasnoyarsk)

Josh Crane - Lions played for GBU in WUGs 2019 (Krasnoyarsk)

Staff:

GBU Men:

Matt Bradbury - Lions (coach) and Panthers (player) GBU in WUGs 2007 (Torino), 2009 (Harbin), 2013 (Trentino), 2017 (Almaty) and 2019 (Krasnoyarsk)

Mike Urquhart - Lions (coach) and Panthers (player / coach) GBU in WUGs 2007 (Torino), 2009 (Harbin), 2013 (Trentino)

Simon Hopkins - Lions (coach)... created GBU (Men 2005 and Women 2007) Team Manager GBU Men in WUGs 2007 (Torino), 2009 (Harbin), 2013 (Trentino), and Assistant Coach GBU Men at WUGs in 2017 (Almaty) and 2019 (Krasnoyarsk)

GBU Women:

Ryan Rathbone - Lions (player) GBU Women Assistant Coach in 2013 (Trentino) and GBU Women Head Coach 2017 (Almaty), 2019 (Krasnoyarsk) and 2023 (Lake Placid).

Others to note:

Alex Karsay - played Lions and Slovakia under 20s and trained with the Panthers mid-00s

Chris Markham - Lions, played Great Britain U18s

Paul Moran - Lions and Panthers, played in pre-WUGs games for GBU (vs EIHL Coventry and EPL Swindon)

Simon Hopkins

Para (Sledge) Hockey (This piece taken from wikipaepia)

Sledge hockey (now known as **Para ice hockey**, or **sled hockey** is an adaptation of **ice hockey designed for** players who have a **physical disability**. Invented in the early 1960s at a rehabilitation centre in **Stockholm, Sweden**, and played under similar rules to standard ice hockey, players are seated on **sleds** and use special **hockey sticks** with metal "teeth" on the tips of their handles to navigate the ice. (Due to lower limb disorders)

World Para Ice Hockey, the **International Paralympic Committee** (IPC) acts as the international sanctioning body for the sport by means of its World Para Ice Hockey division. Para ice hockey has been played in the **Winter Paralympics** since **1994**, and has been one of the most popular events.

Two men from Sweden designed the sledge in the 1960s because they wanted to continue to play hockey despite their **physical disabilities**. Their design included two skate blades on a metal frame that allowed the puck to pass underneath. They completed the ensemble by including two round poles with bike handles for sticks. Although there are many restrictions to the measurements and weight of the sleds used in the **Paralympic Games**, the basic design of modern sleds remains true to the original 1960's simple sleds for kids. These sleds were then made to be used for hockey.

Despite the initial lack of interest and awareness in the few years that followed, competition between sledge hockey teams started up in 1971 that included five teams in **Europe**. In 1981, **Great Britain** established their first sledge hockey team, and that was shortly followed by **Canada** in 1982. It was not until 1990 that the **United States** developed their first ice sledge hockey team. Sled hockey continued to expand when **Estonia** and **Japan** developed their teams in 1993. Sledge hockey was introduced to the Winter Paralympics in **1994**, with Sweden claiming the first gold medal. Since **2010**, sledge hockey has been a mixed-gender event.

The **British Para Ice Hockey Association (BPIHA)** is the national governing body in the **United Kingdom** for **ice sledge hockey**. Formed in 1995, its main objectives are to expand the number of teams active in the UK (and by association the number or participants) and to develop the national team.

Note:
Matt Bradbury ('Matt Bradbury Sports' business) tells me that late 1990's/early 2000s Nottingham had what he believes was the best Sledge (Para) hockey team in the country but they do not have one presently.

Matt on the left here in his playing days for the Trojans stood in the old stadium back corridor where you'd find the changing rooms.
Matt has worked for the club for many years, presently running his own business and still coach of the Nottingham Lions team.
Paul Glossop is assistant coach and head of Nottingham Ice Hockey Club (NIHC)

BALL HOCKEY

A game with increasing popularity, which might be called 'floor or street hockey' for non skaters, is popular in Nottingham. I myself started the local Gym Hockey game (with a plastic puck) in the 80's and it was played in trainers and had some protection but mainly for the net minders and this had sponsors and media attention. It attracted Ice hockey players too.

I visited Southglade Leisure Centre recently in Bestwood to view Ball hockey (see picture) and there was a mix of players of all ages and genders in this club named the Wolves. They train in the complex on Tuesdays 7 till 9.30 and Fridays 6 till 9pm, new recruits are very much invited to join in.

There are seven Nottingham clubs in the area, this one being the biggest which has woman's and junior sections. They play in the central region league which has seventeen teams representing Hull, Leeds, Manchester, Sheffield and Nottingham.

Nationally thirty two teams compete in competitions.

Nottingham area teams are: Greasley Bears (Eastwood), Long Eaton Lightening, Nemesis BHC (Sandiacre), Nottingham Hawks, Nottingham Titans, Nottingham Vikings (all Clifton) and Wolves

From the old Gym Hockey era (oh those were the days)

Above left: The Nottingham Vipers women's team celebrate their 2018/19 Women's Premier League title win. Above right: Laura Urquhart (Source: BBC Sport)

Nottingham Vipers Women's Team

Honours:
Women's Premier League Champions (top tier) 1999/00
Women's Premier League Champions (2nd tier) 2018/19
Divisions 1 North Champions 2005/06, 2007/08,

The Nottingham Vipers women's team were formed in 1987. They originally played in the regionalised British women's leagues until a new national top division – the Women's Premier League – created in 1990. By virtue of their league position at the time, the Vipers were placed in the WPL and went on to win the league title the 1999/00 season.

They were relegated down to Division 1 (D1) North in 2002 following a poor season that saw them win just 1 of their 16 league games and, after 4 seasons in the lower division, they won the 2005/06 title and were promoted via the end of season play offs.

Their stay back in the WPL lasted just one season however as they finished rock bottom of the 10-team table with no wins from their 18 games.

The Vipers won the Division one North title again at the first attempt, but missed out this time on promotion in the play offs and this led to an extended stay of 7 more seasons in the regionalised division.

A restructuring of the women's leagues in 2015 saw the introduction of a new Women's Elite League (WEL) as top tier and this pushed WPL down to second tier status and Division one North & South to third tier.

This move meant that the Vipers were back in the WPL - albeit at the new lower level - where they remained for 4 seasons. A highly successful campaign in the 2018/19 season saw them win the WPL title and, with it, promotion to the WEL for the first time.

As with previously promoted teams, the Vipers struggled with the huge difference in playing standards between the WEL and the WPL and they finished the Covid-curtailed 2019/20 season in bottom place of the table with no wins from 20 league games.

The Nottingham ladies found themselves back in the 2nd tier WPL for the 2021/22 season where they finished in 8th place and, following a re-branding of the women's divisions in 2022, the WPL became Women's North Ice Hockey League (WNIHL) Division 1, in which the Vipers are currently competing at the time of writing.

Over the years, the Nottingham women's team has provided numerous England and GB international players.

Laura Urquhart – wife of former Panthers import Mike Urquhart - is probably the most widely known of those players, having played some 200 WPL and D1 games and also featured for the GB women's team as a player and coach.

She was the first ever woman to be head coach of the national team when she led the Great Britain women in the 2000 World Championship qualifying tournament in Hungary.

CONTACT DETAILS: https://www.facebook.com/nottmvipers/

*Article supplied by Paul Breeze

AD

https://www.britishicehockey.co.uk/

Honours and chosen 'All STARS' team players

Voted awards

Coach of the Year 1987, 1989 Alex Dampier
Coach of the Year 1995 Mike Blaisdell
Player of the Year 1992 Dan Dorian
Net minder % 2006 Curtis Cruikshank

Voted to All-Star teams
1948-49 Chick Zamick
1950-51 Chick Zamick and Les Strongman
1951-52 Chick Zamick and Les Strongman
1952-53 Lorne Smith and Chick Zamick
1953-54 Gerry Watson
1954-55 Chick Zamick and Les Strongman
1955-56 Chick Zamick
1957-58 Chick Zamick
1958-59 Jack Sieman and Vern Pachel
1959-60 Jack Sieman
1980-81 Dwayne Keward (Inter-City League)
1981-82 Frank Killen (English national league)
Mark Kasun (Inter City League / English League South)
1988-89 David Graham and Darren Durdle
1991-92 Dan Dorian
1994-95 Garth Premack / Chuck Taylor and Rick Brebant
1995-96 Garth Premack and Darren Durdle
1996-97 Garth Premack and Paul Adey
1998-99 Greg Hadden and Paul Adey
2000-01 Jimmy Paek and PC Drouin
2002-03 Lee Jinman
2003-04 John Craighead
2006-07 Jan Krajicek
2007-08 Sean McAslan
2009-10 Jade Galbraith
2011-12 Corey Neilson (UK Ice Hockey Writers (UKIHW) + Elite)
2012-13 Craig Kowalski*/Eric Werner/Bruce Graham/David Ling* - *also Elite
2015-16 Juraj Kolnik (UKIHW + Elite)
2019-20 Mark Matheson and Sam Herr (Elite)
2020-21 Jackson Whistle and Mark Matheson (Elite)

My Hall Of Fame –

Paul Adey
Bill Allen
Ollie Betteridge
John Bremner
David Clarke
Gavin Fraser
David Graham
Greg Hadden
Dick Halverson
Simon Hunt
Dwayne Keyward
Robert Lachowicz
Stephen Lee
Marc Levers
Matthew Myers
Corey Neilson
Nigel Rhodes
Bill Ringer
Jack Sieman
Lorne Smith
Les Strongman
Ashley Tait
Graham Waghorn
Gerry Watson
Randall Weber
Kenny Westman
Chick Zamick

SPOTLIGHT ON MATTHEW MYERS

FOUR separate occasions signing for the club

Over 100 Great Britain caps

Over 1,000 games played in domestic Ice Hockey

In his second testimonial season

		Games	Goals	Assists	Points	Penalties
Myers Matt	2004-05	64	5	23	28	89
	2005-06	54	10	5	15	60
	2006-07	58	6	20	26	129
	2007-08	65	10	20	30	74
	2008-09	51	13	33	46	87
	2010-11	64	25	46	71	115
	2011-12	64	20	40	60	50
	2012-13	67	19	29	48	74
	2015-16	67	15	20	35	55
	2021-22	66	16	24	40	49
		620	139	260	399	782

Plus 22-23 seasons statistics to add to the above totals

At time of print

Appearances
650 and 4th in the overall all-time list
Goals
143 and 17th overall all-time (close to 16th)
Assists
271 and 9th all-time
Points
414 and 10th all-time

Penalty Minutes
786 7th all-time (close to 6th)

264

QUIZ TIME (see page 283 for answers)

1. What type of rubber is a puck made from?

2. What are the teams three main colours used as home/away and alternate jerseys?

3. How many seasons did Gary Moran serve as commercial and general manager combined?

4. What was the Hotel that fans stopped in for games in Kirkcaldy
    a) The Fife Flyer b) The Station Hotel or c) The Fife Hotel

5. Who is the clubs all-time penalty player?

6. What was the first bit of silverware won by the team?

7. Which season was the first in the new arena?

8. Who was the last 'player of the year' for the Panthers?

9. What year was Nottingham Panthers named but never played domestic hockey?

10. Have the team ever played in the Knock Out cup?

11. Including this 22-23 season, how many seasons have there been?

12. Who is this?   Picture by Sue Bailey

265

Jerseys (shirts) over time

1946-47

47-48

48-49

49-50

50-51

51-52

52-53

53-54

54-55

55-56

56-57

57-58

58-59

59-60

80-81

81-82

266

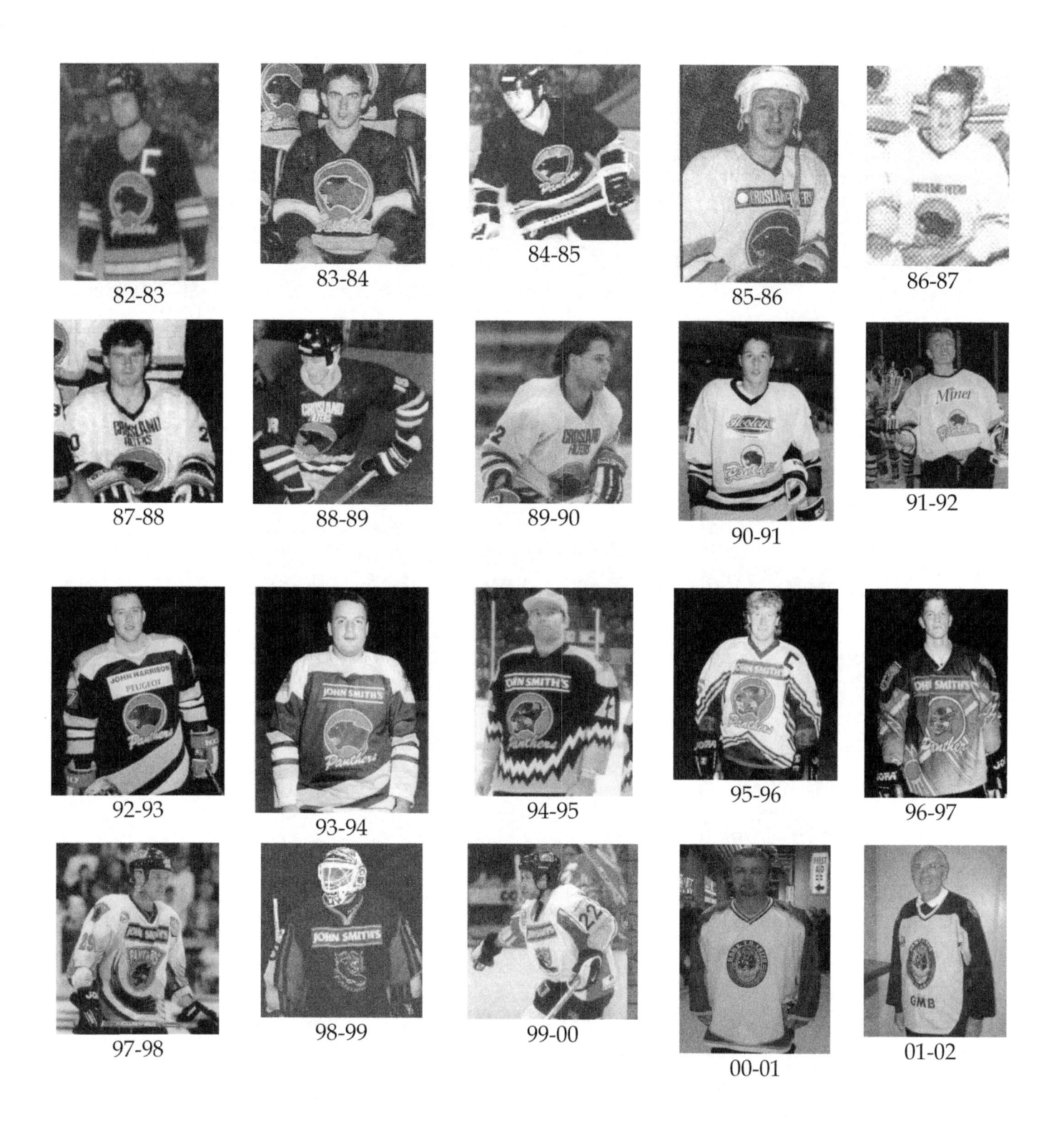

82-83
83-84
84-85
85-86
86-87
87-88
88-89
89-90
90-91
91-92
92-93
93-94
94-95
95-96
96-97
97-98
98-99
99-00
00-01
01-02

The thick woolly type gave way to the more airy jersey of today

Our colours used have been many BUT originally Black and White the colour Gold has been embraced to what we now have as Black, White and Gold.

02-03  03-04  04-05  05-06  06-07

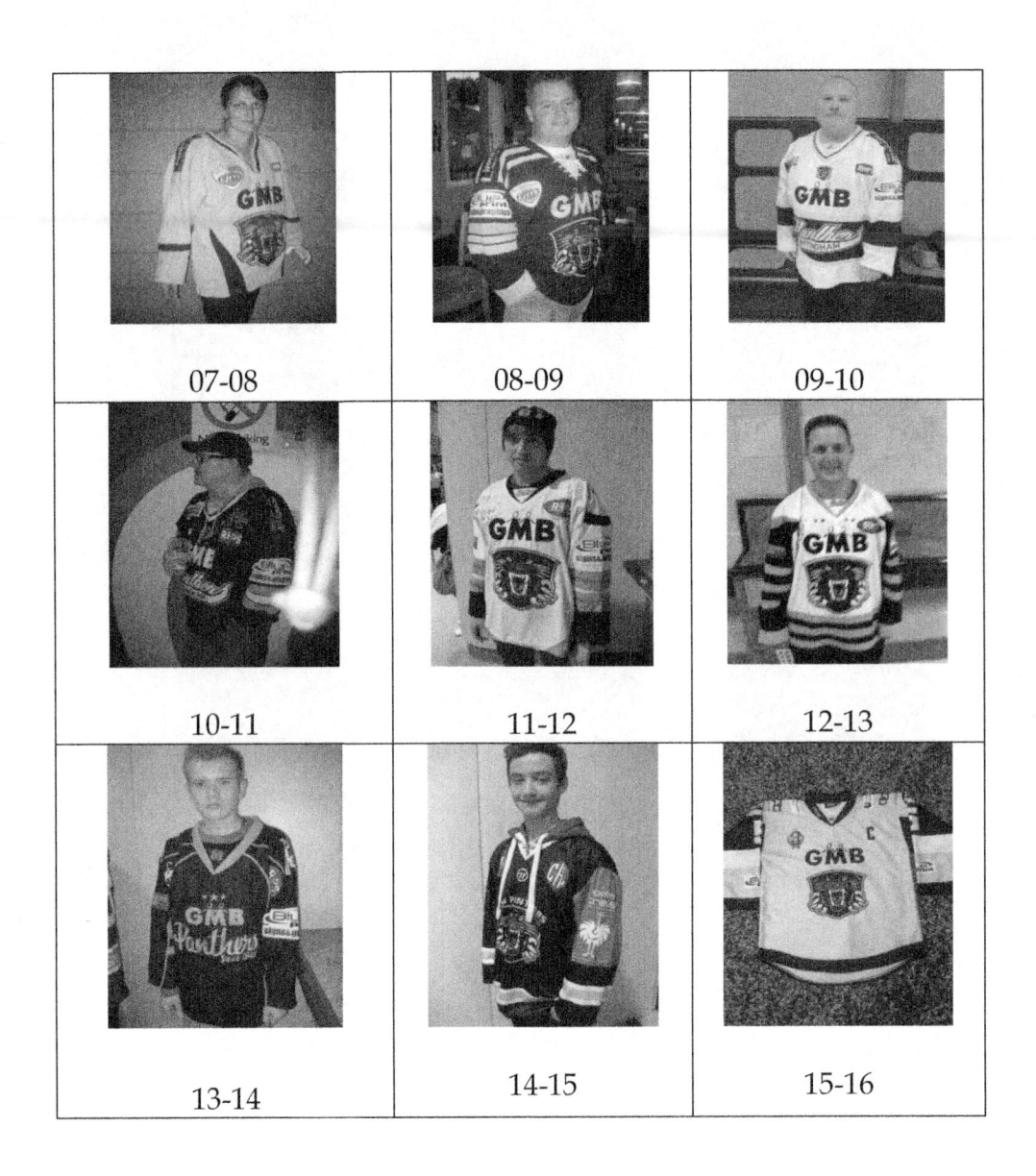

07-08 08-09 09-10

10-11 11-12 12-13

13-14 14-15 15-16

268

16-17	17-18	18-19
19-20	20-21	21-22

22-23

****

AD

The Fox and Grapes public house, Sneinton.

269

WHO's WHO?

Now the club are more interactive with the fans, and are clearly being more transparent with pictures of the 'inner circle' off ice team, we can start to know more of who does what.
Behind club owner Neil Black and Chief Executive officer Omar Pacha are a team who pay service to office chores or are footing it to some event or social need. Freddie Black (finance) Nicola Strachan (Commercial and Sponsorship), Sarah Longdon (Office), Alistair St.Clair (Marketing and Communications), Lisa Rawding (Fan Liasion and Community), Sophie Rouse (Social Media), Chris Ellis (Media) Dan Green (Housing and Webcast with Jono Bullard) are pictured folk in the official websites list of staff. Some are well known others just new to their roles.

One of these whom I have had a long time association with is Jono Bullard who first entered the building as a fan and not long after brought about five fanzine booklets between 2000 to 2003 called 'The Cat's Whiskers' going 'online' with it in 2008.
Later delved into the world of 'live' broadcasts in a text commentary service for all Panthers games that lasted until 2012 when Panthers Hockey Live took up the mantle.

Cat's Whiskers TV started at the beginning of the 2012/13 season with three other fans and Jono fronting the show, then a podcast took over. Jono left the other members to continue that whilst he tended to commentaries on Manchester Storm in that 2021/22 season, which he still does today.

He's joined the Panthers media team this season to co-commentate on all of their home games. He seems the only one who has worked up through to his present position.

Others around the rink
Bar coach Cory Nielson on the bench, there with him you'll find long standing Equipment Manager Adam Goodrich and recently Physio Laura Jo-Bowler.
Sat centre ice announcing is David 'stef' Litchfield along with Ken Feast working the sound system.
Also aside calculating are Fran Wiles the timekeeper, Jaime Howarth doing the live scoring, plus Denise, Jez and Evan Shaw adding up the Face offs and shot count.
At the ends of the ice are Fraser Shaw and Zander Wiles goal judging, whilst Carole Howarth and Jay Crich are stood in their penalty boxes. Floating around is Paws (Ross Bashford) – camped in the corridor is Karl Denham and Adam Gouldson on photography as Panthersimages. Bill Northridge will be looking out for you as regards Away Travel and at the game setting up 'Vision Mix' is on media productions.
So there are a few people working on a match night. Sorry if I missed anyone, but there are bound to be Doctor/Dentist crew and Arena staff personnel including St.Johns Ambulance – too many to name here.
These are the present names and there have been plenty of others over the years.
Recognise these fellow's?

1) Son of the late magazine editor and Panthers chairman Vic Batchelder, here is Alan in the stripes.
2) Then ex-player Jamie Craiper in a different line of work refereeing 3) once English Ice Hockey association chairman and Panthers player is Ken Taggert. 4) and into broadcasting – Chuck Taylor. (pictures by icepix)

Recognise this place below?

Making way for a newer arena

Now you're in here…

272

BITS and PIECES
(Stories and anecdotes from the past)

Southampton Cup – short lived
As the Vikings were not set to play in the autumn of 1957, this tournament was organized between four National League teams. Only one game was played, on October 29, with the Nottingham Panthers defeating the Brighton Tigers 7-4. The Vikings returned by January.

Around and About by George -Hockey Fan Volume 2 Issue 3? Dec 61
It was interesting, after my comments about Nottingham in the last addition, to see in a recent Altrincham programme a reference to a match between the Cheshire Cats and Nottingham Panthers, won by the Cats 6-5. On further investigation, I discovered that the Panthers side was made up very largely of members of the old Nottingham Wolves (second team-ED) team which disbanded several years before their seniors. In case this sounds like a revival of hockey in the Midlands, I would point out that Nottingham boys have to travel to Altrincham in order to practice as they still can't obtain ice time on their own rink.
Now there's dedication for you –ED

Fife v Nottingham
Much has been said about the formation of the Scottish outfit the 'Flyers' in Kirkcaldy, being the oldest club in the country. Of course this is correct, erecting a building and a team playing there since 1938. However, when you look into top flight hockey Nottingham become the longest serving club partaking into 'top flight' competition. 56 seasons played against Fife's 53.

Read all about it
https://en.wikipedia.org/wiki/Nottingham_Panthers

https://en.wikipedia.org/wiki/History_of_the_Nottingham_Panthers_(1939%E2%80%931960)

https://www.the-sports.org/ice-hockey-nottingham-panthers-results-identity-equ5827.html

https://panthersfromthevault.wordpress.com/category/uncategorized/

https://thecageforum.proboards.com/thread/20823/2022-23-fixtures-statistics

Stolen (well, with approval) from Twitter
"Hockey has physiological demands on individual's bodies. For example they use anaerobic energy system, but also need to have a similar endurance to the aerobic system. They also need to be able to throw and absorb hits. There are multiple different energy systems.
Because of that, you need to look at the nutritional needs, but because of how under researched it is, you need to analyse things like sprinters, rugby players and then combine them.
This (hockey) is similar to other sports but it's more to do with a combination of sports rather than one due to the energy systems.
Nb) Muscle glycogen = fuel 60% of muscle glycogen in quads is utilised. In back to back games 'mg' is less……written by AJ.'…girls don't just watch Ice Hockey, we study it too'.
ED: I knew all this of course.

Tennis to Hockey
Bjorn Borg (a keen player in his teens) played ice hockey while on holiday visiting a friend for Malmo in practice. News got around and offers came in from Toronto Maple Leafs and Washington Capitols – publicity interest? However, a Swedish journalist correctly quoted that 'hockey was fun but his tennis was business'.

Governing body error?
'…a misunderstanding arose as regards the accepted number of imports permitted to play for a club.' Despite the body had made it clear to all clubs, in writing, that the maximum of players had to be restricted to three. A number of clubs had committed to more. To alleviate the situation five were eventually allowed to sign but as long as three only dressed for a game. Fred Meredith from British Ice Hockey 'towers' declared this arrangement as ' a result of 'spirit of co-operation and goodwill within the clubs. (If only that happened today – ED)

Walk out Panthers
Durham Wasps leading 8-3 at home, with 8 minutes left on the clock, Nottingham staged a walk out causing a game to be abandoned. Citing 'deliberate intend to injure with sticks' the team were brought off to 'protect them from serious injury'. Durham officials stated 'a dumb trick….they just couldn't take a beating'. Yup that seemed about right.
On another occasion I (ed) recall the minors strike and Nottingham relenting to go back to work and on entering Wasps home the local crowd pitched in on mass with ' Scabs, scabs, scabs' as we strolled to our seats (actually coffin lids – true) as if we were all miners taking a match in on an unpaid holiday.

Rule breaking
'Can the governing body please get together some sort of organisation as regards notifying all, early, their intentions about rules, (and) keeping to them….' ED wrote in a national magazine some forty years ago. (Nothing changes then?)

c2cclothinguk.com

Others stats by David Parker and Bob Hicklin

Attendances for the last five attended League seasons

	2016/17	2017/18	2018/19	2019/20	2021/22	Average
Sheffield Steelers	4955	5352	6127	6610	6693	5947
Nottingham Panthers	5471	5674	5764	5504	4740	5430
Belfast Giants	4616	4525	4332	4387	4155	4403
Cardiff Devils	2969	2986	2964	2978	3041	2988
Braehead/Glasgow Clan	3079	2993	2728	2926	2772	2900
Coventry Blaze	2304	2151	2087	2107	1886	2107
Fife Flyers	1897	1808	1637	1367	1043	1550
Manchester Storm	1352	1592	1437	1365	1417	1433
Dundee Stars	962	1141	1206	1390	1490	1240
Edinburgh Capitals	843	662				753
Guildford Flames		1776	1799	1797	1610	1745
MK Lightning		1626	1665			1646
Average	2872	2690	2877	3043	2885	2933
Average for the nine ever-present clubs	3067	3135	3142	3181	3026	3110

Total attendances for the last five attended League seasons

	2016/7	2017/8	2018/9	2019/20	2021/22
No. of games	260	336	330	239	270
No. of spectators	746,816	904,161	949,539	727,277	778,950

Percentage differences in attendances, 2021/22 vs a) 2019/20, b) 2016/17

	vs 2019/20	vs 2016/17
Sheffield Steelers	+ 1.25%	+ 35.07%
Nottingham Panthers	- 13.88%	- 13.36%
Belfast Giants	- 5.28%	- 9.99%
Cardiff Devils	+ 2.11%	+ 2.42%
Braehead/Glasgow Clan	- 5.26%	- 9.97%
Coventry Blaze	- 10.48%	- 18.14%
Fife Flyers	- 23.70%	- 34.47%
Manchester Storm	+ 3.81%	+ 4.81%
Dundee Stars	+ 7.19%	+ 54.88%

Days for Panthers home games for the last five attended seasons (all games, excluding play-offs)

	2016/17	2017/18	2018/19	2019/21	2021/22
Saturday	13	20	17	13	10
Sunday	8	5	9	11	16
Midweek	3	7	6	7	4
Friday	5	1	2	1	1
Bank holiday	2	1	2	2	3

Panthers' points percentages and League positions for the last five full/near-full seasons:

2016/17: 0.56 (fourth)   15 pts behind third-place team; 23 pts behind winners
2017/18: 0.63 (fourth)   Equal pts with third-place team; 13 pts behind winners
2018/19: 0.58 (third)   22 pts behind second-placed team; 22 pts behind winners
2019/20: 0.63 (fifth)   2 pts behind fourth-placed team*; 6 pts behind winners
2021/22: 0.51 (fourth)   19 pts behind third-placed team; 33 pts behind winners

* Fourth-placed team had played two games more, in a season truncated by between 5 and 8 games

Panthers' points percentage in the League-winning season of 2012/13 was 0.82.
In 2008/09 and 2011/12, we were also above 0.70 (0.72 and 0.74 respectively).

When I asked Bob and David about jersey player numbers: they looked at point scoring lines, and the highest numbers combined.

Penny, Waller and Sanford at Cardiff would come close this season (90, 91, 96) at 277, while Panthers' Chamberlain, Dineen and Boivin from 2021 (90, 92 and 94) at 276 are just one behind them. Rheault, Bulmer and Deutsch (88, 92 and 95), at 275, from 2019-20 before are one behind the latter trio.

276 was also reached by Callum Boyd (89), Igor Valeyev (92) and Jaris Upitis (95) of the Caps in 2017-18 and by Jaroslav Hertl (89), Michal Dobron (91) and Yevgeni Fyodorov (96) of the Caps in 2016-17. Where do they get these facts from?

MOST TITLES WON – one I can do is work out the clubs who have been 'League' winning successful. It isn't easy though with UK history as many factors causing barriers to be able to. Like a changing format/structure so you can't just list them. For example, England/Scotland had separate competitions at one time and regional leagues had several winners and some types had play-off games to decide a title.

Therefore for this list we have the 'major' leagues, 1904-1955 to 1970 and 1983 to present for evidence, including the Northern league 1967-70. The reason to miss regional leagues is that other leagues took precedent is the easiest way to say it.

Team	
Sheffield	9
Cardiff	6
Belfast	5
Durham	5
Coventry	4
Nottingham	4
Paisley	4
Dundee	2

This is followed by many on one win.

Manchester, Ayr, Bracknell, Brighton, Harringay (Racers), London Canadians, Murrayfield, Streatham and Wembley Lions.

In regionalised hockey: Murrayfield and Streatham have 12 each, Fife 9, Dundee 8, Glasgow and Whitley Bay 4, Altrincham (Manchester), Blackpool, Paisley and Wembley Lions all on 3….On 2 are Ayr, Bridge of Weir, Brighton, Harringay (Greyhounds), Harringay (Racers), Kelvingrove (Glasgow), Oxford Uni, Perth and Sussex. Then six on one being – Birmingham, Grosvenor House Canadians, Liverpool, London Phoenix Flyers, Sheffield Lancers, Solihull.

Do you know your players?   One last quiz

FERRARA – GAGNON – WELSH   – HAMMOND ....QUIZ TWO

Which player has played in both France and Poland in the same season?
 (A, for both Bordeaux and Cracovia Krakow in 2020-1)

And which of the other players was a team-mate in the same season in Poland?
 (C)

Which two players are British-born?
 (A, – Peterborough; B, – Brighton)

Can you rank the players in height order, tallest first?
 (C, 6'3", D, 6'2" - A, 5'11" - B, 5'10")

Which two players have played for Brampton Beast in the ECHL?
 (B – 2015-16; D – 2016-17, 2018-19)

Which two players were on the same team in the Elite Series of 2020-21?
 (A, and B – Coventry)

Who is the only one of the four players to have played in Slovenia?
 (D – HDD Jesenice in 2018-19)

Who is the only one of the four players to have played in Denmark?
 (B – Odense and Frederikshavn in 2020-21)

Who is the only one of the four players to have played in Czechia?
 (C – HC Dynamo Pardubice, 2018-19)

Which player played at Midget level for Montral Canadiens?
 (D, 2008-09)

- Answers bottom of page 283 -

Do you know your players?
(Bonus points if you knew these)

Which former Panthers forward was on the Carolina Hurricanes squad when Jeremy Welsh made his NHL debut for the team?
 (Anthony Stewart, 2011-12)

Which former Panthers defenceman was in the Vancouver Canucks squad when Jeremey Welsh played 19 games for the team in 2013-14?
  (Yann Sauvé)

Which former Panthers defenceman was in the same Fort Wayne Komets ECHL as Mathieu Gagnon in 2012-13?
  (Brent Henley)

Which current (2022-23) Dundee stars defenceman was in the Kelowna Rockets WHL squad when Mike Hammond made his debut for them in 2006-07?
  (Colin Joe)

Which player did Mike Hammond beat to the EIHL scoring title by 2 points in 2017-18?
  (John Dunbar – Hammond had 83 (32+51) for Manchester, Dunbar 81 (22+59) for Guildford)

Which of Luke Ferrara and his brother James scored most goals for Peterborough Phantoms in their time there?
  (James – 164; Luke scored 113)

Which record did Mathieu Gagnon hold in the Alberta Junior Hockey League in 2012-13?
  (Most Penalized Player – 259 min)

On the way out   Coming in

Coach's – who'd be one?

Some points about Nottingham's officials who stand on the bench

I think we have had some 19 different coaches' over the history of the team.
The longest term being from Corey Nielson with ten straight seasons.
Most seasons' altogether is Alex Dampier with eleven, so Corey will equal that coming back in 2022.
Only coaching in one season were Jim Haldane/Reg Howard/Terry Gudzuinas/Kevin Murphy/Peter Woods/Richard Chernomaz/Dave Whistle/Gary Graham

APPENDIX

1. Hockey History
2. Cup Competition
3. League play
4. Play offs

Hockey History

1875   Organised hockey was arranged at McGill University in Montreal and at this time a Capt.Creightons McGill team played Capt Torrance's Victoria Team at the Victoria Skating rink on 3rd March as the first recorded Ice-Hockey game. It developed in middle and lower classes.

1889   Pierre Coubertin of France (founder of the modern Olympic Games) had travelled to North America and noted various winter sports. He was impressed by the Canadian version of Ice-Hockey yet it was years before this game bore influence on the big version 'bandy' type played over in Europe.

1893   Stanley Cup introduced which authenticated the game.

1894/1897   George Meagher (Champion Skater) of Kingston, Ontario had visited Paris realizing that they Did not know the Canadian version of the game and he revisited at the Palais de Glace, Paris In 1987 with new equipment and played friendly Ice-Hockey with the French versus visiting 'Bandy' clubs from London and Glasgow. At this same time Major Patton was doing the same with puck and flat bladed sticks in London.

1900   Varsity games began between Oxford and Cambridge.

1902-03   At Princes Skating Club, Knightsbridge, London-Canadian Club formed (Captained by .Donald Higgston-Montreal) when real Ice-Hockey games were being played. Mainly Medical and Law students were introducing the Canadian style to the Princes players. The aristocrat and high society of Europe were the growth here as opposed to waves of public interest in Sweden and Bohemia/Czechoslovakia.
            Major Patton is president of a British domestic league of 5 teams.

1904 (25/1) Patton takes Princes to France beating Lyon 2-11 and 2-0 in France.
            One other game score unknown.
            First real International Ice-Hockey game in Europe.

1905   Although Princes played earlier games in Lyon/Paris a Club match FPB Brussels v CP Paris (Club de Patineurs de Paris)- where the difference in rules were highlighted- Was advertised as *Belgium v France* in March 05.... 3-0 and 4-2 results.
            This division in rules frustrated (game in Les Avants 15/1/05) a Louis Magnus,he wanted a 'solution this year' however the Ice Skating Union were not interested in the issue and it was ignored. Louis Magnus of Paris enthralled by this sport as opposed to European bandy had founded CP Paris (officially club de Patineurs De Paris)…

1906   Oxford Canadians formed – mainly Canadian Rhode scholars (Touring Europe), beating many an opponent in Europe.

15/16th May 1908   1st LIGH Congress at 34 Rue de Provence, Paris (sports club) with Belgium (Eddie De Clerq and Edward Malaret), France (Magnus-The organiser, Robert Planque and Robert van Der Hoeven), GB (E.E.Mavrogodato of the National Skating Association) and Switzerland (Euard Mellor and Louis Dufour) were represented. Louis Magnus was voted unanimously president.

3rd-5th Nov 1808   First international club tournament was played in Berlin. Final score .. CP Paris 2 Princes 3. Also taking part were Berliner SC and Berliner HC of Berlin, Germany.

15th Nov 1908   Bohemia were added as members to the LIHG at Louis Magnus's home. with Planque as general secretary they codified the sport separate from other games.

23rd-25th Jan 1909   Second international club tournament (Chamonix) - with second Congress held debating format and player rules. Princes win. Third club tournament played in Berlin .Akademischer sc 1906 win.

(Months prior to the 1st LIGH European Championship 1910, the format and use of foreigners were debated. France is opposed to use of foreigners in teams and the Swiss wanted a Round Robin of games when Magnus wanted direct elimination.

1910   First of England v Scotland clashes start.
4th Club tournament played in Chamonix. Winners CP Paris.

9th Jan 1910   Third congress …13 reps from 5 nations decided a Round Robin format and the use of no foreigners to be used by 1911 this made Magnus furious.

10th-12th Jan 1910   ★1st LIHG European (Country) Championship (Les Avants Switzerland) – although club teams represented nations.
Belgium (Brussels IHC and Federation des Patineurs de Belgique)-were a combination of two
teams, Germany, GB (Princes) and Switzerland.
Nb. France/Bohemia had withdrew
'Oxford Canadians' played but "out of competition" representing Canada for the first time. They were the best of their time.
GB won the tournament (Tommy Sopwith (air ace) in goal)
5th Club tournament (Berlin) CP Paris win, 6th Club Tournament (Lannoy) CP Paris win. 7th club tournament (Brussels) were Oxford Canadiens win.

14 Mar 1911   LIHG 2nd European Championship. Adopted Canadian rules. Winners Bohhemia.
8th Club Tournament in Avants and Oxford Canadiens win,

At the 9th in Chamonix Oxford take the title again s well as the 10th in Brussels.

NB…During 1912-14 LIHG European Championships and
An "Open" World type LIHG Championat were played where foreigners were allowed in teams.
The newspapers were saying that the Championat was more prestigious than the European championships.

Early 1912 ★European Championship – annulled (Austria participated but were not a member of LIHG & other teams had played with import foreigners) Bohemia (part of Austrian Empire) president Emil Procchazka resigned because of this.

March 1912 ▶First LIHG Championat/open- at Palais de Glace saint sauveur Brussels… Belgium, France, Germany and Switzerland (who, however had to play x3 Belgium's) and Oxford (Canada) Magnus had asked Brussels IHC to organise this due to the European annulment earlier that year. Allemagne champions.

5th Congress- accepts Austria, Luxembourg and Sweden. (Austria and Germany try to exclude Bohemia as it was part of the Austrian empire—but Bohemia president Adolf Dusek convinced LIGH to keep them as an Independent member) New LIGH president was elected 'Henri Van den Bulcke'.

1913 A letter by Oxfords captain Gustav Lanctot says "Bohemia has 11 hockey clubs, Switzerland 7 to 8, GB/Germany have two new ice rinks and news that Austria, Holland, Hungary, Russia to take up the game.

★ 3rd European Championship played. Belgium win.
▶ 2nd LIHG Championat open –St Moritz, Germany, England, France. Germany winners in view of most goals scored when all 3 countries had the same record.

Jan 1914 ▶ 3rd (last) LIHG Championat open – Chamonix GB (Princes) are winners.
7th Congress (and last) in Berlin- re-elected Henri president after two hours but not before 2 others had been elected also at that time Magnus and Patton.
11th club tournament in Avants where Princes triump.

1914 ★ 4th European Championships…. Bohemia, Germany, Belgium,(Switzerland played outside comp with some Berlin club players). Bohemia win.

WAR interrupted the sport by 1920 with new president elect Max Sillig of Germany, Canada had joined LIGH as they and the USA had played in the summer (Antwerp, Belgium) Olympics. The first time North American and Europeans had played against each other in competition. Hosts Belgium declared they would put hockey and figure skating in as demonstration events if Canada (Winnipeg Falcons) participated. Czechoslovakia, France, Sweden, Switzerland and Belgium themselves were the other teams. Count de Lannoy served as the Belgium president.

The tournament was controversial by its format, whereas the modified Magnus elimination system had a tournament (A) bringing about a winner. Tournament (B) had teams who lost to the winner replay for a second place and again a Tournament for the Bronze medal by those beaten by the silver medallist. Yet France for example only got to play one game .A 0-4 loss to Sweden who went on to play 6 games in all. The start of hockey's complicated tournament complexities. Winners are Canada denoted as World Champions.

1921-24	European Championship played. Winners are Sweden, Czechoslovakia, Sweden and France. (From 1922 to 1947 Pail Loicq of Belgium was the most recent president of LIGH)…
1924	Olympic winter games played.(Canada win)
1925-27	European Championships.(Czechoslovakia , Switz, Austria)
1928	Winter Olympics (Canada)
1929	European Championships (Czech)
1930	LIHG World championships independent of the Olympics this year. Another odd format as with 1920, Canada seeded to the final playing Germany and winning 6-1. University of Mukden, Manchuria participated in the Worlds representing Japan.
1930s	Continents Asia, Africa, Oceania have all active leagues.
1931	World Championships. (Canada)
1932	Olympics at lake placid USA had only Germany and Poland affording to send squads. Canada took the title. Last European Championships were played with Sweden going out winners.
1933-35	World Championships played.(USA , Canada , Canada)
1935	16 players signed by passing CAHA. 'Foster and Archer' included. Suspended by LIGH but allowed to complete Olympics which GB actually won.
1936	Olympics in Germany…GB win over Canada 2-1 in earlier round which proved decisive. Complaints from Canada about the GB team players not being legitimate. Canadians wanted the results from the earlier round not to be carried forward as they had lost 0-1 to GB (i.e., play again), LIGH voted against

	this.
Sept 1936	British University teams Oxford and Cambridge play in South Africa. However, the first South African team has 8 Canadians 2 Germans and 1 Austrian…As in 1937 when an Austrian side Wiener EV play, there is little room for 'home grown' talent.
1937-39	World Championships played.(Canada win all 3 in a row)
1940	Nazi occupation averted people's attention with International winter sports weeks in GarmisPartenkirchen…Bohemia/Moravia beating Hungary in this first event.
1941	Germany edge Sweden in another tournament. Sweden/Swiss sports authorities having no moral qualms at this time travelling to Germany.
1946	LIGH changed its name to IIHF in New York meeting LIGH had a new rival…the 'International Ice Hockey Association' which included Scotland.

A new era of hockey starts with the Nottingham Panthers

QUIZ ANSWERS from page 265

1. Vulcanised
2. Gold/White and Black
3. 24   *If you got 10-12 you're an old goat
4. b) Station Hotel   If you got 6-9 you know your stuff
5. Simon Hunt   If you got 4-6 'not bad'
6. English national League 1951   If you got 1-3 you're a young newbie
7. 00-01
8. David Ling
9. 1939
10. No
11. 57
12. Alex Dampier - Coach

**Answers to 'Do you know your players' Questions from page 277

All with letter A = Ferrara, B = Hammond, C = Welsh, D = Gagnon

The CUP
A short history….
The Ice-Hockey programme is well known for its cup, league then play-off schedule. In 1936-37 Earls Court Rangers were Knock-Out Champions in England.
By 1939-40 Dunfermline Vikings picked up the tournament prize denoted as the Scottish Cup.
From 1946-47 both countries played out regular Autumn Cup competitions of their own through to the 1953-54 season. Thereafter the cup campaign took on its British mantle as both associations merged.
At this time 1946-47 to 1949-50 a brief National Tournament was held on a similar basis having foreign teams participate in its third season.
Likewise a Midlands Cup from 1980-81 to 1982-83 and again in 1989-90 had a short shelf life.
Due to constant change in our sports history the 1960's brought about regional contest. The Northern League had cup winners from 1968 until 1982. The other associations down south, the Inter-City/English South League and the Midland/English North brought forth competition from 1980. From this the Southern Cup within the Inter-City/English League south lasted only two seasons due to the fact that there was a return to a British National schedule with interest to a singular countrywide Autumn Cup once again.

This Autumn Cup was the format from 1983 but that ceased in 2000-2001 as two competitions (Autumn and Challenge Cup) which had overlapped between 1998 and 2001 had the Challenge Cup become the major choice of the two to continue. (Who knows why?)
NB) the Icy-Smith Knock-Out Cup played 1966-75 nationally, turned into what is now the British Championship Play-offs. Its title was also played as a minor competition in latter years once again, Nottingham involved in 1989/90.

Other than these domestic affairs Panthers have represented Britain as a team in the Ahearne Cup in 1955, 2002, 2003 and 2006 and in the European Continental Cup by merit in years 1999, 2005, 2006, 2013, 2016/17, 2019 and Champions Hockey League 2014, 2018
Sub note: - Apart from local invitational cups played home or away, or tri-team tournaments. These, mentioned above, were the major cup/tournaments over British ice-hockey history that Panthers have entered. Only in the first ever season of the earlier Autumn Cup in 1946/47 plus the 2005/06 to 2008/09 Knock-out Cup have the club not taken part.

It seems an affliction with this countries game to disregard uniformity in the sport.
Unlike soccer. for example. whose competitions have run for years alongside its main league. Could you see the Football Association Cup being cancelled in favour of another competition?

In the first era (47 to 60) the National Tournament survived for four seasons as a sideshow with the regular Autumn Cup and League campaign (also played 1935-36 to 1939-40 previously) deciding to bring in French opposition in the 48/49 season for an international affair.

The second era saw the return of the Autumn Cup by 1983 but the regional league set up, prior to this (on Panthers return to hockey in 1980), had a Cup competition of its own named the Southern Cup. It was at this time that a Midlands Cup competition was played for (v Solihull) in three seasons, then again in 1990 including two other sides, Telford and Trafford, but never Peterborough?

What have Nottingham done?
46/47 English Autumn Cup did not play, National Tournament R/U of 4 teams
47/48 English Autumn Cup 5th place of 6 teams National Tournament 5th of 7
48/49 English Autumn Cup 6th of 8 teams, International Tournament R/U of 8
49/50 English Autumn Cup 3rd of 7 National Tournament 6th and last
50/51 English Autumn Cup 4th of 6

51/52 English Autumn Cup R/U of 6
52/53 English Autumn Cup 4th of 6
53/54 English Autumn Cup 5th and last
54/55 British Autumn Cup 5th of 12
55/56 British Autumn Cup Winners of 5
56/57 British Autumn Cup 5th and last
57/58 British Autumn Cup 3rd of 5
58/59 British Autumn Cup 5th and last
59/60 British Autumn Cup 3rd of 5
80/81 No Autumn Cup competition, Southern Cup - 4th of 6, Midlands Cup - winners 81/82 No Autumn Cup competition, Southern Cup + Play-off-R/U of 6, Midlands Cup – winners
82/83 No Autumn Cup competition, Midlands Cup – winners
83/84 British Autumn Cup group stage only
84/85 British Autumn Cup group stage only
85/86 British Autumn Cup semi final
86/87 British Autumn Cup winners
87/88 British Autumn Cup group stage only
88/89 British Autumn Cup group stage only
89/90 British Autumn Cup group stage only, Midlands Cup – winners, Icy- Smith Cup – group stage
90/91 British Autumn Cup group stage only
 91/92 British Autumn Cup winners
92/93 British Autumn Cup semi-final
93/94 British Autumn Cup semi-final
94/95 British Autumn Cup winners
95/96 British Autumn Cup runners up
96/97 British Autumn Cup winners
97/98 British Autumn Cup quarter final, Express/Challenge Cup – semi final
98/99 British Autumn Cup winners, Challenge Cup – R/U
99/00 British Autumn Cup quarter-final, Challenge Cup – R/U
00/01 British Autumn Cup group stage only, Challenge Cup – did not qualify
01/02 Challenge Cup – semi final
02/03 Challenge Cup – runners up,
03/04, Challenge Cup – winners
04/05 Challenge Cup – semi final
05/06 (British Knockout Cup – did not enter), Challenge Cup – semi final
06/07 (British Knockout Cup – did not enter), Challenge Cup – quarter final
07/08 Challenge Cup - Winners
08/09 Challenge Cup - quarter final
09/10 Challenge Cup - winners
10/11 Challenge Cup - winners
11/12 Challenge Cup - winners
12/13 Challenge Cup - winners
13/14 Challenge Cup - winners
14/15 Challenge Cup - semi final
15/16 Challenge Cup - winners
16/17 Challenge Cup - semi final
17/18 Challenge Cup - semi final
18/19 Challenge Cup - semi final
19/20 Challenge Cup - semi final
20/21 Elite 'series'   - winners
21/22 Challenge Cup - semi final…..what for 2023?

Autumn Cup Runners up Medal

The reverse side detailing Bill Ringer as the recipient

The LEAGUE

Most of the season is dedicated to the lengthy league programme. But the history is chequered since 1898 when Niagara was the first "nominated" English club champions. It appears sides were "seen as" being the best and thus more likely "elected" champions from the culmination of the entire regular period of play. This continued up until the year 1929.

Thereafter, club sides from England, and a separate Scotland, made up competitive schedules, although this was pitted by faults. 1929-30 had London Lions (Wembley) top of an incomplete league and again denoted the "leading club" side in the year 1931 prior to a full season of play in 31-32.

Leagues continued until 1935-36 when Birmingham Maple Leafs gained an English League title in our records before a more professional set up was to commence, starting in that 35/36 season as the English National league.

Thus after 1935-36 the story became a little clearer. National Leagues embarked on a healthy period both north and south of the border and is remembered more for its ice hockey history in what is known as the "Golden Years". Later our own Nottingham Panthers picking up English trophies in 1951 and 1954. As the two countries then amalgamated to a British League by 1954-55, Panthers had silverware in the cabinet by 1956.

The tale again has the competition fold by 1960 as the League becomes defunct. 1966-67 saw a regional "Northern Association" return with both Scottish and North Eastern English teams. This continued until 1982.

A Southern Association section held a similar League from 1970. This was split into two regional divisions from 1975 with a Southern section and Midland section. In 1978, the Southern section became the Inter-City League (later English League South) and the Midland section later became English League North. Both, however, ceased competition after the 1981/82 season. During this final season a strange situation saw both English and Scottish National Leagues run alongside these regional set ups and ice hockey then felt confident enough by its success to promote a return to British League play, which has existed to the present day.

This more professional scene highlighted by the names Super and Elite in preference to the term British (United Kingdom) League. Perhaps we may include Southern Ireland (EIRE) in the future.

Sub note:- Apart from the hiccups in 'quiet' years of the 60's to 80's when Hockey was striving to find a foothold in a sporting calendar. The Leagues have generally been English/Scottish or British orientated.

What have Nottingham done?
46/47 English League 7th and last
47/48 English League 6th of seven
48/49 English League 4th of eight
49/50 English League 6th of seven
50/51 English League 1st of six Champions
51/52 English League 6th and last
52/53 English League 3rd of six
53/54 English League 1st of five Champions
54/55 British League 2nd of twelve - runners up
55/56 British League 1st of five - Champions
56/57 British League 5th and last
57/58 British League 2nd of five - runners up
58/59 British League 4th and last
59/60 British League 2nd of five - runners up

80/81 Inter-City League 4th of nine
81/82 English League 2nd of eighth - runners up plus second in English League South,
82/83 British League 4th in section b in a tri-league 15 team format
83/84 British League 8th of nine
84/85 British League 8th of ten
85/86 British League 6th of ten
86/87 British League 3rd of ten
87/88 British League 6th of ten
88/89 British League 3rd of ten
89/90 British League 6th of nine
90/91 British League 6th of ten
91/92 British League 2nd of ten – runners up
92/93 British League 3rd of ten
93/94 British League 4th of twelve
94/95 British League 3rd of twelve
95/96 British League 4th of ten
96/97 British ISL 4th of eight
97/98 British ISL 4th of eight
98/99 British ISL 3rd of eight
99/00 British ISL 6th of eight
00/01 UK ISL 8th of nine
01/02 UK ISL 4th of seven
02/03 UK ISL 3rd of five
03/04 UK Elite 2nd of seven – runners up
04/05 UK Elite 4th of seven
05/06 UK Elite 3rd of eight
06/07 UK Elite 5th of ten
07/08 UK Elite 3rd of ten
08/09 UK Elite 3rd of ten
09/10 UK Elite 3rd of ten
10/11 UK Elite 4th of ten
11/12 UK Elite 3rd of ten
12/13 UK Elite winners
13/14 UK Elite 4th of ten
14/15 UK Elite 4th of ten
15/16 UK Elite 5th of ten
16/17 UK Elite 4th of ten
17/18 UK Elite 4th of twelve
18/19 UK Elite 3rd of eleven
19/20 UK Elite 5th of ten
20/21 void/covid: 19
21/22 UK Elite 4th of ten
22/23 UK Elite

The PLAY-OFFS

Both Cup and League have been won but the highlight and culmination of the Ice Hockey season ends with a traditional play off. Teams have to qualify (most seasons) by League placing. Then "drawn" groups of teams play out a series of games and the quarter-finals bring about the last four teams, a finale of games making the big FINALS weekend. This is a semi-final then Final Knock-Out event.

1929-30 saw the first playoffs which had the London Lions engraved into history.
Scottish National play then took on board Play-Offs from 1939-40 when the Kirkcaldy Fliers became the first of nine champions of Scotland.
England testing the Play-Off water again for just one season in 46-47 as Harringay Greyhounds lifted the Trophy.

By the end of the "golden" era of hockey, Brighton Tigers took the honour of British Play-Off Champions for a third time only, yet Play-Off hockey would now disappear until the late 1960's.

Leagues held out Play-Offs from the now regional hockey era that Britain played. The Northern Association comprising of the two countries teams who held an end of league competition from 1968 through to 1979 whereas all the winners happened to be Scottish.

The Southern and Inter-City Association teams in 1976, 77, 78, 80, 81, 82 saw its own title holders. Streatham Redskins being the bookies bet for winners.

But, the long established tournament from 1966 called The Icy-Smith Cup (it was played for from 1966-81 by the strong Northern League) "became" the British Championships and the 1976 winners and subsequent winners to 1981 were heralded as the British Play Off Championship winners and play off champions have added to this list of winners since then to the present day.

Sub note:- This competition is the last of the three main tournaments where the best teams, sometimes all of the teams, take part. Only in 80/81 and 81/82 was it played for from regional set ups.

1980/81 only had a regional format anyway but in 1981/82 teams, again from their regional leagues qualified for it, although a stronger English/Scottish National League was in place that same season.
All the northern association teams played until the semis where they were then joined by Streatham (from the Inter-City League) and Blackpool (from the Midland league).

So organisers had surprisingly took regional winners rather than the 'best' national teams.. Nottingham being runners-up in both the English National League and regional English League South were left out in preference to Blackpool only 5th in the English National League. Three places below us.

What have Nottingham done?
46/47 English League non qualifiers
59/60 British League runners up
80/81 Inter-City League non entrants to Icy-Smith Championship
81/82 English & ELS non qualifier although 2nd in English League regional league winners chosen i.e.: Blackpool (Panthers r/up)
82/83 British League non qualifier

83/84 British League non qualifier
84/85 British League non qualifier
85/86 British League group stage only
86/87 British League group stage only
87/88 British League group stage only
88/89 British League Championship
89/90 British League semi-finalists
90/91 British League group stage only
91/92 British League runners up
92/93 British League semi-finalists
93/94 British League semi-finalists
94/95 British League semi-finalists
95/96 British League runners up
96/97 British ISL runners up
97/98 British ISL group stage only
98/99 British ISL runners up
99/00 British ISL group stage only
00/01 UK ISL group stage only
01/02 UK ISL group stage only
02/03 UK ISL semi finalists
03/04 UK Elite runners up
04/05 UK Elite runners up
05/06 UK Elite group stage only
06/07 UK Elite winners
07/08 UK Elite quarter final
08/09 UK Elite runners up
09/10 UK Elite semi final
10/11 UK Elite winners
11/12 UK Elite winners
12/13 UK Elite winners
13/14 UK Elite quarter final
14/15 UK Elite quarter final
15/16 UK Elite winners
16/17 UK Elite quarter final
17/18 UK Elite semi final
18/19 UK Elite semi final
19/20 Void covid: 19
20/21 Void covid: 19
21/22 UK Elite quarter final
22/23

MY plan for a better season based on 10 teams.

A Cup followed by a League schedule which in turn reflects upon the Play-Offs.

CUP
a round robin affair with the ten teams split into two groups of five, playing two times home and away. The top two from each group go into a knock out semi final stage over two legs, home and away. This also happens in the final... at this point successful teams would have played either two or four games more than the ones who had just played the 16 round robin matches.

LEAGUE
- the importance is to gain as better position from this schedule by seasons end to make life better for you at Play Off time.
A 36 game (18 home and 18 away) series. At this point the fewest games you could have played this season is 52 against a possible 56 as a Cup finalist as above.

PLAY-OFFS
(strap yourself in to read this one) - Teams denoted as 'top four', 'middle table' or 'bottom four'.
As per the Australian rules type of season.

Stage one
Includes ALL teams from the league but whereas those at the bottom would have not normally qualified, they do here.
The bottom FOUR play out between themselves for the right to enter stage two when all other league teams join in.
(not decided myself, but you could have a round robin, series of 3 games or an A v D and B v C knock out - could be less games as explained later**. BUT the two qualifiers of Round Robin groups or the top two will gain a place to stage two with the other six teams who finished above them in the league. This basically give's an exciting dog fight for all lower teams for this stage two.

Stage two
The two qualifiers from stage one above now play the 5th and 6th placed teams in a two legged knock out BUT the 5th/6th team have the home advantage in the return leg (should they want it)...another reason to gain a better league place.

Whilst this happens, the top four play each other. Over two legs again home and away and as a result the winners go to the semi final whilst the losers (reason for interest in league to get a better position) have a second chance in 'Stage Three' against the winners of the….. '5th/6th v bottom 4 winners' match up.

League placing advantage explained.....1) Bottom four play a 3 game series to gain the right to play a middle league team (5th/6th) then it would be a third stage ONE OFF game versus a top four loser for a semi final place against the top four, two winners.
2) The 5th and 6th teams just need to beat the bottom four team qualifiers over 2 legs for a one off game v a top four loser for that semi final place.
3) The top four losers only have to beat the 5th/6th or a bottom club qualifier in stage 3 in order to make the semi's.
4) The top four winners by rights of good play in the league season and winning the stage 2 (first round

for them) games go to the finals weekend - understand that his happens anyway in a simple quarter final clash presently.
THIS new format not only makes winning league games SO much more important each week but gives lower teams more games and opportunity having already lost out earlier in Cup/League competitions.

Therefore, in this play off competition. Some will play 4 (top four winners) or 5 (top 4 loser/5th and 6th team) games through 3 or 4 rounds of play.
Another team could end up playing 6**/8 games (bottom four - in 5 rounds)...** the bottom four series can be reduced to a one off KO or just a two legged aggregate if need be.

By seasons end the 'fewest' games to have been possibly played is 55 with a 'highest' team total of 64, dependant on success/failure.
To note here also as an example - Nottingham, in winning everything in season 2012-13 - played 67 games with others *at least* 59...
This domestic season also allows possible challenge game additions if clubs so wish.

(If I could design a reference diagram here to explain I would)...pen this to paper yourselves and you'll see my idea.
Avoids 'double up' games with Cup dates and improves upon a 'just win 4 games ONLY' Play off competition. Here someone may actually raise their game and win after playing from the bottom and it would be deserved too because of the structure.

SIGNING OFF …

Name: Michael Andrew Chambers

Age: 63

Panthers Fan since: Inception of second era (was only one year old in the first ever domestic season of the first)… Blast missed it.

Favourite Panther
Current: Never had one. It's a team sport so have no favourites though I know when players aren't trying. That's about it.

All-time thoughts: Miss the old days of the eighties when there was major British content in the squad who fought for their lives in games.

Best ever Panthers game: Poor memory, but anything to do with big Cup final wins. I even cried in 1989 would you believe it?

Best Panther moment: Seeing us turn around a losing game in 2001 and whoop the Steelers after Barry Nieckar nearly fought all-comers from the opposition. You know which game I mean.

Favourite other sports: Any team sports.

Favourite hockey film: 'I see Ice' with George Formby. They don't make like that anymore. Ha-Ha.

Favourite book: Any old 1930's/40's book in order to research the old days of Ice-Hockey. Like Major BM Patten's loosely titled piece called 'Ice Hockey'.

Greatest Achievement: Glad to have written three books on the Panthers in 2001, 2007 and 2022. I've worked on other books too about the GB national team, UK Ice Hockey's history and a fictional hockey story.

Best hockey mate: All those lovely fans and authors (home and abroad) who have given me their time for my own ventures in writing, Thanks to them.

ONE OF THOSE PHOTOS YOU LIKE OF YOURSELF ha-ha

Previous books by Michael A Chambers

Nottingham Panthers Statistical Guidebook

Out of stock

Nottingham Panthers Factual Scrapbook

Out of stock

Great Britain Ice Hockey – A Tournament History

Originally sold by Ice Hockey UK – governing body
Contact the organisation for possible purchase.

Ice Cold Murder (Fictional Story)

Copies in hand for sale, email spikc2004@yahoo.co.uk
£4 plus postage

UK ICE HOCKEY - Its history and Competitions Winners
Available on AMAZON.CO.UK £14.99p

UK Ice Hockey -
Its history and competition winners

Michael A Chambers

X Thank you to everybody who has purchased over the years. X

The old Cricket Players but with hockey adorned interior.

Sadly gone with the past.

Top: Ghostly picture of what we play over today

Bottom: A game on the ice

In the bowls of the new arena

Top: I think this is where the ice goes

Bottom: Storage

Picture: Stephen Buckley

I've enjoyed many a game in the Stadium and here. Like to sit back in my seat and watched from block five the ups and downs, the offence and defence, power play and short handed stuff. I have been annoyed by those that sit forwards in their seats and block the view, annoyed by referees. Winge, winge.

Seen the fights and great goals, poor play and frustrated by club affairs but all in all glad I have been involved. Wished I had done more but appreciated the ride and satisfied of what I have contributed.

1980 to 2023   Hope you enjoyed the read like these two ex-players

WIN PANTHERS BOOK!

Panthers star of the fifties Bill Ringer gave the faithful a wave as he was heralded during the home fixture versus Manchester. Here he is in shot here reading our columnist's Mick Chambers' latest publication 'Nottingham Panthers Factual scrapbook' Bill said: ' hit harder, I have still reason to believe that the game in my day was more entertaining as a spectacle, I mean players were on the ice longer and the game flowed a little better." To win one of five copies of Mick's book containing the entire history packed with stats and facts from 1939 to the present day just name the Panthers only goal scorer against Manchester.
Send your answer by e-mail to editorial@nottinghamjournal.com or on a postcard to: Panthers Competition, Editor, Nottingham Journal, Unit 3, Grove House, Bridgford Rd, West Bridgford, NG2 7NN. Closing date is Monday November 10.

...

...

Printed in Great Britain
by Amazon

47132239R00170

Air Fryer Cookbook for Beginners 2022

Ease Your Life with Over 850 Quick, Easy, And Affordable Air Fryer Recipes That Will Make You Fry, Grill, Roast And Bake Delicious Meals Every Day | + Tips & Tricks